Investment Planning

by Keith R. Fevurly

D1406768

ISBN: 978-0-9726772-8-8

CFP®, CERTIFIED FINANCIAL PLANNER™ and CFP® are marks owned by Certified Financial Planner Board of Standards, Inc. These marks are awarded to individuals who successfully complete CFP Board's initial and ongoing certification requirements.

Kaplan University does not certify individuals to use the CFP®, CERTIFIED FINANCIAL PLANNER™ and CFP® marks. CFP certification is granted only by Certified Financial Planner Board of Standards to those persons who, in addition to completing an educational requirement such as this CFP Board-Registered Program, have met its ethics, experience and examination requirements.

TABLE OF CONTENTS

Cash + Cash Equivalents

Chapter 1: The Estate Planning and Transfer Process

Chapter 2: Bonds and Debt Securities

Chapter 3: Stocks and Stock Attributes

Chapter 4: Mutual Funds and Managed Investments

Chapter 5: Insurance-Based Investments

Chapter 6: Real Estate and Real Estate Investment Trusts (REITs)

Chapter 7: Alternative Investments

Chapter 8: Sources of Investment Risk

Chapter 9: Measurements of Investment Risk

Chapter 10: Portfolio Management Theory and Portfolio Development

Chapter 11: Measures of Investment Return

PREFACE

In the financial planning process, investment planning is likely the most important subject matter area since it is the "engine" behind the process. Specifically, investment planning (if done properly) *builds investor wealth*. As such, it provides the lump sum capital needed to accomplish other common investment and/or financial planning goals, such as a comfortable retirement and distribution of one's wealth to other family members at death.

Since this book addresses only those topics in CFP® Board's 2004 Job Analysis Study relating to investments (specifically, topic numbers 34-43), it may not discuss some concepts historically considered in traditional college or university investment courses. In addition, the book covers numerous theoretical concepts (such as the underpinnings of modern portfolio theory or "MPT") that the investment practitioner may or may not use when constructing a portfolio for his or her client. Nevertheless, the subject matter covered throughout the course is both informative and useful to readers preparing to take and successfully complete the CFP® Certification Examination.

This book is designed to serve primarily as the textbook for the second or third course of a personal financial planning program registered with Certified Financial Planner Board of Standards Inc. (CFP® Board) and satisfying the educational component of CFP Board's requirements for earning the CERTIFIED FINANCIAL PLANNER ™ certification*. The book has been written at the upper undergraduate (junior and senior) levels and may also be successfully used in introductory investment courses at traditional colleges and universities. Each of the 18 chapters opens with an introduction of the chapter subject and a list of learning objectives. At the end of each chapter, there is a list of important concepts, questions for review, and suggested additional readings.

Finally, this book is also used as the sole textbook for Investment Planning, the third course in Kaplan University's Online Certificate in Financial Planning Education Program and in Kaplan University's accelerated classroom education program. In the online course, the book is supplemented by brief online readings, exercises, quizzes at the end of each of the 10 lessons, and a Final Examination consisting of 50 multiple choice questions similar to those appearing on CFP Board's Certification Examination. Students in Kaplan University's online financial planning education program also have the use of a message board where they can pose questions online to qualified practitioners/instructors.

---

*CFP®, CERTIFIED FINANCIAL PLANNER™ and CFP® are marks owned by Certified Financial Planner Board of Standards, Inc. These marks are awarded to individuals who successfully complete CFP Board's initial and ongoing certification requirements.

Kaplan University does not certify individuals to use the CFP®, CERTIFIED FINANCIAL PLANNER™ and CFP® marks. CFP certification is granted only by Certified Financial Planner Board of Standards to those persons who, in addition to completing an educational requirement such as this CFP Board-Registered Program, have met its ethics, experience and examination requirements.

ACKNOWLEDGMENTS

The author is indebted to all the academicians and personal financial planning practitioners who have created the body of knowledge covered in this text. These individuals have not only taught or practiced investments in an exemplary manner, but have also participated in several CERTIFIED FINANCIAL PLANNER™ job analysis studies conducted by CFP® Board of Standards Inc. delineating the investment topics that are the basis of examination.

I particularly thank J. Alan Bennett, MBA, CFP®, for his technical review of the manuscript of this text and significant additions to its content. J is also the instructor for the Investment Planning course within Kaplan University's Certificate in Financial Planning Education Program and, therefore, hears "first hand" from students studying for the CFP® Certification Examination about their concerns and suggestions for improvement of the course material. J., you are the best!!

In addition, I wish to thank Kaplan University's Daniel Moore and John Howard who endured several rounds of revisions and produced the final document in a highly professional manner.

Keith R. Fevurly
MBA, JD, L.L.M (Taxation), CFP®, RFC

ABOUT THE AUTHOR

Keith R. Fevurly, MBA, JD, L.L.M. (Taxation), CFP®, RFC is currently the Assistant Dean of Kaplan University's Certificate in Financial Planning Education Program and directs both their online and accelerated (classroom) offerings. The Certificate in Financial Planning Education Program is part of the School of Continuing and Professional Studies (CAPS) at Kaplan University, a subsidiary of Kaplan Higher Education Corporation, which in turn is wholly-owned by Kaplan, Inc. Kaplan, Inc. is a wholly-owned subsidiary of The Washington Post Company. Prior to this position, Mr. Fevurly served as Chief Operating Officer for a private business as well as holding the Academic Director and Vice President of Education positions at the College for Financial Planning, Denver, Colorado. He has also served on CFP Board of Standards Board of Examiners (1994-1996). He has been involved in traditional and distance education for over 20 years.

Mr. Fevurly holds graduate degrees in law, business, and taxation as well as the CFP® financial planning certification. He has written numerous articles and books in the field of financial and estate planning as well as presenting seminars and keynote presentations before many financial services firms. He is the author of *Estate Planning*, used in the last course of Kaplan University's Certificate in Financial Planning online and accelerated program, and is the co-author of *Individual Income Tax Planning* (2nd edition), used in Kaplan University's Income Tax Planning course. He also currently serves on the Board of Editors for the *Journal of Financial Planning*, the major professional journal for practicing financial planners. He is recognized in both *Who's Who in American Law* and *Who's Who in American Education*.

Mr. Fevurly lives in Centennial, Colorado with his wife, Peggy, and two children, Rebecca Dawn and Grant

SAMPLE INVESTMENT FORMULAS

(Note: These formulas will be provided to all candidates taking the CFP(r) Certification Examination, although without titles specifying the meaning and use of each formula.)

Constant Growth Dividend Discount Model

$$V = \frac{D_1}{r - g}$$

Expected Return Form of Dividend Discount Model

$$r = \frac{D_1}{P} + g$$

Covariance Between Two Sample Assets

$$COV_{ij} = \rho_{ij}\sigma_i\sigma_j$$

Standard Deviation of a Two Asset Portfolio

$$\sigma_p = \sqrt{W_i^2\sigma_i^2 + W_j^2\sigma_j^2 + 2W_iW_jCOV_{ij}}$$

Beta Coefficient of Sample Asset

$$\beta_i = \frac{COV_{im}}{\sigma_m^2} = \frac{\rho_{im}\sigma_i}{\sigma_m}$$

Population for Standard Deviation of a Single Asset

$$\sigma_r = \sqrt{\frac{\sum_{t=1}^{n}(r_t - \bar{r})^2}{n}}$$

Sample for Standard Deviation of a Single Asset

$$s_r = \sqrt{\frac{\sum_{t=1}^{n}(r_t - \bar{r})^2}{n-1}}$$

Conversion Value of a Convertible Bond

$$CV = \frac{Par}{CP} \times P_s$$

Capital Asset Pricing Model

$$r_i = r_f + (r_m - r_f)B_i$$

Capital Market Line

$$r_p = r_f + \sigma_p\left[\frac{r_m - r_f}{\sigma_m}\right]$$

Sharpe Index of Portfolio Performance

$$S_p = \frac{r_p - r_f}{\sigma_p}$$

Jensen Index of Portfolio Performance

$$a_p = r_p - \left[r_f + (r_m - r_f)\beta_p\right]$$

Treynor Index of Portfolio Performance

$$T_p = \frac{r_p - r_f}{\beta_p}$$

Macauley Duration/Duration

$$D = \frac{\displaystyle\sum_{t=1}^{n}\frac{c_t(t)}{(1+i)^t}}{\displaystyle\sum_{t=1}^{n}\frac{c_t}{(1+i)^t}}$$

Macauley Duration/Duration

$$D = \frac{1+y}{y} - \frac{(1+y) + t(c-y)}{c\left[(1+y)^t - 1\right] + y}$$

Estimate Change in Price of a Bond

$$\frac{\Delta P}{P} = -D\left[\frac{\Delta(1+y)}{1+y}\right]$$

Meaning of Symbols used by CFP Board in Sample Formulas Sheet:

V = Intrinsic Value of Stock as used in Constant Growth Dividend Discount Model

D_1 = Next Year's Dividend payable by Stock in Constant Growth Dividend Discount Model

r = Required Rate of Return in Constant Growth Dividend Discount Model; also used to mean Expected Rate of Return in Expected Return Form of Dividend Discount Model

g= Growth Rate of Dividends in Constant Growth Dividend Discount Model

P= Purchase Price of Targeted Stock using Expected Return Form of Dividend Discount Model

COV_{ij} or COV_{im} = Covariance between Two Sample Assets ($_{ij}$) or Covariance between One Sample Asset and Market or Market Index ($_{im}$)

P_{ij} or P_{im} = Correlation Coefficient between Two Sample Assets ($_{ij}$) or Correlation Coefficient between One Sample Index and Market or Market Index ($_{im}$)

σ_i = Standard Deviation of First Sample Asset

σ_j = Standard Deviation of Second Sample Asset

σ_p = Standard Deviation of a Portfolio

W_i = Weighting Percentage of First Sample Asset in Standard Deviation of a Portfolio Formula

W_j = Weighting Percentage of Second Sample Asset in Standard Deviation of a Portfolio Formula

2 = Number of Sample Assets in Standard Deviation of a Portfolio Formula

β_i = Beta Coefficient of Sample Asset

σ_m = Standard Deviation of Market or Market Index

σ_r = Population for Standard Deviation of a Single Asset

$\sum$ = Greek Sigma meaning multiple number (n) of actual returns

r = Average or Mean return among multiple number of actual returns (in standard deviation formulas)

s_r = Sample for Standard Deviation of Single Asset

CV = Conversion Value of a Convertible Bond

Par= Par Value of Bond (normally $1,000)

CP= Conversion Price of a Convertible Bond

P_s = Current Market Price of Underlying Stock used in Conversion Value of a Convertible Bond Formula

r_i = Required Rate of Return in Capital Asset Pricing Model

r_f = Risk Free Rate of Return in Capital Asset Pricing Model, Capital Market Line Theory, Sharpe, Jensen, and Treynor index measures of portfolio performance

r_m = Market Rate of Return in Capital Asset Pricing Model

β_i = Beta Coefficient of Sample Stock or Asset in Capital Asset Pricing Model

r_p = Portfolio Rate of Return in Capital Market Line Theory, Sharpe, Jensen, and Treynor index measures of portfolio performance

S_p = Sharpe index measure of portfolio performance

a_p = Jensen index measure of portfolio performance; also known as "alpha"

β_p = Beta Coefficient of Sample Portfolio in Jensen and Treynor index measures

T_p = Treynor index measure of portfolio performance

D = Macauley Duration of a Bond

ΔP = Change in Bond Price given a respective change in market interest rates (Δy)

Cash and Cash Equivalents

• • •

This is the first of seven chapters describing the characteristics of various investment vehicles or assets. This chapter considers the most fundamental of these vehicles, cash, although it also addresses those assets that may easily be converted into cash without any significant loss of the amount invested (also known as the investor's "principal").

In this introductory chapter, we discuss the estate planning and transfer process, including the members of the estate planning "team" of advisors.

Upon completing this chapter, you should be able to:

- Describe the use of cash and cash equivalents in the financial planning process
- Explain investment assets primarily offered by banks, such as certificates of deposit (CDs), money market deposit accounts, and passbook savings accounts
- Explain cash equivalents offered by the U.S. Treasury, including Treasury bills and U.S. "savings bonds"
- Describe the use of corporate commercial paper and bankers' acceptances
- Define *Eurodollars*
- Explain the features and use of the investment policy statement in the financial planning process

CASH AND CASH EQUIVALENTS IN THE FINANCIAL PLANNING PROCESS

Most individuals believe that they have a clear understanding of what is meant by the term *cash*. That is, "it is green and you can see it." However, in the world of financial planning, cash has a very specific meaning. It refers to those investments that have a high level of *liquidity*.

By definition, an investment is *marketable* if it can be sold relatively quickly. In contrast, an investment is liquid if can be sold or redeemed quickly, *but at a known price or without a significant loss to principal*. Typically, investments that are liquid are also marketable, *but not always*. For example, a stock listed on the New York Stock Exchange is most definitely marketable, but it may not be very liquid since its price may have declined from what the investor initially paid for the stock. Conversely, while a savings account is very liquid, since it may be converted to cash without a significant loss to principal, it is not *marketable*. In fact, a savings account is *redeemable*, meaning it must be converted to cash only by the issuer of the investment, in this case, the bank. Recognizing the difference between liquid, marketable and redeemable investments is critical for the financial planner, because all three definitions are part of the *risk/ reward tradeoff*, that is, *the greater the risk assumed by the investor, the greater the return expected!*

All cash and cash equivalent investments share the same characteristic of liquidity. Accordingly, since little, if any, risk (via loss of principal) is assumed, the return on these investments is relatively small. Since their ultimate return of principal is ensured, cash and cash equivalents are most suited to the satisfaction of short-term investment and emergency needs. Indeed, when establishing an *emergency fund* for a client, you should advise him or her that only cash and cash equivalents should be used for this purpose. The cash investments that clients most often use to constitute such a fund are checking accounts (preferably interest-bearing), passbook savings accounts, money market deposit accounts, money market mutual funds, and certificates of deposit (CDs) with a maturity of one year or less. Regardless, all of these investments are also part of what is known in the investment marketplace as the "capital market" (as contrasted to the "investment market") since the maturity date on any, if it applies at all, is *one year or less*.

All individuals need some amount of liquid assets, if for no other reason than to pay current expenses and for aforementioned emergency funds. However, some individuals, by virtue of an extreme risk-averse temperament, may tend to overemphasize them. If you have such a person as a client, it is important to acknowledge their concern over losing a portion of their principal, but it is imperative to educate them concerning the investment risk inherent in holding a great amount of cash and cash equivalents in an inflationary economy. One of the most damaging financial mistakes that senior citizens make is to put too much of their investment portfolio in cash and cash equivalents only to find, not so many years later, that their capacity to buy necessities of living (purchasing power) is eroding. This is what financial planners refer to as *purchasing power* or *inflation risk*.

For example, let us posit that the economy is currently experiencing a 4% annual rate of inflation and that passbook savings accounts are returning to the senior citizen a rate of 2% annually. Thus, each year, this investor is losing 2% of his or her purchasing power. Further, in five years, he or she will have lost 10% of relative purchasing power. In 10 years, he or she will have lost 18% of purchasing power. (Note: The keystrokes on your financial function calculator to solve for this future value are: PV= negative 1; N= 10; and I/YR is a negative 2.) To put this into budgetary terms, if the senior citizen is living on a $2,000 fixed monthly income, he or she will have lost nearly $200 of purchasing power after five years and $366 after 10 years. Therefore, unless the senior has some monetary surplus in his or her budget, where accommodations can be made, he or she will be forced to make sacrifices to his or her quality of life.

It should also be recognized in the above example that the senior citizen's financial situation may be made even direr when the effect of income taxes is taken into account. Nonetheless, the overall point is clear: *all investors,* with the possible exception of those that are terminally ill or those that have more monthly income than they could possibly spend, *need a growth component in their portfolio.*

PASSBOOK SAVINGS ACCOUNT

A passbook savings account is established with a commercial bank or savings and loan (S&L) and is a *redeemable* investment. The account usually has no minimum balance and features a penalty-free withdrawal of funds at any time. The account generally does not include (or has only very limited) check-writing privileges and returns a relatively low rate of interest.

CERTFICATES OF DEPOSIT (CDs)

Certificates of deposit or CDs (also sometimes known as *time* deposits) are deposits made with a bank or S&L for a specified period of time, usually a minimum of three to six months. The financial institution generally pays a fixed rate of interest for the term of the certificate, with rates increasing the longer the term. Usually, an investor who wants to redeem (liquidate) a CD prior to its stated expiration date must pay a substantial penalty in the form of either a one-time fee or a lower overall interest rate. The practical effect of this penalty for early withdrawal is somewhat mitigated by the availability of an *above-the-line* income tax deduction (a deduction from an individual's *gross income* to reach his or her *adjusted gross income*), but it still lowers one's investment return.

It is usually recommended that investors with a relatively large amount of money to invest in CDs purchase *multiple* certificates rather than investing in only *one* certificate. This makes it possible to redeem part of the investment without accessing the other certificates or paying the penalty for early withdrawal on the total amount. In addition, a viable investment strategy is to *ladder* the maturity dates of the multiple certificates in order to more effectively manage interest-rate risk. For example, if interest rates increase, dividing an investment in CDs into 6-month, 12-month, 18-month, and 24-month maturities will yield a higher overall interest rate than investing all of the individual's money in the 6-month maturity CD. Then, as each 6-month CD matures, it may be reinvested at the then-higher interest rate and, if so desired, keep extending by another 6 months the overall investment beyond the 24-month original ending date maturity.

Finally, not all CDs are insured by the federal government (specifically, the Federal Deposit Insurance Corporation or FDIC) and, even if they are insured, amounts in excess of $100,000 per account are *not* covered. Accordingly, if the investor wishes to ensure that a large investment is covered, he or she should invest in CDs offered by different financial institutions, and in no more than an amount of $100,000 in any one institution. An alternative strategy is for the investor to purchase certificates in the names of a spouse or children so that no one certificate exceeds the $100,000 limit. Fortunately, these investments may be made jointly with others or using the other investor's own names.

Negotiable CDs

Issued in exchange for a deposit of funds by most American banks, the *negotiable* CD is a marketable deposit of the issuer, who also stands ready to sell new CDs on demand. The deposit is maintained in the bank until maturity, at which time the investor receives his or her deposit back plus interest. However, these CDs are *negotiable* since they may be sold in the secondary market before maturity. Broker/dealers in securities (for example, Merrill Lynch) then make a market in these un-matured CDs.

MONEY MARKET FUNDS AND DEPOSIT ACCOUNTS

A money market mutual fund is a fund offered by an open-end investment company (mutual fund) that invests in high quality, short-term investments, such as Treasury Bills, commercial paper from various corporations, and large or *jumbo CDs* from large commercial banks. All of these investments will mature within one year and generally have an average maturity of 30 to 90 days. The typical minimum investment is $1,000 and funds may be withdrawn from the account at any time without penalty by writing a check on the account. Most funds also offer shareholders the ability to wire transfer money from the fund to the investor's bank account. The rate of return paid by the fund is highly sensitive to changes in short-term rates due to the short maturity of the investments within the fund.

There are also money market funds that specialize in short-term, *tax-exempt* investments. The payments received by investors from these funds retain their federal income-tax-free status, although the payments may be taxable for alternative-minimum-tax purposes. National tax-exempt funds are diversified in many state obligations and are exempt from federal tax, but subject to state tax. Other funds that are invested in a single state's obligations are exempt from federal and state tax for investors who also reside in the state that issued the security.

Many commercial banks and S&Ls offer *money market deposit accounts (MMDAs)*. The interest paid on these accounts is normally less than that paid by money market mutual funds for the simple reason that the MMDA is federally insured subject to the $100,000 per account limit (accordingly, the investor assumes less risk). MMDAs are essentially a variation of the passbook savings account offered by banks, with the investor paying a service fee if his or her balance falls below a minimum amount. Still, MMDAs are a popular cash-equivalent alternative since they are convenient and the balance may be obtained at the same location where the investor banks. Typically, six pre-authorized transfers are permitted from the account each month, up to three of which may be by personal check.

TREASURY BILLS

A Treasury bill (T-Bill) is a short-term debt security offered by the federal government with a maturity of either 4, 13 or 26 weeks. The Treasury Department discontinued the 52-week T-Bill in July, 2001. T-Bills are purchased in a minimum amount of $1,000 and are issued "at a discount," meaning that they are sold at *less* than their par or face value. At the time of maturity, the investor then reports the difference between the discounted purchase price and the value of the T-Bill at maturity as accrued interest (ordinary income). The interest earned, however, is income-tax free at the state and local level under the *doctrine of reciprocity* of federal tax law.

Because of their lack of default risk and high degree of marketability, T-Bills are often used as the proxy for a risk-free investment in modern portfolio theory (see chapter 10). Specifically, the 13-week (90-day) T-Bill is frequently cited as the risk-free rate. T-Bills are offered by the Treasury Department according to a regular schedule, with 13- and 26-week bills offered every week. Every Thursday the offering is announced publicly in *The Wall Street Journal* and any investor who wants to purchase a new-issue T-Bill directly from the U.S. Treasury submits a standardized form known as a "tender" either by mail or in person at the appropriate Federal Reserve Bank. The bills are auctioned on the following Monday. In addition, individual investors may purchase a T-Bill from their local bank or brokerage firm, although a commission will be charged as well as a premium on purchases under $100,000.

(Note that the other predominant forms of Treasury Department securities, the Treasury note and Treasury bond, will be discussed in chapter 2 of this textbook.)

SERIES EE AND SERIES HH SAVINGS BONDS

Also known as *savings bonds*, Series EE bonds are cash investments that, with recent changes, may provide a relatively high interest rate and, sometimes, a tax advantage. EE paper bonds are purchased at 50% of their face amount and range in face value from $50 to $10,000 (therefore, they may be purchased for as little as $25). They generally have a maturity date of 30 years, after which the bond stops paying interest. The investor may defer payment of any federal income tax until he or she redeems the EE bond or may choose to accrue and pay this interest annually on his or her IRS Form 1040 (or similar form). The interest earned on the bond is exempt from state and local income tax and there are special tax benefits available for bonds used in payment of higher education expenses for the taxpayer, his or her spouse, or any dependent of the taxpayer for whom the taxpayer is allowed a dependency exemption.

EE bonds that are issued from May 1, 1997 through April 30, 2005 pay interest based on a *floating rate* equal to 90% of the average return on the five year Treasury note. They increase in value every month, instead of every six months, and interest is compounded semi-annually. They cannot be redeemed at any time within the first six months from date of purchase and a three month interest penalty applies to any bond that is cashed in prior to five years from the purchase date. This rewards longer term bond holders who then benefit from the higher 5-year interest rates over the remaining term of the bond.

EE bonds that are issued on or after May 1, 2005 earn a *fixed rate* of interest, with this fixed rate applying for the full 30-year term of the bond, which includes a 10-year extended maturity period. Interest accrues monthly and is compounded semi-annually. The EE bond must be held a minimum of one year from date of purchase and a three- month interest penalty applies to bonds that are held less than five years from the issue date. The Treasury Department also guarantees that the bond's value will double after 20 years (meaning that, under the *Rule of 72* the minimum interest rate on the bond will be 3.6% annually).

Series HH bonds, which are no longer offered but may be otherwise encountered in a financial planning practice, pay interest every six months at a fixed rate established when the investor purchased the bonds. This interest rate is then reset on the 10th anniversary of the bond's issue date. (Note that HH bonds issued from January, 1980 to the present have a 10 year maturity date.) Unlike EE bonds, the investor who purchases HH bonds has *no* tax deferral election and must report the interest annually on his or her income tax return. However, prior to September 1, 2004, upon redemption, the investor in EE bonds could exchange at least $500 of the bonds for Series HH bonds and continue the tax deferral on the EE bond interest until the year in which the HH bond reached final maturity or was redeemed. Beginning September 1, 2004, this option is no longer available (that is, the investor must separately redeem his or her EE bonds and pay the income tax due on the accrued interest at that time).

COMMERCIAL PAPER

Commercial paper is a negotiable, short-term, unsecured promissory note issued by large, well-known, and financially strong companies. The name refers to the actual piece of paper on which the borrower's (the corporation's) obligation of repayment is printed. Denominations start at $100,000, with a maturity date of 270 days or less. Such paper is normally sold at a discount and is rated by a rating service (such as Standard & Poor's) as to quality. Because it has a somewhat greater risk than Treasury bills and other government securities, commercial paper normally offers higher interest rates as well.

BANKER'S ACCEPTANCES

Banker's acceptances are short-term (30- to 360-day maturities) drafts that are drawn by a non-financial firm on a major bank used to finance imports and exports. Before a foreign exporter will ship goods to the United States, it wants assurances that the funds are ready for payment when the goods arrive. Accordingly, the exporter will request that a banker's acceptance be drawn on its behalf in the currency of choice.

> **Example 1-1:** XYZ Foreign Cars is purchasing three German automobiles for sale in its showroom. Since it cannot pay for the automobiles in advance, XYZ goes to its bank and arranges for a draft made payable to the German manufacturer one week from receipt of the autos

(thereby providing for sufficient time to inspect the quality of the delivery). XYZ's bank knows from past experience (or from XYZ's account on file at the bank) that it is "good for the money" so therefore it honors the draft (in the form of a banker's acceptance) and sends it on to the German manufacturer. The exporter/manufacturer now knows that it will be paid for the automobiles.

Banker's acceptances are typically traded at a discount from their face value on the secondary market.

REPURCHASE AGREEMENTS (REPOs)

Dealers in government securities use repurchase agreements (also known as *repos)*. In order to improve liquidity (get cash), such a dealer will *sell* some of those securities to another dealer with an agreement to buy them back at a later date at an agreed-upon price. The buyer of the repurchase agreement then receives the equivalent of a fixed yield or return on its investment. Such repurchase agreements are included in the context of *money market securities* since the term of the agreement is typically less than one year. Indeed, the standard repo may only have an *overnight* maturity. The short-term maturity and government backing means that repos provide lenders with extremely low risk.

The opposite of the repo is the *reverse repurchase agreement (or reverse repo)*. In a reverse repo, the dealer buys government securities from an investor and then sells them back at a later date at a higher price.

Repos and reverse repos also have importance in open market operations conducted by the Federal Reserve Bank *(the Fed)*. If the Fed is attempting to stimulate or expand the economy, it will sell securities in the secondary market, thereby putting money into the system (the equivalent of a repo). Conversely, if the Fed is attempting to contract or tighten the money supply, it will buy securities (the equivalent of a reverse repo), thereby taking money out of the system.

EURODOLLARS

Contrary to its name, Eurodollars have very little to do with European countries. Rather, Eurodollars are simply U.S. dollar-denominated deposits at banks *outside* of the United States. The average Eurodollar deposit is very large (in the millions) and has a maturity of less than six months. Therefore, the market is obviously way out of reach for all but the largest financial institutions and the only way for individuals to invest is indirectly through a money market mutual fund.

A variation on the Eurodollar time deposit is the Eurodollar certificate of deposit (Euro CD). A Eurodollar CD shares the same characteristics with its U.S. counterpart, except that the Eurodollar obligation is a liability of a *non-U.S. bank*. Accordingly, it is less liquid (due to the exchange-rate risk assumed by the investor) and, thus, offers a slightly higher yield than that of the obligation of the domestic bank. In addition, the Eurodollar market is relatively free of government regulation, thereby potentially lessening the safety of the obligation.

THE INVESTMENT POLICY STATEMENT IN THE FINANCIAL PLANNING PROCESS

The *investment policy statement* has three purposes in the financial and investment planning process:

1) To articulate and confirm the investor's policy objectives and tolerance for risk

2) To define how the portfolio will be monitored and how progress toward the stated investment objectives will be measured

3) To define the investor's target asset allocation, which studies have confirmed to be the single most important component in whether the client actually meets his or her investment planning goals

An investment policy statement will normally include the facts of the client's financial situation. It will also include information not unlike the following:

- The client's investment objectives, in order of priority
- The client's time horizons for meeting these objectives
- The client's risk tolerance level
- A preferable *expected* rate of return on any investments that are made
- The client's projected cash flow needs (or surplus)
- An investment strategy or asset allocation guidelines
- Standards or *benchmarks* for the performance measurement of the portfolio

The statement will eventually arrive at a suggested or recommended portfolio of investment assets, of which cash and cash equivalents may be a part. However, cash equivalents (most notably, money market mutual funds) are typically used only as a *sweep account* to deposit monies until a more productive use (namely, a higher yielding investment) for them may be found. While an investment policy statement is *not* a required element in sound investment planning, most investment advisors do prepare such a statement and refer to it often as the guideline for managing the portfolio of an investor.

IMPORTANT CONCEPTS

Cash equivalent

Passbook savings account

Certificate of deposit (CD)

Negotiable certificate of deposit

Money market mutual fund

Money market deposit account (MMDA)

Treasury bill

Series EE savings bond

Series HH bond

Commercial paper

Banker's acceptance

Repurchase agreement (repo)

Reverse repurchase agreement (reverse repo)

Eurodollar

Investment policy statement

QUESTIONS FOR REVIEW

1. What is the importance of cash and cash equivalents in the financial planning process?

2. Define the following three terms:
    • Liquidity
    • Marketability
    • Redeemable

3. Explain the *laddered* CD investment strategy.

4. What is a negotiable certificate of deposit (CD) and what attribute does it possess that is not present with a CD issued by a bank or savings and loan (S&L)?

5. What is the primary purpose of the money market mutual fund in the investment planning process?

6. What is meant by the term *money market* in finance and investments?

7. Contrast a money market mutual fund to a money market deposit account (MMDA). Which one is insured by the FDIC and up to what amount?

8. How is interest paid on a U.S. Treasury bill?

9. What are the maturities of a U.S Treasury bill? Which maturity date is typically used as the proxy for the risk-free rate of return in modern portfolio theory?

10. How is the interest rate computed on Series EE savings bonds for those issued prior to May 1, 2005? How is this rate computed on such bonds issued on or after May 1, 2005?

11. Who issues commercial paper and what is its maturity date?

12. What is the primary use for a banker's acceptance?

13. Contrast a repurchase agreement (repo) to that of a reverse repurchase agreement (reverse repo). In what context are both of these obligations used by the Federal Reserve Bank (the Fed)?

14. What is a Eurodollar and how does an individual investor purchase this obligation?

15. What are three purposes of the investment policy statement in portfolio management? How are cash equivalents reported on this statement and how do most financial planners and/or money managers use them?

SUGGESTIONS FOR ADDITIONAL READING

Tools and Techniques of Investment Planning, Stephen R. Leimberg, Robert T. LeClair, Robert J. Doyle, Jr., and Thomas R. Robinson, The National Underwriter Company, 2004.

Investments: An Introduction, 7th edition, Herbert B. Mayo, Thomson/ South-Western, 2002.

Investment Analysis and Portfolio Management, 7th edition, Frank K. Reilly, and Keith C. Brown, Thomson/South-Western, 2003.

The Wall Street Journal Guide to Money and Investing, 3rd edition, Kenneth M. Morris, and Virginia B. Morris, Fireside Publishing, 2004.

CHAPTER TWO

Bond and Debt Securities

• • •

A bond is a loan that an investor makes to corporations or governments. The obligation pays interest over a fixed term (or *maturity*), at the end of which the *principal* of the bond, or original investment amount, is also repaid to the lender or bond holder. Typically, the rate at which interest is paid and the amount of each payment is *fixed* at the time the bond is offered for sale. The percentage rate specifying this amount of interest (as computed on the original issue or *par value* of the bond) is known as its *coupon rate*. Since the amount of each payment and percentage rate of interest is fixed, bonds are sometimes referred to as *fixed income securities*. A bond's interest rate must be competitive when issued, which means that the rate it pays must be comparable to what other bonds being issued at the same point in time are paying. However, as market interest rates fluctuate up or down, the market value of the bond will also fluctuate in an inverse relationship (that is, if interest rates increase, the value of the bond will decrease and vice-versa). Therefore, if the investor sells the bond in the secondary market prior to the bond's maturity, he or she will realize a capital gain or loss on the bond if the prevailing interest rate at the time of the sale differs from the bond's coupon rate.

Upon completing this chapter, you should be able to:

- Explain the characteristics and uses of U.S. Treasury notes and bonds in investment planning
- Identify the types of bonds issued by state and local governments (also known as *municipalities*)
- Describe each of the various forms of corporate bonds, including convertible and callable issues
- Describe the suitability of foreign bonds as a possible investment
- Explain the features of zero coupon bonds

There are essentially three types of bonds or *debt securities*. There are securities offered by the U.S. government through the Treasury Department (known as *Treasury bonds or Treasury notes*), those issued by municipalities (known as *municipal bonds or munis*), and those issued by private corporations or businesses (corporate bonds).

U.S. GOVERNMENT SECURITIES

The U.S. government issues five major types of securities, one of which, the Treasury bill (T-Bill) is discussed in chapter 1. The other major types of securities are:

1) The Treasury note
2) The Treasury bond
3) The Treasury STRIP
4) Treasury Inflation Protected Securities (TIPS)

They differ from each other in their maturities, in the interest that they pay, and in the manner in which this interest is paid. However, unlike (for example) corporate debt securities, government securities all share the characteristic of safety. That is, as is often said, only the government may "print more money," meaning that it can always reimburse the investor for any debt obligation incurred. Accordingly, since the investor here assumes comparatively less risk, U.S. government securities also offer less return than those issued by a private corporation or business.

Treasury Note

A Treasury note is a medium-term debt security, paying interest semi-annually, and issued in a minimum denomination of $1,000. They are auctioned by the government every four weeks. Notes have a fixed maturity date greater than one year and not more than 10 years in length from date of issue (actually they are issued with terms of 2, 5, or 10 years). Unlike T-Bills that are issued at a discount, notes are issued at their stated par value and then trade in the secondary market like other debt securities, including corporate bonds. All interest payable from the note is subject to federal income tax as ordinary income at the highest marginal rate of the taxpayer/investor. Interest from the obligation, however, is *exempt from all state and local taxes*. If the note is sold before maturity on the secondary market, gain or loss is treated as capital gain or capital loss.

A note may also be part of a mutual fund that restricts its portfolio to issues of the U.S. government. Although such a fund is not insured by the FDIC (like a corresponding bank obligation), it is fully invested only in government debt, therefore providing a high degree of safety. Accordingly, an extremely conservative investor who needs certainty of income and who is unwilling to accept the risk inherent in a mutual fund investing in stocks or corporate bonds, may find a government securities mutual fund to his or her liking. However, Treasury mutual funds should generally be compared with money market mutual funds, since the return on money market funds may rival that of Treasury funds, but with much greater liquidity.

Treasury Bond

A Treasury bond is a long term debt security with a fixed maturity date of more than 10 years. The Treasury discontinued issuance of the so-called *long bond* (30 year maturity date) in October, 2001, but recently, begining in February 2006, resumed auctioning the long bond as an additional tool to finance the expanding federal deficit. Historically, the 30 year bond has been the benchmark against which to measure conventional home mortgage interest rates, but, during its suspension, the 10-year Treasury note took on more importance as the standard long term interest rate barometer. The minimum denomination for the Treasury bond, like the Treasury note, is $1,000 and it also returns interest semi-annually to the investor. Taxability of bond interest and principal is also the same as that of the Treasury note.

Prices for Treasury bonds (and notes) on the secondary market are quoted as a percentage of par value. The fractional component of the quote is given in 32nds, rather than 100ths, of a percentage point. Each 1/32 equals 31.25 cents (or the $1,000 par value divided by 32), but the fractional part is dropped when the price is quoted. For example, a bond quoted at 103:15 would have a price that is 103% of par, plus 15/32, or 103.4688%. If the bond's par value was $1,000, the bond's price would therefore be $1,034.69 ($1,000 times 1.0346880. Prices are also quoted as *bid* and *asked*, rather than with a final closing price like a stock. This is necessary because all Treasury issues are traded "over the counter," in thousands of electronic (and telephone) transactions between the investor (and his or her broker/dealer) and the U.S. Treasury. Such issues are not traded on the major exchanges like individual stocks and/or mutual funds. In addition, the bid and ask is from the standpoint of the *seller*, so that the ask price (the price the seller wants for the bond) will always be *higher* than that of the bid (the price that the buyer is willing to pay for the bond), so as to allow for necessary transaction costs.

Treasury STRIP

A Treasury STRIPs (standing for *Separate Trading of Registered Interest and Principal of Securities*) is the U.S. Treasury form of a *zero coupon bond*. Stripped bonds are created when investment bankers buy large blocks of coupon-paying bonds (typically U.S. Treasury issues) and separate them into the coupon and principal amounts. Each component is then sold separately, with the principal (*or stripped bond*) sold at an adequate-enough discount to provide a competitive market yield until the date of the bond's maturity. An investor who wants to eliminate any risk associated with the reinvestment of the coupon payments from a regular bond will be interested in a stripped bond since the reinvestment rate is guaranteed. (In other words, reinvestment rate risk is eliminated with the purchase of a Treasury STRIP or any other form of zero-coupon bond).

STRIP prices are always less than par, since they are issued at a deep discount. Those closest to maturity trade at higher prices since they can be redeemed at par value relatively soon (that is, at their date of maturity). However, prices of STRIPs (as with any zero coupon bond) are more sensitive to interest rate changes than prices of coupon-paying bonds of the same quality and maturity, This is because of a concept known as *bond duration* that we will discuss in chapter 13 of this text. Since the *duration* of a zero coupon bond (including a Treasury STRIP) is equal to its maturity, and interest rate sensitivity is measured by duration, the *greater* the maturity of the bond, the *greater* the price change of a zero coupon bond, given a corresponding change in market interest rates. (Note that we will discuss other forms of zero coupon bonds, specifically those issued by municipalities and corporations, later in this chapter).

Finally, the income tax consequences of an investment in STRIPs (and zero coupon bonds generally) are very important. The discount on STRIPs is treated as taxable income and *earned annually*. This is the case even though the investor in a STRIP does *not* receive any cash interest at the same time. Therefore, a cash flow problem arises: specifically, the investor must pay taxes on interest for which he has not received any cash. This is known in the financial planning world as *phantom income* and leads to an important investment conclusion: Taxable STRIPs are very suitable investments to be placed in a retirement plan or any tax -deferred type of account, but, under most circumstances, they should *not* be part of a taxable portfolio. The exception to this rule is where a tax-exempt STRIP is purchased by the investor. Tax-exempt STRIPs are excellent vehicles for children under age 18 who are subject to their parent's tax rate on unearned income (that is, where the *kiddie tax* applies and the child pays only very little tax on the accrual of STRIP interest).

Treasury Inflation Protected Securities (TIPS)

A unique group of securities issued by the U.S. Treasury are Treasury Inflation Indexed or Protected Securities, often simply referred to as *TIPS*. These securities were first issued in early 1997 and are now auctioned by Treasury four times each year. As the name indicates, TIPS are designed to offer protection against the effects of inflation. They are marketable securities and are traded on the secondary market subsequent to issue. The face value of TIPS is adjusted semiannually to keep pace with inflation as measured by the Consumer Price Index (CPI) over the previous six-month period. Like other Treasury securities, TIPS pay a fixed rate of interest; however, this rate is not applied to the par value, but rather to the inflation adjusted principal. Therefore, the higher the inflation rate, the higher the face value of the bond and the higher the semiannual interest payment.

> **Example 2-1:** John pays $1,000 for a TIPS security (10 year inflation-indexed note) that carries a 3% coupon on January 2, 2005. At mid year, the Consumer Price Index (CPI) measures that inflation has increased by 1% during the first six months of the year. Therefore, the principal or face value of John's note is increased to $1,010. In addition, instead of receiving a semi-annual interest payment of $15 (half the 3% times the $1,000 par value) John now receives an interest payment of $15.15.

Of course, as may be anticipated, TIPS are very useful when an investor is particularly concerned with the effects of inflation (loss of purchasing power) on his initial investment.

Simply stated, the investor is taxed annually on the interest payment *plus* the appreciation in face value. However, only federal tax applies since TIPS, like other Treasury securities, are exempt from state and local taxes. In Example 2-1 above, the $15.15 in interest income (received in cash) plus the $10 increase in principal would each be taxed at the investor's ordinary income tax rate. Further, the $10 increase in face value constitutes *phantom income* (like the Treasury STRIP interest accrual) that is not collectible until the bond is sold or matures. Also, like the STRIP bond, this income is taxable in the year that it is *accrued* as the Internal Revenue Code makes *no* distinction between real and phantom income. Therefore, TIPS are also best positioned in a tax-deferred or tax-advantaged account.

I Bonds

Series I Bonds are a new type of inflation-indexed security issued by the U.S. Treasury for the individual investor who does not have a great deal of money to invest. They are essentially the TIPS equivalent of the Series EE savings bond (see chapter 1) and generally share the taxable consequences of TIPS. They are sold at face value, starting in denominations as low as $50, and earn interest for up to 30 years. An individual may buy up to $30,000 of paper I bonds in any one year and an additional $30,000 in electronic bonds, with separate purchases of Series EE bonds unaffected. While Series EE bonds cannot be exchanged for Series I bonds, an investor may cash in (redeem) the EE bonds and use the proceeds to buy I bonds. The interest earned, however, on the EE bonds must be reported on the investor's federal income tax return for the year in which such bonds are redeemed.

Mortgage Backed Securities

The U.S. Treasury also directly guarantees or implicitly backs (indirectly guarantees) debt-type securities that are secured by a pool of mortgage obligations. In the financial world, these are sometimes collectively known as *asset backed securities*, although the term "asset backed" can include securities that are secured by obligations other than home mortgages.

Three of the best known mortgage backed securities are obligations (*certificates*) issued by the Government National Mortgage Association (GNMA), the Federal National Mortgage Association (FNMA), and the Federal Home Loan Mortgage Corporation (FHLMC). GNMA is a wholly-owned U.S. government corporation that buys Federal Home Administration (FHA) and Veterans Administration (VA) insured mortgages from banks and places them into mortgage pools and then issues pass-through certificates representing an individual interest in the pool. FNMA is a government-sponsored corporation owned entirely by private stockholders that buys conventional mortgage obligations and repositions them into mortgage pools. FHLMC is owned by the twelve Federal Home Loan Banks, but also purchases and collateralizes conventional mortgages into pools with corresponding pass-through certificates. The securities that each of these three organizations issue are appropriately nicknamed, *Ginnie Maes, Fannie Maes*, and *Freddie Macs*, respectively.

Ginnie Maes are a *direct guarantee* of the U.S. Treasury. The minimum size of an individual GNMA sold to an individual investor is $25,000. While there is no default risk (such issue is, after all, backed by the U.S. government), an investor does assume interest rate risk given that the obligation is a type of fixed income security. A GNMA certificate also carries reinvestment rate risk, since the investor has to assume a reduced certainty of monthly payments due to homeowners who have financed their purchases with FHA and VA mortgages repaying those loans early when market interest declines. Still, an investor who desires a relatively high rate of return with a commensurate high level of liquidity may strongly consider the purchase of a GNMA pass through certificate either directly or by investing in mutual funds that specialize in such securities.

In contrast to Ginnie Maes, the U.S. Treasury does *not* directly guarantee the repayment of either Fannie Mae or Freddie Mac certificates. Rather, it backs those issues only indirectly or implicitly. It does this by giving both agencies a legislated priority in purchasing conventional mortgages in the secondary market. In addition, it is virtually inconceivable that the government would not step in if either agency experienced a *liquidity crunch* in making good on its obligations to investors. However, because both Fannie Mae and Freddie Mac obligations are not officially guaranteed by the U.S. Treasury, they are considered riskier than Ginnie Maes. Also, because they are not as liquid as Ginnie Maes, both obligations typically provide a slightly higher rate of return or yield to the investor.

MUNICIPAL BONDS

A municipal bond, also known as a *muni bond*, is a debt instrument issued by a state, county (or parish), city, or other non-federal governmental agency. Generally, any municipal bond shares the characteristic of generating *tax-free income* to the investor for federal income tax purposes. Some municipal bonds are also insured by either the American Municipal Bond Assurance Corporation (AMBAC) or by the Municipal Bond Insurance Association Corporation (MBIA). The reason that an issuer would also incur the cost of insuring its bond is to achieve a higher quality rating by a rating agency (such as Standard & Poor's), thereby increasing the attractiveness of the issue in the open market. Of course, the insurers guarantee payment of the bond's interest and principal should the issuer let the bond default.

As noted, generally, the interest earned on a municipal bond is exempt from *federal* income tax. However, this interest is subject to state and local tax (unless the bond is purchased by a resident of the state that has also issued the bond-- also referred to as a *double barreled bond*). Capital gains (or losses) realized on the sale of a municipal bond are subject to normal capital gain (or loss) tax treatment. Special rules apply to municipal bonds issued at a discount and that are known as *original issue discount* (OID) bonds (see chapter 18 of this textbook). Compared to an alternative investment generating taxable income, municipal bonds may produce a *higher* after-tax return. In this case, the *tax equivalent yield* (used for comparison purposes with the tax-exempt yield quoted on the municipal bond) is computed with use of the following formula:

$$\text{Tax Equivalent Yield} = \frac{\text{Tax Exempt Yield}}{(1- \text{marginal tax rate})}$$

> **Example 2-2:** Richard owns a municipal bond that features a tax-exempt yield of 5%. He is in the 35% federal marginal income tax bracket. Accordingly, the tax-equivalent yield (T.E.Y.) on a taxable investment is 7.69% [or .05 divided by (1-0.35)]. This means that Richard would need to purchase a taxable investment returning him at least 7.69% annually to exceed the equivalent 5% tax-free return generated by the municipal bond.

As one can easily see, the *higher* an investor's marginal income tax bracket, the *greater* the advantage to him or her of investing in an asset that returns federally tax-exempt income. Conversely, if an investment already features tax-exempt income (such as a qualified retirement trust), a municipal bond investment providing an additional exemption is unwise as the investor will unnecessarily suffer a reduction of possible return.

There are three types of municipal bonds-*general obligation (G.O.) bonds, revenue bonds, and private purpose bonds*-each of which will now be discussed.

General Obligation (G.O.) Bonds

General obligation (G.O.) bonds are normally issued to finance the general operations, functions, and programs of the issuer (municipality).

A general obligation municipal bond is backed by the full faith, credit, and taxing power of the municipality. This means that the municipality promises to increase taxes on its citizenry without any limit if needed to pay off the bondholders. In the unlikely event of default (or no risk of default if the bond is insured), G.O. bondholders have the right to force a tax levy or legislative appropriation to make payment on the debt. Because of this, G.O. bonds are generally considered to be the *safest* type of municipal bond (and, accordingly, will reflect the lowest stated or nominal yield).

Revenue Bonds

Revenue bonds are normally issued to finance public capital projects (such as an airport or bridge) or public services (such as a sewage treatment plant) where user fees or specific assessments are intended to repay the debt.

A revenue bond is one that is backed by a specific source of revenue to which the full faith, credit, and taxing authority of the municipality is *not* pledged. Therefore, bondholders must rely on the adequacy of the fees or tolls received by the municipality to pay interest on the bonds. Revenue bonds are usually junior to the municipality's general obligation bonds (meaning that they are paid only after the G.O. bonds are paid), so revenue bondholders assume a greater amount of credit risk. Revenue bonds also generally have longer terms of maturity. Accordingly, they trade at higher yields than do general obligation bonds.

Private Purpose Bonds

Private purpose bonds are issued to finance certain activities that do *not* constitute the normal functions of a municipal government (such as the development of an industrial park). Typically, the bonds are used in the trade or business of individuals or entities other than the state or local government (municipality).

The important feature to note about a private purpose bond is that its interest is *not* tax-exempt for federal income tax purposes (although it may be from the issuing municipality's income tax). Such interest is also a *tax preference* item for alternative minimum tax purposes, meaning that it is added back in the computation of alternative minimum taxable income (AMTI) under that system of taxation. As a result, the yield quoted on the bond is higher still than either a general obligation or revenue bond, so as to take into account the generally disadvantageous tax consequences to the investor.

Finally, rather than purchasing all of these types of municipal bonds separately, some investors prefer the greater diversification available in a *municipal bond unit trust*. Such a trust is a fixed, unmanaged portfolio, meaning that there is no *active management* (trading) of the assets. A *unit trust* is also *self-liquidating*, which means that when the asset values drop below a certain point (normally 20% of the initial investment), the fund terminates and unit holders receive their proportionate share of the current value of the portfolio. Therefore, unit trusts are best for long-term bondholders who wish to receive a certain amount of fixed *income*. As the trust's holdings reach their maturity date, the bondholders are paid on a pro-rata basis.

CORPORATE BONDS

Bonds issued by corporations are, by far, the greatest component of the secondary bond market. In order to understand them, however, we first need to define some bond vocabulary that applies to all types of corporate bonds:

Par Value: The stated value of the bond at date of issuance and the amount that is returned to the investor when redeemed; usually a $1,000 minimum; also referred to as *principal*.

Coupon Rate: The stated rate of interest on the debt obligation (bond); the interest paid by the corporation on the bond (unlike a dividend declared on stock) is income tax deductible as an "ordinary and necessary" business expense. It should be noted here-- in anticipation of confusion by some readers-- that the coupon rate on a fixed rate bond does *not change*. A bond's coupon rate is sometimes confused with its yield. The former never changes, but the latter frequently does, as will subsequently be shown.

Indenture: The formal written agreement between the issuer of the bond and the trustee of the bond acting on behalf of the bondholders; also called a *deed of trust*.

Sinking Fund: A bond provision that requires the issuer to either:
- Redeem some or all of the bond systematically over its term rather than in full at maturity, or
- Set aside sufficient capital in a separate account, over the life of the bond issue, which will ultimately pay off the total bond principal at the bond's maturity.

Mortgage Bond: A bond that pledges specific assets such as buildings or equipment; generally, a secured bond where the assets pledged are used to pay off the bondholders in the event of default.

Debenture: A bond that promises payments of interest and principal but pledges no specific assets; generally, an *unsecured bond.*

Call Feature: When a bond is *callable,* the issuer has the right to redeem the bond at a predetermined price at a date prior to maturity; an issuer is most likely to call a bond early if interest rates have *declined* in the market (thereby making it possible for the issuer to replace the bond that is called with one paying a lower interest rate).

Investment Grade Bond: A bond that is rated BBB or higher by the Standard and Poor's rating agency; generally, a high-quality bond with little risk of default by the issuer.

High Yield Bond: A bond that is rated BB or below by the Standard and Poor's rating agency; generally, of lower quality with a greater risk of default by the issuer than an investment grade bond; also known as a *speculative grade* or *junk bond.*

Convertible Bond: A bond with the added feature that the bondholder has the option to turn the bond back into the issuer in exchange for a specified number of common stock shares of the issuer.

Discount Bond: A bond sells at a discount when its par value exceeds the bond's purchase price on the secondary market; also known as a *market discount bond;* contrast to an *original issue discount bond* (OID bond) where the bond is issued at a discount or reduction to its stated par value.

Premium Bond: A bond sells at a premium when the bond's market price exceeds the bond's par value.

Zero Coupon Bond: A bond that pays its par value at maturity but has *no* periodic interest payments (i.e. pays a 0% coupon rate); offered by both corporate and government issuers.

Characteristics of Corporate Bonds

In most corporate bond issues, income and principal repayment are relatively safe. Of course, ultimately, the security of both interest and principal payments depends on the financial strength of the issuer corporation, but bond rating agencies (such as Standard and Poor's and Moody's) may provide some assistance in making this determination by the investor. Bonds normally pay interest income on a semi-annual basis and, once begun, cannot be changed in either amount or timing regardless of the financial condition of the issuer. In other words, unlike the payment of dividends on stock that is made only at the discretion of the corporation's board of directors, interest payments on bonds are a *fixed legal obligation* of the issuer. Accordingly, where the investor's objective is a secure and consistent cash flow of income, an investment in (preferably) investment grade corporate bonds is warranted.

While the interest payments on bonds are fixed in amount, their ultimate purchasing power may be eroded by inflation. This is referred to as *purchasing power risk* and is an inherent disadvantage of an investment in any type of fixed-income security (with the exception, of course, of those designed to avoid it, such as TIPS). In addition, inflation will also reduce the purchasing power of a bondholder's principal. Further, the *longer* the period of time before the investor has to wait for repayment of his or her principal in the bond, the *lower* the amount of those dollars in present value terms. For example, assume that Joe purchases a 10 year corporate bond for $1,000. At a 2.5% rate of inflation, the $1,000 par value/ principal repayment he will receive at maturity is equivalent to only $781.20 in present value terms. This effect may be minimized with an investment of only shorter term bonds (or, perhaps, an investment in a bond mutual fund), but the risk of a loss in purchasing power cannot be eliminated when inflationary pressures are present within the overall economy.

Bond prices also fluctuate with changes in current market interest rates. If interest rates paid on newly issued bonds *increase*, older bonds will be less attractive to current investors and, accordingly, the market prices of those older bonds will *fall*. For example, if market interest rates increase from 10% to 12%, a 25-year semi-annual bond with a stated coupon rate of 10% would fall in price to $842.38. This is because the price of the 10% bond must be reduced until it produces a *yield to maturity* (YTM) equivalent to the yield of the new 12% bond. (Note that *yield* to maturity will be further discussed in chapter 13 of this textbook, but that it is defined as "the average annualized rate of return that an investor will earn if a bond is held until its maturity date"). Similarly, the reverse effect is also true: if market interest rates decrease, the price of previously issued bonds will *rise*. This risk of a change in bond price, given a corresponding change in market interest rates, is known as *interest rate risk* and consists of two parts: 1) *price risk* (or the relationship between bond prices and the investor's required rate of return) and 2) *reinvestment rate risk* (or the uncertainty about the rate at which any future income generated by the bond may be reinvested).

Finally, most corporate bonds that are issued today are issued as debentures, meaning that they are an unsecured credit obligation of the issuer corporation. Further, most bonds offered in this form are *subordinated* in security (safety) to all other corporate creditors, including its general creditors. Because of the greater risk associated with *subordinated debentures*, they pay a higher interest rate than those of either mortgage bonds or non-subordinated debentures. Still, as debt obligations, even subordinated debentures have a security preference over any equity shares (common and preferred stock) issued by the corporation and, therefore, carry less investor risk than common stock.

(Note that the taxation of bonds will be covered in chapter 18 of this textbook when discussing the "Taxation of Investment Vehicles.")

Convertible Bonds

An investor who is interested in combining the certainty of semi-annual income payments with the opportunity for significant capital gains may be interested in a *convertible bond*. Such bond actually offers *two* opportunities for capital appreciation. The first is through the conversion of the bond into ownership of the common stock of the issuer corporation. The second is through the appreciation in the market value of the convertible bond that occurs as the market price of the underlying common stock increases. As the underlying stock value increases above the value of the convertible as a fixed income investment, the convertible bond's price will increase in almost perfect lock-step with that of the common stock.

> **Example 2-3**: A bond convertible into 40 shares of common stock will sell for at least $1,400 if the underlying common stock increases in price from $30 per share to $40 per share ($10 per share increase multiplied by 40 shares of common stock).

Most forms of convertible bonds also offer some protection in the event that the price of the underlying common shares decline below a specified point. This concept is often referred to as providing a *floor* under the price of the convertible security and, accordingly, a convertible bond will always sell for *no less than* the larger of a) its bond value or b) its conversion value. If the price were to decline to below this value, bond investors would buy the convertible since its yield to maturity would be *greater than* alternative comparable bonds.

> **Example 2-4**: Debbie owns a $1,000 par convertible bond with a coupon rate of 7% (with semi-annual interest payments). The bond matures in 10 years and the bond is convertible into the common shares of ABC Company at $44 per share. The current market price of the shares is $34 and the convertible bond is selling for $1,200 on the secondary market. Comparable debt currently yields 6%. Accordingly, the floor value of the convertible bond is $1,074.39 computed as follows using keystrokes for the HP 10 B II calculator:

2, Shift, P/YR (This sets up the calculator for a semi-annual bond payment, i.e., 2 payments per year)

$1,000 FV

$70 divided by 2=$35 PMT (Note: $70 is the annual interest payment on the bond or 7% coupon _ $1,000 par value)

10, Shift, X P/YR (alternatively, of course, you can do this in your head and enter "20 N")

6 I/YR

PV= $1,074.39

(NOTE: Sometimes, students will derive an answer in a time-value-of-money computation that is within a few dollars of the actual answer. This is because most often they have their calculators set in BEGIN mode. This is rare in investment practice so, unless the problem indicates otherwise, your calculator should always be set to END mode or its default setting.)

Note that because a convertible bond is like a straight bond combined with an option contract, an investor pays a *conversion premium* when he or she buys a convertible bond. This premium (here, $125.61) is the difference between the floor value of the bond (here, $1,074.39) and its current market price (here, $1,200).

There is a separate formula for computing the *conversion value* of the convertible bond, namely its value if converted into common stock at the stock's current market price. This formula is as follows:

CV= [PAR divided by CP] times Ps

where PAR is the par value of the bond, CP is the conversion price and Ps is equal to the current market price of the underlying stock.

> **Example 2-5:** Continuing with the facts of Example 2-4, the conversion value of Debbie's $1,000 par convertible bond is $772.73 computed as follows:

CV= [$1,000/44] x $34= $772.73

Note that, alternatively, you may be told in a problem that a specified convertible bond is convertible into so many shares of common stock. Given the facts above, for example, the problem might have told you that this convertible bond could be converted into 22.73 shares of common stock, without any mention of the conversion price of $44. Nonetheless, in such a problem, the conversion price is implicitly provided, since it is found by dividing the bond's par value, $1,000, by the number of conversion shares or 22.73.

Another important characteristic when evaluating convertible bonds is the *payback period* (sometimes also known as the *break-even time*). This period measures how long the higher interest income from the convertible bond (compared to the dividend income from the common stock) must continue to make up for the difference between the price of the bond and its conversion value. The formula used to compute this period is as follows:

$$\text{Payback} = \frac{\text{Bond Price less Conversion Value}}{\text{Bond Income less Income from Equal Investment in Common Stock}}$$

> **Example 2-6:** Again using the facts of Examples 2-4 and 2-5, and assuming that Debbie sells the bond for a price of $1,200.00 and that ABC stock's dividend yield is zero, the payback period for her convertible bond is 6.10 years computed as follows:

$$\text{Payback} = \frac{\$1,200.00 \text{ less } \$772.73}{\$70.00 \text{ less } \$0.00} = \frac{\$427.27}{\$70.00} = 6.10 \text{ years}$$

Finally, rating agencies such as Standard & Poor's evaluate convertible bond issues and assign quality ratings in much the same manner as regular corporate bonds. However, there are very few convertible bonds with ratings of A or higher. This is because the rating agencies tend to award ratings to convertible bonds (given its convertibility to higher risk equity) that are one level *below* that of the issuer's non-convertible debt. As a result, most convertibles have a rating in the BBB or even BB range. The BB or below rating equates the convertible issue with that of high-yield bonds generally.

Callable Bonds

So-called *callable bonds* do not always run their full term. If the bond does not run full term, the issuer has "called" the bond, meaning that it pays off the obligation before the bond's maturity date. In turn, this process is known as *redemption*. The first date that a bond is vulnerable to being called by the issuer is listed at its time of issue, with call or redemption announcements published regularly in such financial newspapers as the *Wall Street Journal*.

Issuers may wish to call a bond if interest rates drop. If they pay off their outstanding bonds, they may then *float* another bond at the lower rate. Sometimes, however, only part of a specific bond issue is redeemed, rather than all of this same issue. In that case, the particular bonds actually called are chosen by a lottery drawing at the issuer's headquarter offices.

Callable bonds are usually less attractive to a potential investor than those that cannot be called. This is because an investor whose bond has been called is now confronted with reinvesting the bond proceeds at a now lower, less attractive market interest rate. Therefore, to protect investors who expect and rely on long term steady income from the bond, call provisions usually specify that a bond may not be redeemed before a certain number of years have passed, usually ten. Finally, callable bonds also typically carry a slightly higher interest rate compared to similar, non-callable bonds, so as to compensate investors for the possibility of a potential future call event.

FOREIGN BONDS

A foreign bond has three distinct characteristics:

1) The bond is issued by a foreign entity (such as a government, municipality, or foreign corporation; note that if the bond is issued by a foreign corporation, but is denominated in U.S. dollars, it is referred to as a *Yankee bond*)
2) The bond is traded on a foreign financial market
3) The bond is denominated in a foreign currency

Of these three characteristics, the major risk to a domestic investor is that of the denomination of the security in a foreign (non-U.S dollar) currency. As such, the domestic investor is subject to *currency* (or *exchange rate*) risk. Simply defined, currency risk is the potential for loss due to fluctuations in currency exchange rates. This risk may turn a profit on a foreign investment into a loss or vice-versa.

Example 2-7: Sharon, a U.S. citizen, purchases a 1,000 U.K. pound par value bond with a 5% coupon rate. At the time that she made the investment, the currency exchange rate was 1.50 U.S. dollars to 1.00 U.K. pounds. This means that Sharon paid $1,500 in U.S. currency for the U.K. bond. Several years later, the bond matured and Sharon was issued a check for 1,000 U.K pounds (the par value of the foreign bond). Unfortunately, when she goes to convert the pounds to U.S. dollars, she finds that the currency exchange rate has adjusted to a standard of 1.40 U.S. dollars to 1.00 U.K. pounds (or the dollar has "strengthened" against the pound). As a result, Sharon incurs a loss of $100 due entirely to the currency risk fluctuation (that is, she only receives $1,400 for a bond that she purchased for $1,500).

Of course, it is also possible to profit from currency risk. In the example above, if the dollar had "fallen" against the pound (for example, the exchange rate adjusted to 1.80 U.S. dollars to 1.00 U.K. pounds), Sharon would have received $1,800, or $200 more than she had paid for the foreign bond.

There is also *political risk* associated with the purchase of a foreign bond. An investor that owns the bonds of a corporation in his or her home country has specific legal recourse in the event of default. Foreign bonds, however, offer no such protection. Rather, a radical political movement--such as that of the radical Islamists in Iran during the late 1970's--could come to power and immediately disavow all foreign debts and claims. A foreign country may also become engaged in a military conflict (as is now going on in Iraq) and prohibit its currency from circulating outside its borders.

Finally, there is a difference between so-called Eurobonds and foreign bonds generally. A Eurobond is one that is issued and traded in a country *other than* the one in which the currency is denominated. An example is General Electric (G.E.) issuing a bond denominated in U.S. dollars in the German financial markets. Therefore, a Eurobond does *not* necessarily have to originate or end up in Europe, although most debt instruments of this type are issued to European investors by non-European entities.

ZERO COUPON BONDS

We have previously discussed a type of zero coupon bond issued by the U.S. government, the Treasury STRIP. However, corporations and municipalities also issue zero coupon bonds. Such bonds are sold at a deep *original issue discount* (OID) from their face value, with investors then receiving the difference at maturity rather than in the form of periodic interest payments. Zeros, as they are often called, may be issued either in taxable form (for example, by corporations) or as a tax-exempt obligation (by municipalities). These securities are frequently used to meet specific investment goals, particularly when the date of a future need is known well in advance, such as a child's entry date into college or a planned retirement date.

As we know, an investor purchasing zeros must generally include accruing interest in his or her tax income annually, even though no cash is received until the bond matures, is sold, or is called. This leads to the conclusion that taxable zeros are usually only appropriate if positioned within a retirement plan or other tax-deferred account. Tax-exempt zeros are suitable investments for high-income-tax-bracket taxpayers who want to accumulate wealth, have little need of immediate cash, or are not concerned about reinvestment of cash flows. Although investors in a zero-coupon bond are guaranteed that they will receive a reinvestment rate equal to the bond's yield to maturity (assuming that they do not sell the bond or the bond is not called prior to that date), they achieve this advantage at the expense of sacrificing the opportunity to reinvest earlier cash flows if market interest rates increase during the term of the bond. Conversely, of course, the investor will be very pleased if he or she is locked into a high implicit rate of return during a time of declining interest rates.

Bond issuers like zeros because they have an extended period to use the money they have raised *without* paying periodic interest. Thus, they can be an effective cash flow management instrument for the issuer. Investors like zeros because the heavily discounted price means that they can purchase more bonds with the same amount of investment monies, and that they can purchase bonds of different maturities, timed to coincide with anticipated expenses. In reading the bond quotes as published in financial newspapers, the investor will recognize that the bond being traded is a zero by the inclusion of the symbol "zr" next to the bond issuer, whose symbol is immediately followed by the scheduled maturity date of the bond.

PROMISSORY NOTES

Promissory notes are *private transactions* between a lender and borrower primarily used to finance business operations or expansion. Since these notes are private and are not marketable, they are not really "investments" in the meaning attributed to them here. Nevertheless, at times a financial planner is asked by a client to assess the quality and/or terms of such note and should generally be aware of its characteristics and importance as a financing mechanism for the small business owner client.

The written execution of a promissory note may be very helpful in avoiding the treatment of the transaction as a gift, subject to federal gift taxation. While the interpretation of a gift in lieu of what was intended to be a loan is not a significant issue in non-family transactions, it is a potential pitfall where family members are the only parties to the transaction. Further, in the event that the note fails to provide for interest or provides for interest below certain market rates, interest may be imputed to the lender and considered paid by the borrower under the so-called *below market loan rules*. These rules (unless a de-*minimus* rule applies) re-characterize a transaction as an *arms length* loan requiring payment of interest at the applicable federal rate (APR) as published by the Treasury Department on a monthly basis. All of the interest from a promissory note (whether imputed or stated) is fully taxable to the investor at ordinary income tax rates.

Promissory notes tend to be highly customized to reflect the intent of the parties to the agreement; however, most include one of the following types of repayment schedules:
1) Equal monthly payments
2) Equal monthly payments with a final *balloon* payment (which must be paid off in a final lump sum usually reflecting a shorter time period than that of a month)
3) Interest-only payments (this type of note is becoming more popular in real estate/home mortgage financing as a means of permitting a first-time homebuyer to enter the market; of course, the significant disadvantage of the interest-only note or loan is the fact that little to no equity is accumulated in the property purchased)
4) A single payment of interest and principal (this type of repayment schedule is normally only for loans that are less than one year in time)

A promissory note should also specify whether the borrower has the right of prepayment on the note and, if so, whether a penalty is in effect. Such a provision may be a valuable inducement for the borrower to execute the note and substantially lower the total interest cost of the loan. You should note that in the context of home mortgage financing, pursuant to the provisions of the Truth in Lending Act, the lender is *required* to provide to the borrower a written statement indicating the total amount of interest that is paid over the term of the loan, in addition to informing the borrower of any prepayment penalty associated with paying off the note before its stated term of expiration.

IMPORTANT CONCEPTS

Debt security

Treasury note

Treasury bond

Treasury STRIP

Treasury Inflation Protected Security (TIPS)

Series I bond

Mortgage backed security

Government National Mortgage Association Certificate *(Ginnie Mae)*

Federal National Mortgage Association Certificate *(Fannie Mae)*

Federal Home Loan Mortgage Corporation Certificate *(Freddie Mac)*

Municipal bond

Tax equivalent yield (T.E.Y.)

General obligation (G.O.) bond

Revenue bond

Private purpose bond

Par value

Coupon rate

Mortgage bond

Debenture

Investment grade bond

High yield bond

Convertible bond

Conversion value

Payback period

Callable bond

Foreign bond

Yankee bond

Zero coupon bond

Promissory note

QUESTIONS FOR REVIEW

1. What is the most common example of a *debt security* that is issued by a corporation or government?

2. Why might the *floating* of a debt security by a corporation be a more preferable financing mechanism than merely issuing stock?

3. What is the term of maturity of a Treasury note? What is the term of maturity for a Treasury bond?

4. A Treasury STRIP is what type of debt security? If purchased, where should it be positioned within an individual's portfolio?

5. What is the major advantage of an investment in U.S. Treasury securities (from the standpoint of the individual or institutional investor)?

6. What characteristics are important to an investor who is considering an investment in Treasury Inflation Protected Securities (TIPS)?

7. How is the semi-annual interest payment on a TIPS investment computed?

8. What is a Series I bond?

9. Which government or quasi-governmental agency issues each of the following *pass through* certificates?

    • Ginnie Mae

    • Fannie Mae

    • Freddie Mac

    Which one of these is a direct guarantee of the U.S Treasury?

10. Explain what is meant by the term *mortgage backed security*? What is the primary investment risk associated with such security?

11. There are three primary types of municipal bonds. What are they and which has the least amount of investor risk? Why?

12. Who (what type of taxpayer) is most suited to make an investment in municipal bonds? Why?

13. What is the measure used to compare the yield from a municipal bond with its taxable equivalent?

14. What is a major disadvantage of purchasing a private purpose or private activity municipal bond?

15. Define the following terms:

    • Par value of a bond

    • Coupon rate

    • Indenture

    • Sinking fund

    • Investment grade bond

    • High yield bond

16. In what form are most corporate bonds issued today?

17. If a bond investor is primarily interested in safety, would she purchase a mortgage bond or debenture? Why?

18. What are the two advantages of investing in a convertible security?

19. Give an example of how to compute the conversion value of a convertible security. Why is determining this value important?

20. Why does an investor pay a premium when he or she purchases a convertible security?

21. If you are a potential investor, everything else being equal, would you prefer to purchase a callable or non-callable corporate bond? Why?

22. What are three distinct characteristics of a foreign bond? Which one is likely the most important to an investor?

23. How is a *zero coupon bond* (a *zero*) different than a regular corporate bond? Where should a zero be positioned within an investor's portfolio and why?

24. What is a *Eurobond*?

25. Why might it be advantageous to execute a promissory note between family members?

26. If no interest or a below market interest rate of interest is charged in executing a promissory note among family members, what tax consequence is likely to occur? Explain.

27. What is a *balloon payment*?

SUGGESTIONS FOR ADDITIONAL READING

Tools and Techniques of Investment Planning, Stephen R. Leimberg, Robert T. LeClair, Robert J. Doyle, Jr., and Thomas R. Robinson, The National Underwriter Company, 2004.

Investments: An Introduction, 7th edition, Herbert B. Mayo, Thomson/ South-Western, 2002.

Investment Analysis and Portfolio Management, 7th edition, Frank K. Reilly and Keith C. Brown, Thomson/South-Western, 2003.

The Wall Street Journal Guide to Money and Investing, 3rd edition, Kenneth M. Morris and Virginia B. Morris, Fireside Publishing, 2004.

CHAPTER THREE

Stocks and Stock Attributes

• • •

Stocks are what most individuals think of when considering the possibility of a financial asset that may generate a significant return. However, as we shall learn, with the possibility of increased return, there is also increased investor risk.

Upon completing this chapter, you should be able to:

- Analyze the advantages and disadvantages of an investment consisting of equity ownership in a corporation (stock) versus that of debt ownership (bonds)
- Describe the characteristics and uses of common stock in investment planning
- Describe the characteristics and uses of preferred stock in investment planning
- Distinguish various forms of stock attributes, such as warrants, stock rights, and/or stock options
- Discuss when it may be appropriate to use stock or stock attributes as equity-based compensation for executives or other valued corporate employees
- Identify the use of American Depository Receipts (ADRs) in the financial marketplace

EQUITY VS. DEBT

The term that is most frequently used to refer to a stock issue in the primary marketplace is *equity*. Accordingly, each equity owner (referred to as a *shareholder)* is entitled to a proportionate share of the assets and profits (dividends) of a corporation. As an added incentive to become such an owner, shareholders are given voting rights associated with their stock whereby they exercise control. While most shareholders are only a small minority of the total number of shareholders, they nonetheless are entitled to "vote their shares," most often in the form of a proxy sent to them by the corporate secretary prior to the shareholder's annual meeting.

As a comparison to debt issued by a corporation, equity has one major advantage: it does not become an ongoing liability of the business (therefore, depleting much-needed cash). However, equity has one major disadvantage: Unlike interest paid on debt, the corporation does *not* get an income tax deduction for any dividends declared and paid on shares of stock. Therefore, it is more expensive to the corporation to issue stock than debt (at least from an income tax perspective). In addition, dividends on stock are generally taxed as *ordinary income*, thereby leading to a double taxation effect on distributions of corporate profits. While, under tax legislation passed in 2003, certain *qualifying dividends* (generally those paid by domestic corporations and some foreign corporations) are entitled to a tax-favored rate similar to capital gains, other dividends are subject to much higher ordinary income tax rates.

Finally, there may be a distinct dislike of additional equity ownership (stocks) where a corporation is *closely held* (not publicly traded). In these corporations, which are numerous in the small business marketplace of today, stock is held only among a small number of shareholders, typically family members. Normally, these entities do not desire additional owners with the attendant voting rights and to whom they are ultimately responsible. As a result, to reward existing owners/employees for their efforts in growing the business and making it successful, closely held corporations will often structure executive compensation arrangements that are payable in *cash*, rather than in stock or stock rights. An alternative financing mechanism to stock for a closely held corporate owner is, of course, debt in the form of a bank loan, although usually a *personal guarantee* of repayment is a condition of the loan.

COMMON STOCK

Common stock represents units of ownership in a publicly traded corporation. Owners are entitled to vote on the selection of the Board of Directors of the corporation, and other important matters, as well as to receive any dividends that are declared on their shares. In the event that the corporation is *liquidated* (terminates business with its assets converted to cash) the claims of secured and unsecured creditors and owners of bonds and preferred stockholders take precedence over the common stockholders.

Common stocks are typically purchased through a stock brokerage firm, often referred to as a *broker/dealer*. This term is appropriate because not only may the firm purchase stock for other investors, but it also purchases shares for its own account and, therefore, acts as a "dealer" in those stocks. Once an account is established with the investor, brokers purchase or sell common shares through a variety of orders, the most common of which is a so-called *market order*. Such order is a direction by the investor/customer to buy or sell securities at the best obtainable price during the market activity of that day. In other words, in a market order, the price is basically determined by the market. Conversely, a *limit order* is a direction by the customer to buy or sell securities at a specified price determined by the customer (not the market). It is increasingly common for these orders to be placed using personal computers via online brokerage accounts.

Many investors, however, prefer to own common stocks *indirectly* as part of a *mutual fund* or *open end investment company*. Such a fund provides a number of advantages, but most notably diversification of risk and the professional management of assets. Mutual funds and managed accounts are the subject of chapter 4, in this textbook.

Some believe that payments of dividends on common stocks (that is, a distribution of corporate profits for that year) are not guaranteed. Quite the contrary! A number of so-called *growth stocks* (for example, Microsoft) have historically not paid a dividend and have reinvested profits back into the corporation for future capital appreciation. Therefore, an investor who is considering an investment in an individual common stock (or a stock mutual fund) is likely to be more interested in the possibility of appreciation in the underlying value of the shares of stock rather than regular income from the payment of dividends. This motivation is further encouraged by two consequences of income taxation: first, the shareholder may choose when to *recognize* his or her gain for tax purposes and second, once recognized (the stock is sold or otherwise disposed of), and assuming a requisite holding period is met, any gain is taxable at preferential long term capital gain rates, currently no higher than 15%. See chapter 18 for more on the taxation of common shares.

Finally, common stocks are highly *marketable*. This means that they may easily be converted to cash, if necessary, as there are usually a substantial number of interested buyers. However, common stocks are not considered liquid because the investor is not likely to receive an amount equal to or greater than that paid for the shares originally. Rather, the market price of common stock shares may change significantly throughout the course of a trading day or series of days. It is also possible that the investor could lose *all* of his or her initial investment. The risk that an investor takes in purchasing common shares is collectively referred to as *market risk*, which may be minimized (but not entirely eliminated) by proper asset allocation and diversification of the investor's portfolio of securities.

Stock Dividends and Stock Splits

A *stock dividend* is a dividend paid in *additional shares* of company stock, rather than in cash. Since all common shareholders receive their proportionate share of the dividend, the total value of all the common stock of the company is unchanged. However, when such a dividend is declared and paid, the value of each common stockholder's shares is proportionally reduced. Unless the stockholder has the option to receive the declared dividend in cash rather than stock (which would entail *constructive receipt* (meaning that the dividend is taxable) a stock dividend is generally *not* taxable for federal income tax purposes.

So who is entitled to a stock (or cash) dividend? This is determined by referencing those who are listed as stockholders on the corporate books as a *holder of record* as of the *date of record* when the dividend is declared. The date of record is the second business day after the *ex-dividend date*. Accordingly, for an investor to be entitled to a dividend, he or she must purchase the stock *before* the ex-dividend date.

> **Example 3-1:** If Friday, August 19, 2005 is the date of record of the corporation, when must the investor purchase the stock of XYZ Company in order to be entitled to its stock dividend? Answer: Count back two business days from August 19, 2005 to determine that the ex-dividend date is Wednesday, August 17, 2005. This means that the investor must purchase the stock of XYZ Company no later than Tuesday, August 16, 2005 to be entitled to its stock dividend declared by the corporate board of directors.

A *stock split* is defined as a distribution of more than 25% of the outstanding common shares of the corporation designed to lower the stock's price per share (and, thereby, make it more attractive for purchase by new investors). In a split, the par value of each share of stock is reduced and the number of common shares is increased proportionately. For example, if a stock were selling for $120 per share before a 2 for 1 split, then after the split, each shareholder would have twice the number of shares held previously, but the price per share would be $60. Unsophisticated investors typically love stock splits since they believe they now own more of the corporation for no more investment money expended. However, you should note that the investor owns *exactly* the same percentage of the corporation as before; all that has happened is that each share now represents a correspondingly smaller percentage of the company. Because of this mere "shuffling of the ownership cards," stock splits are *never* taxable to the shareholder.

The opposite of a stock split is a *reverse split*. In a reverse split, the company reduces (rather than increases) the number of shares outstanding. Such a variation of the normal split is usually initiated by companies wanting to increase the price per share of each outstanding share because the company is about to be acquired. In this manner, the company may "fend off" an interested, but unwanted, acquirer.

Book Value vs. Fair Market Value

The *book value* of a corporation will be further considered in chapter 12 of this textbook when discussing how to value equity securities (stocks). Such value is defined as the accounting value of the equity as shown on the corporate balance sheet and is the sum of the common stock outstanding, any capital in excess of par, and any retained earnings. It is similar to the *net worth* computation performed in preparing a statement of personal financial position. Generally, a low book value may indicate that the company's assets are underestimated, and that its stock is a potentially good value for prospective investors.

Book value is frequently used when analyzing certain ratios that may aid in determining a proper amount to be paid for a stock as well as by appraisers in estimating at what multiple a closely held corporation should be purchased. However, it should be noted that such value is rarely, if ever, the single most appropriate method to value a corporation that features a number of individual security investments on its balance sheet. Rather, that corporation should be valued after adjusting those investments to their current *fair market value* as determined by the market price for the date of valuation. Since book value, by its very nature, reflects only a *historical cost approach*, it is only one of several factors to consider in valuing any business.

Return on Equity (ROE)

Stock analysts oftentimes examine the components of a company's profitability in order to determine whether the stock should be purchased. A primary component or ratio that analysts evaluate is that of a company's *return on equity* (ROE). Indeed, this ratio is the key component in determining the earnings growth of a company (and, therefore, the expected price increase in the value of its common stock). ROE is calculated with use of the following formula:

$$\text{ROE} = \frac{\text{Earnings available for common shares (EPS)}}{\text{Common equity (net worth or the company's book value)}}$$

> **Example 3-2:** Assume that you have determined that a company has a book value of $100 per share. It has earnings for the year of $2.0 million and has 500,000 common shares outstanding. All of its earnings are distributed to the shareholders in the form of dividends. Therefore, the earnings per share (EPS) is $4.00. Thus, the company has a return on equity (ROE) of 4% ($4.00 divided by $100).

Of course, the higher the return on equity of a company, the better it is as an indicator of the company's financial strength. However, the more important analysis is the *direction* of this ratio; in other words, if it is increasing in percentage, it usually means that the company's earnings per share (EPS) are growing and, accordingly, so are the prospects for the future market value of its stock.

Dividend Payout Ratio

A corollary ratio to that of return on equity (ROE) is the *dividend payout ratio* (DPR) of a company. This ratio is the percentage of earnings per share that a company uses to pay out a dividend to its common shareholders and is computed as follows:

$$\text{DPR} = \frac{\text{Common dividends paid per share}}{\text{Earnings available for common shares (EPS)}}$$

The normal range for this ratio is usually 25% to 50% of a company's earnings per share, although this range may be increasing given the legislative incentive to pay out dividends under the 2003 Tax

Act (JGTRRA). In general, however, the *higher* the dividend payout ratio, the *more mature* the company is with respect to number of years in business operation. By contrast, younger companies or particularly profitable companies with good growth prospects (and thus a great need for cash) will tend to retain most, if not all, of their earnings.

Initial Public Offerings (IPOs) and Secondary Offerings

If a small business finds that its product or service is in great demand, the owners may decide to *go public* and do an *initial public offering* (IPO) of its stock. To do this, first, the owners engage an investment banking firm to *underwrite* the stock offering; that is, to purchase all the public shares at a pre-established price and then resell them to the public (presumably at a significant profit). The proposed stock sale is publicized in the financial press with ads commonly known as *tombstones* since they are in heavy print with a notable black border. The day before the actual sale of the company's shares to the actual public, the underwriter typically *prices the issue*, or establishes the price that it will pay for each share. This may be done either on a *firm commitment* basis (the underwriter will purchase any shares that remain unsold) or using the underwriter's *best efforts* (the underwriter will make every effort to sell all the shares, but the company does not receive any money for unsold shares). Technically, when the investment banker agrees to sell the company's stock using best efforts, the banker does not underwrite the securities at all because it does not buy any securities. Rather, the banker acts only as a broker to sell whatever stock it can at the stipulated price.

With an IPO, there is a general expectation of underpricing of the newly offered shares. Therefore, there may be an investment opportunity for sophisticated investors. But, if so, how great is the underpricing on average and how fast does the market adjust the price for the underpricing? Studies have tried to answer both these questions. With respect to the first, there is an average underpricing of approximately 18 percent, but it varies according to the year in which the IPO occurred and other factors. The major variables that tend to cause differential underpricing seem to be risk measures associated with the company or industry; the size of the company; the prestige of the underwriter; and the status of the company's accounting firm. In answer to the second question, studies indicate that the market adjusts to the underpricing within one day after the offering. Accordingly, this leaves a very short period of time for either an individual or institutional investor to take advantage of any market inefficiencies.

If a company has already issued shares, but wants to raise additional capital through the sale of more stock, it does so by what is called a *secondary offering*. Companies are often loath to issue more stock, since the larger the supply of stock outstanding, the less valuable each share is that has already been issued (not to mention the commensurate reduction in earnings per share). This is called *dilution*. For this reason, a company typically issues new shares *only* if its stock price is considered to be too high in the secondary marketplace. Alternatively, to raise needed capital, the company may decide to issue bonds, or, sometimes, convertible bonds or preferred stock (to be subsequently discussed).

Private Placements

Instead of incurring the time and expense of an IPO, some small businesses choose to sell stock privately. In such an arrangement, referred to as a *private placement*, the company designs an issue and sells it to a small group of institutions or sophisticated individual investors. Since the transaction is exempt from registration with the SEC, the company enjoys lower issuing costs. In addition, the institution that purchases the issue typically benefits because the company passes some of these cost savings on to the institution in the form of a higher investment return. In fact, the purchasing institution should require a higher rate of return since there is no secondary market for the stock, thereby resulting in a greater market risk.

A private placement may also be offered to certain individual investors after disclosure through an *offering circular* (instead of a prospectus, which technically is only relevant for a public offering). Specifically, the placement may be sold to a maximum of 35 non-accredited investors and an unlimited number of *accredited investors*. An accredited investor is currently defined as a purchaser who has a net worth of $1.0 million or an individual with an annual income of $200,000 or a couple with a joint income of $300,000. If an investor does not satisfy any of these criteria (in other words, he or she is a *non-accredited investor*), the investor must be sophisticated (experienced) and sign an investment letter acknowledging that he or she is aware of the investment risks associated with purchasing a non-registered security. Further, if he or she cannot evaluate the offering independently, Regulation D of the Securities Act of 1933 requires the use of an agent such as a lawyer or accountant.

PREFERRED STOCK

Preferred stock is really a type of hybrid security since it combines features of both debt (bonds) and equity (common stock). As its name implies, preferred stock carries a preference with respect to the earnings of the corporation. Dividends on such stock must be paid *before* any dividends can be paid to holders of common stock. However, like common stock, there is no requirement that a dividend be declared on preferred stock at any time. Nevertheless, preferred stock differs from common stock in that it pays a *fixed rate* once a dividend is declared and that these dividends are *cumulative* in nature (meaning that any preferred dividends that are not paid as scheduled must subsequently be accumulated and paid at some future date). Finally, owners of preferred stock have precedence over common stockholders if a corporation liquidates its assets.

Like a bond, preferred stock is issued at a par value, although instead of $1,000 par value as in the case of a bond, preferred stock normally carries a par of $100. Then, as noted, preferred stocks pay a fixed dividend rate based on a stated percentage of the stock's par value. This fixed percentage is normally higher than that of bonds, however. This is because preferred stock dividends are only paid *after* the company satisfies its bond interest obligations. Since this reduced legal obligation increases the uncertainty of returns, preferred stock investors demand a higher rate of return for this enhanced risk.

The typical purchaser of preferred stock is *not* the individual investor. Rather, it is a corporate treasurer with excess funds to invest. If the treasurer were to buy bonds, all of this interest is taxable to the corporation. However, a favorable tax privilege is available if the treasurer buys preferred stock instead. Generally, a corporation is entitled to deduct 70% of the dividends it receives from other domestic corporations from its taxable income. Therefore, only 30% of the dividends received by the corporate purchaser are subject to federal income tax. This tax advantage stimulates the demand for preferred stocks by corporations as purchasers.

Preferred stock is a *perpetuity* because, unlike a bond, it has *no* specified maturity date. Accordingly, to recover their initial investment, investors must sell their preferred shares. In addition, because of the perpetual time frame of the security, the prices of preferred stocks are extremely sensitive to changes in interest rates. When market interest rates increase, the prices of preferred shares tend to decline, irrespective of any corporate quarterly earnings results that primarily impact common stock issues. Obviously, the inverse relationship between interest rates and preferred share price also holds when rates increase, but preferred stocks generally exhibit the price volatility characteristic of long term bonds rather than shorter term fixed income investments.

Some preferred stocks are also *convertible* into common stock. This means that they may be exchanged at a specified rate for the common stock of the corporation at a time chosen by the preferred stockholder. Usually, it will be advantageous to convert when the price of the common shares is increasing relative to the fixed rate of exchange. However, once converted, the preferred stockholder sacrifices the preference in dividends and corporation liquation that are the hallmarks of the security form.

Perpetuity Valuation

Because preferred stock is a *perpetuity,* an investor may compute its proper value simply by dividing the stated annual dividend by the investor's *required rate of return* (see chapter 10 of this textbook) on the preferred stock. In formula terms, this is written as follows:

$$V = \frac{\text{Dividend}}{k_p}$$

Example 3-3: Assume that a preferred stock has a par value of $100 and has a stated dividend rate of 7% (or, in this case, $7 per year). Because of the expected rate of inflation and the uncertainty of the dividend payment, the investor's required rate of return on the stock is 9%. Therefore, the proper value of the preferred stock to the investor is $77.78 (or $7 divided by .09). Given this proper value (what the investor *should* pay for the preferred stock), if the stock's current market price is $80, the investor would likely *not* purchase the stock. Conversely, if the stock's current market price is $70, the stock is probably a good buy.

WARRANTS

A stock warrant is essentially a long-term *call option* (see chapter 7 of this textbook) to purchase the stock of the corporation issuing the warrant. That is, like a call option (or *call*), warrants give the owner the right to purchase a specified number of common stock shares for a specified period of time at a specified price. However, unlike a call where the owner has the right to purchase a *round lot* of shares (100 shares), warrants generally do not give the owner the right to buy nearly as many shares. In addition, there are other important differences between a call and a warrant. These are as follows:

- A warrant is issued by a corporation, whereas a call is created by an individual.
- A warrant is *customized* to fit the needs of the issuer and owner, whereas a call includes standardized terms as required by the Options Clearing Corporation (OCC).
- A warrant typically has a maturity date (or date by which it may be exercised) of at least several years, whereas a call normally expires at the end of nine months if not exercised before that date.

Warrants guarantee, for a small premium, the opportunity to buy stock at a fixed price during a particular period of time. In essence, they are a bet that the future price of the issuer's stock is going to increase. Thus, investors buy warrants if they are optimistic or bullish regarding the prospects for the stock.

> **Example 3-4:** David purchases a warrant for $1 per share that gives him the right to buy 50 shares of KRF stock at $10 per share for a period of five years from date of purchase. Assume that KRF stock goes up to $14 per share after three years and David exercises the warrant. Accordingly, he makes a profit of $150 on the 50 shares [50 x {$14-($10+$1)}].

If the price of the warrant is *below* the specified price when the warrant expires, the warrant is worthless. However, since not much money has been expended for the warrant (in the above example, only $50), and because it has a longer right of exercise than a regular option, warrants are actively traded in the secondary market.

If corporations issue warrants at all, they usually do so in conjunction with new bond issues or preferred stock issues. These warrants give the bond or stock purchaser what is known as an *equity kicker*, making the particular issue more attractive to buyers. In addition, issuing the bonds or preferred stock with a warrant will usually lower the coupon or dividend rate necessary to sell the issue. Why? Because the purchaser is willing to accept a lower rate given the opportunity to buy appreciated common stock. In turn, the corporation's cost of debt service is reduced. Therefore, the use of warrants is especially useful for a younger company that anticipates rapid growth but needs to hold onto as much cash as possible to finance future expansion.

Warrants are taxed under the same general rules as options, when acquired other than as an employment incentive and in lieu of compensation. Specifically, no gain or loss is recognized when the warrant is acquired and the owner does not incur a taxable event until a) the time that the warrant period ends and the warrant expires unexercised or b) the time the option is sold. When a warrant is sold or expires unexercised, the character of the gain or loss is generally as a capital asset with a preference for gains if the warrant is held for more than a year from date of purchase. If the warrant is exercised, there is usually no taxable event until the sale of the underlying stock that is acquired. Warrants received as an employment incentive are generally taxable as ordinary income at their fair market value on the date of receipt.

STOCK RIGHTS

A stock right, sometimes called a *subscription right* is issued by a corporation that plans to raise funds by issuing new stock to the public. Each current shareholder is usually given one right for each share of stock that they own. These rights give the current shareholders the opportunity to buy new shares of the new stock issue, thereby maintaining their overall percentage ownership of the corporation. Shareholders who do not wish to exercise their rights may sell them for cash before they expire. If they do not sell them before they expire and do not exercise them, they expire worthless.

Like a warrant, a stock right gives the owner the right to purchase common shares. However, in contrast to the warrant, the life of a stock right is *very short*, usually for only a very few weeks, and thus equates to a short term call option. Since the time until expiration is generally very small, a stock right typically has little or no speculative premium like other options. Accordingly, the value of the right may be determined with use of the following formula:

$$V = \frac{(\text{Market price of the current stock less Subscription price of the new shares})}{(\text{\# of rights required to purchase one new share of stock} + 1)}$$

> **Example 3-5:** Assume that the market price of ABC current stock is $50 and that the subscription price of the new shares is $44. Further assume that, under the terms of the rights offering, it takes seven rights in addition to a set price for the stock to buy one share of any newly issued common stock. Therefore, as long as the price of ABC stock remains at $50 a share, the value of each right is $.75 [($50-$44) divided by (7+1)]. For each seven rights that the investor has, he or she can contribute an additional $44 and buy a share of stock currently worth $50.

The financial marketplace occasionally confuses the terms *warrant* and *stock right*. However, in actuality, the controlling difference is how the option to purchase shares of common stock was obtained. If the option was received as part of the purchase of a bond or preferred stock and for the purpose of purchasing existing shares, it is a *warrant*. If the option was distributed to a current shareholder as an opportunity to purchase additional shares, it is a *stock right*. Sometimes investors receive a stock right designated as a warrant. Nonetheless, to most, it is a distinction without a difference.

STOCK OPTIONS

Stock options are of two basic types: 1) those options that are purchased for investment (or sometimes speculative) purposes and 2) options used as executive compensation benefit to reward performance. The first of these will be considered when discussing derivative investments in chapter 7 of this text and the second has already been addressed in the second course, *Insurance and Employee Benefits*, of Kaplan University's Certificate in Financial Planning Program. You should also note that options purchased for investment purposes may be written and traded on any *listed* stock of a recognized exchange, whereas options granted in lieu of executive cash compensation is usually in the form of *employer* stock.

With respect to the first (or investment) type of stock option, several points need to be made here. First, options are a form of *derivative* investment vehicle; that is, their value is based on (is a derivative of) the price of the underlying stock on which the option is written. There are both options to buy the underlying stock (known as a *call*) and to sell such stock (known as a *put*). Of course, which of these options (if either) the investor purchases depends on his or her expectation of what direction the stock (and the broader overall stock market) is likely to take; for example, if there is an expectation that the price of the stock is likely to *increase*, he or she may purchase a call and, conversely, if there is an expectation that the price of the stock is likely to *fall*, the purchase of a *put* option is likely appropriate. Regardless, many investors use stock options only for purposes of *hedging*, broadly defined as an investment strategy that aims to reduce the risk of loss associated with price movements in the underlying stock. In addition, some investors use stock options as a short-term strategy designed to produce income, such as the writing of what is known as a *covered call* (see chapter 7).

Some individuals, however, *speculate* with stock options. Specifically, *Barrons* defines speculation as "an activity that offers the possibility of a significant reward (rate of return) but with the assumption of a higher than average possibility of a significant loss." Practically, speculation is also accomplished over a very short time frame, often mere hours or days. If recommending stock options as a possible strategy for their clients, financial planners should deemphasize (*indeed, discourage*) the speculative aspects of the strategy and, instead, focus on options as a method of risk management (hedging). In other words, stock options as a financial planning technique should be understood as an alternative *investment*, taking into account the possibility of measurable return only in the context of measurable risk assumed by the investor. Only then will the financial planner (and, specifically, the CFP® certificant) comply with his or her *fiduciary duty* to the client.

STOCK AS EQUITY-BASED COMPENSATION

Like stock options used for executive compensation, employer stock shares (or a variation thereof) may also be used as an equity-based incentive for performance. Again, the use of employer stock for this purpose has been previously discussed in the *Insurance and Employee Benefits* course. However, you should be aware that a company's stock may not only be traded on an exchange, but also offered as an employee benefit.

There are three major types of stock used as equity-based compensation. They are:

1) Restricted stock

2) Phantom stock

3) Stock appreciation rights (SARs) (Note: These should not be confused with stock rights or stock *subscription rights* discussed earlier in this chapter.)

A *restricted stock plan* is an arrangement to compensate employees (almost always executives of the company) by awarding them shares of employer stock subject to certain restrictions. Such plan permits the employer to grant the executive an equity interest in the company, but withdraw it if the executive leaves before a certain period of time or goes to work for a competitor (this restriction is known for tax purposes as a *substantial risk of forfeiture*). If the executive satisfies the terms of the restriction, he or she then defeats the risk of forfeiture and becomes *substantially vested* in the stock, at which time a taxable event occurs. When the executive becomes substantially vested in the restricted stock, its fair market value at that time (less any amount that the executive has paid for the stock, which is usually nothing or very little) is taxed as compensation income. Gain on any subsequent sale of the stock is generally taxable as capital gain income, at preferential long term capital gain rates. Alternatively, an executive may elect to recognize income as of the date he receives the restricted stock, rather than waiting to become substantially vested. This election, known as a *Section 83(b) election* under the Internal Revenue Code Section number that provides for the same, must be made within 30 days of receiving the restricted stock or it is not effective.

Because of recent Financial Accounting Standards Board (FASB) rules, it is anticipated that the use of restricted employer stock as a compensation technique, in lieu of stock options, will significantly increase. Specifically, FASB has ruled that the value of any unexercised compensatory stock options must be shown as an expense on the corporation's income statement. Accordingly, there will be a reduction in earnings generated by the corporation, which in turn is likely to temporarily depress the trading value of its stock. Since the restricted stock alternative does not have this same accounting disadvantage, while still providing much the same employment incentive, it is likely to be increasingly used as a deferred compensation technique.

Phantom stock and *stock appreciation rights* (SARs) use different benefit formulas to accomplish the same objective of rewarding an executive for superior performance. In both, no actual stock is set aside, nor are any shares of stock actually distributed. The value of the employer stock is simply the measure that is used to determine the amount of executive benefit awarded. *A phantom stock* benefit generally refers to a plan formula based on a number of shares of hypothetical stock, whereby the employee receives a cash amount equal to the difference in the value of that stock when the agreement is entered into and when the benefit is payable. A *stock appreciation right* (SAR) formula provides that the executive's future benefits are to be determined by a formula based on the appreciated value of the company's stock over the period between adoption of the plan and the date of payment. Both of these compensation techniques are used where the company does not wish to have additional shareholders (for example, in a closely held corporation among family members).

AMERICAN DEPOSITORY RECEIPTS (ADRs)

American Depository Receipts (ADRs) are receipts for the stock of a foreign-based corporation held in the vault of a U.S. bank and entitling the shareholder to all dividends and capital gains. Therefore, instead of buying shares of foreign-based companies in overseas markets, Americans can buy shares in the form of an ADR. Indeed, such receipts were introduced as a result of the difficulties involved in buying shares in foreign countries and, particularly, the difficulties associated with trading at different market prices and with different currency values.

ADRs are priced in U.S. dollars and investors can buy or sell them in the same way that they trade American stocks. Any dividends paid on the foreign stock are also paid in U.S. dollars. ADRs are listed on all the major U.S. exchanges, including the New York Stock Exchange (NYSE), but may also be the subject of a private placement. The concept of ADRs has also been extended to other geographical markets, including the European exchanges, where foreign stocks to that region are traded in the form of European Depository Receipts (and denominated in the Euro currency).

Foreign taxes on any declared dividends are generally withheld before being passed through to the ADR holder. The holder will then receive a foreign tax credit on his or her U.S. income tax return (IRS Form 1040) for income tax paid to the foreign country. The 15% maximum tax rate for *qualified dividends* is generally applicable to U.S. individual investors in ADRs that are issued by entities that satisfy the definition of a *qualified foreign corporation*. Such corporation includes any foreign corporation that a) is eligible for the benefits of a comprehensive income tax treaty with the United States or b) has issued stock that is readily tradeable on an established securities market in the United States.

Typically, investing in ADRs is the simplest way in which a U.S. investor may engage in international investing. However, alternatives to ADR's, for the purpose of achieving international diversification of an investor's portfolio, include investing in international or global mutual funds, international exchange-traded funds (see the upcoming chapter 4 of this textbook), or investing in multi-national corporations listed on the U.S. stock exchanges.

IMPORTANT CONCEPTS

Equity	Secondary offering
Common stock	Private placement
Cash dividend	Preferred stock
Stock dividend	Perpetuity
Ex-dividend date	Warrant
Stock split	Stock (subscription) right
Reverse split	Stock option
Book value	Restricted stock
Return on equity (ROE)	Phantom stock
Dividend payout ratio	Stock appreciation right (SAR)
Initial public offering	American depository receipt (ADR)

QUESTIONS FOR REVIEW

1. What is one major advantage in financing future business expansion through equity ownership rather than debt obligations? What is a major disadvantage of equity ownership?

2. What does the purchase of common stock represent? How is this type of stock typically purchased?

3. Contrast a *market order* to purchase stock to that of a *limit order* for the same.

4. Why does an investor typically purchase common stock?

5. Are common stocks both *marketable* and *liquid*? Explain.

6. What is the difference between a stock dividend and a stock split? Which one is *never* taxable?

7. How does a corporation determine which stockholders are eligible to receive a dividend?

8. What is a *reverse split*? Why would a corporation do this?

9. Define the term *book value* of a corporation.

10. If a company has an EPS of $23.50 and a book value of $150 per share, what is the company's *return on equity* (ROE)?

11. What is the normal range of DPR for a company? If a company has a high DPR, what is this likely to represent?

12. Explain the difference if an investment banker uses a firm commitment agreement in an IPO versus that of its *best efforts*. If you are the issuer of the stock, which do you prefer and why?

13. How long have studies shown that the market adjusts to the general expectation of under-pricing of shares offered as part of an IPO?

14. What is a *secondary offering* of a company's stock?

15. Which individuals are permitted to purchase stock that is sold as part of a private placement?

16. How does preferred stock differ from common stock?

17. Why is the coupon rate that is stated on preferred stock normally higher than that of bonds?

18. Who is the typical purchaser of preferred stock and why is this the case?

19. What formula is used to determine the proper value of preferred stock?

20. What is a *warrant* and why is it typically offered by a corporation?

21. Specify three differences between a warrant and a call option.

22. A stock right is also sometimes known as a *subscription right*. Why is this term appropriate?

23. Warrants and stock rights are sometimes confused in the financial marketplace. How can an investor tell the difference?

24. Stock options are of two basic types. What are they?

25. Should a financial planner *speculate* with stock options? Why or why not?

26. Explain each of the three major types of stock that are used as equity-based compensation.

27. Why is restricted stock expected to increase in importance in future years as a preferable method of executive deferred compensation?

28. What is an American depository receipt (ADR)? Why would an investor be interested in purchasing an ADR?

29. Which types of foreign corporations issuing dividends qualify for the favorable tax rates established under the 2003 Tax Act (JGTRRA)?

SUGGESTIONS FOR ADDITIONAL READING

Tools and Techniques of Investment Planning, Stephen R. Leimberg, Robert T. LeClair, Robert J. Doyle, Jr., and Thomas R. Robinson, The National Underwriter Company, 2004.

Investments: An Introduction, 7th edition, Herbert B. Mayo, Thomson/ South-Western, 2002.

Investment Analysis and Portfolio Management, 7th edition, Frank K. Reilly and Keith C. Brown, Thomson/South-Western, 2003.

The Wall Street Journal Guide to Money and Investing, 3rd edition, Kenneth M. Morris and Virginia B. Morris, Fireside Publishing, 2004.

CHAPTER FOUR

Mutual Funds and Managed Investments

• • •

An open-end investment company (popularly referred to as a *mutual* fund) is likely the most favored form of investment asset for the small or individual investor. It provides both the advantage of diversification as well as access to professional management. However, there are several other forms of managed investment vehicles. The purpose of this chapter is to describe such vehicles and identify their appropriate use for the potential investor.

Upon completing this chapter, you should be able to:

- Describe the types of mutual funds and their use in investment planning for the individual investor
- Identify the characteristics of closed-end investment companies and/or unit investment trusts (UITs)
- Explain the recent innovation of exchange traded funds (ETFs) and/or hedge funds in the secondary marketplace
- Distinguish privately managed accounts from separately managed accounts and identify the characteristics of investors who may be interested in either type of account
- Explain what types of investments have been traditionally structured as a limited partnership investment and why this is the case

OPEN-END INVESTMENT COMPANIES (MUTUAL FUNDS)

Open-end investment companies are most frequently referred to as *mutual funds*. These funds continue to sell shares to investors after the initial sale of shares that first capitalizes the offering (thus, the term *open-end*). The make-up of the fund then continuously changes as new investors buy additional shares, while other existing investors or shareholders cash in by selling their shares back to the company (*redeeming* the shares). However, the shares are otherwise non-negotiable and may only be liquidated by the company offering the fund. As a result of the constant redemption and cashing out of existing shareholders who wish to sell their shares back to the company, the fund must be prepared to raise cash as need be to meet redemption requests.

Mutual funds are an excellent investment vehicle for the so-called *small investor*. They provide instant diversification and permit the investor to take advantage of a skilled, professional investment manager that the investor could otherwise likely not afford. In addition, due to the very large number of mutual funds available to the investor (over 15,000 at last count), there are many options available to satisfy the investor's financial goals at a reasonable cost.

Mutual funds may be purchased directly by the investor (for example, by telephone or over the Internet) or through a broker-dealer. They also may be purchased net of a sales charge, known as a *load,* or without a sales charge, a so-called *no load fund*. In both instances, however, annual management fees and administrative charges imposed by the fund apply. These management fees typically equal anywhere from 1% to 3% of net assets under management by the fund. In addition, for those funds that are professionally managed by broker-dealers and positioned in a so-called *wrap account*, sales charges that may typically be imposed are waived in lieu of an asset management fee, normally expressed as a percentage of assets managed. In broker-dealer language, this percentage is expressed in a number of *basis points,* which is 1/100th of a percentage point. For example, a million dollar managed portfolio that carries a 100 basis point management fee (1%) would incur an annual charge of $10,000. Investors should generally search for those funds with good past performance records (for example, those that exceed a *benchmark index,* such as the Standard & Poor's 500) on a consistent basis, as well as those that charge relatively low management fees and administrative charges (or *expense ratios*). The reader should note, however, that there are relatively few mutual funds with long-term performance records that are consistently above the benchmark index. This fact gives credence to the *efficient market hypothesis,* as subsequently discussed in chapter 9 of this textbook.

Finally, all mutual funds are priced according to their *Net Asset Value* (NAV) per common share as determined at the end of market trading for that particular day. Specifically, this value is computed by dividing the total market value of all holdings in the fund (stocks or bonds) by the number of common shares of the fund outstanding. Further, unlike *exchange traded funds* (ETFs) that are discussed later, open-end mutual funds may only be redeemed at the end of the trading day and *not* throughout the day. This means that the mutual fund investor may experience significant fluctuation in the value of his or her shares during the course of a trading day. In addition, mutual fund managers must make redemption of shares in cash and not with additional stock or property in-kind.

Types of Mutual Funds

As noted earlier, today there are over 15,000 different mutual funds that are available to investors. All can be segregated according to the investment objective of the fund as well as the size of companies in whose securities the funds invest (for example, small, midsize, or large market capitalization stocks). The most common types of mutual funds based on their respective investment objectives are:

1. Growth Fund: A fund that primarily invests in securities that *in turn* offer potentially significant capital appreciation (that is, an increasing share price that is in excess of other securities). A subcategory of this type of fund is an *aggressive growth fund* investing in securities of considerable risk, but also offering the possibility of maximum capital appreciation.

2. Income Fund: A fund that specializes in securities that pay higher-than-average dividends (if investing in stocks) or frequently invest a high percentage of their assets in bonds.

3. Growth and Income Fund: A fund that invests in securities offering potentially increasing value. You should note that this type of fund is primarily interested in so-called *value stocks* or stocks that are underpriced relative to a stock that exhibits similar risk and return characteristics.

4. Balanced Fund: A fund that is relatively conservative when it comes to investing in common stock; accordingly, the fund has as its primary objective the preservation of an investor's capital and moderate growth of income and principal. Usually, a balanced fund diversifies its investments among both stocks and bonds and may provide its investors with significant protection during market downturns.

5. Tax Exempt (or Municipal Bond) Fund: A fund that operates principally to provide high income tax bracket taxpayers with significant after-tax returns. Such fund generally limits its investments to municipal securities of other types of issues providing tax-sheltered income.

6. Money Market Fund: A (typically) no load fund that invests exclusively in short-term (money market) investments such as Treasury bills, corporate commercial paper, and high-grade certificates of deposit (CDs). Money market funds are known for their relative safety and ability to provide immediate liquidity to the investor.

7. Bond Fund: A fund that invests only in (typically) investment grade bonds. The fund possesses several advantages over a direct investment in bonds, most notably that fund investors have a greater chance of optimizing their rate of return due to their ability to reinvest any distributions as they are received. In addition, a bond mutual fund offers greater liquidity since an investor may take money out of a no load fund without incurring excessive unfavorable bond price changes.

8. High Yield Fund: A bond fund that invests in non-investment grade bonds (BBB or lower). There is greater potential income associated with such a fund, but also an assumption of greater risk.

9. Sector Fund: A fund that restricts its investments to a particular sector of the market, such as energy or health care. Such fund tends to be more volatile than a more diversified fund and/or portfolio.

10. Asset Allocation Fund: A fund that is created to provide diversification in asset categories not traditionally offered by conventional mutual funds. Specifically, the fund invests not only in the traditional asset categories of stocks and bonds, but also the nontraditional asset categories of foreign stocks and bonds, real estate securities, and commodities. Also may invest in money market securities to manage investor risk.

11. Commodity Fund: A fund that is designed to allow the small investor to invest in the commodities market, such as oil and gas. Usually, this type of fund is organized as a limited partnership, a type of professionally managed asset that will be discussed later in this chapter.

12. Global Equity Fund: A fund that invests in securities that are traded worldwide, including those of U.S. issues.

13. International Equity Fund: A fund that invests in securities of companies that are located outside the U.S. (in other words, unlike a global equity fund, securities of companies based in the U.S. are *not* included.)

14. Hedge Fund: A fund (often loosely regulated) that uses the most aggressive investment techniques, including high leverage and *selling short* (see chapter 15). In addition, options may be used to achieve the maximum growth of principal. Such a fund is usually for only wealthy investors and for those investors who are willing to assume some amount of speculative risk. Because of the growing importance of hedge funds, they are given additional attention later on in this chapter.

Index Funds

Index funds are mutual funds that try to replicate (or match) the performance of a particular market index (such as the Russell 2000 index of small capitalization growth stocks). For example, the Vanguard 500 Index Fund (currently the largest mutual fund in terms of invested dollars) seeks to provide investment results that track or correspond to the price performance of publicly traded stocks as represented by the Standard & Poor's index of 500 stocks). There are approximately 700 index funds in the marketplace today.

Index funds implement what is known as a *passive management or passive investor technique*, since the investor only wants to achieve the same rate of return as the market index that is used as a benchmark. As such, they differ from the majority of other mutual funds, which employ *active management* in an attempt to outperform the benchmark index or broader secondary market. Studies have shown, however, that, on average, approximately 75% of all common stock growth mutual funds fail to outperform the Standard & Poor's index of 500 stocks. If listening to market experts, this is due primarily to four factors as follows:

1) Management costs that are associated with the traditional mutual fund

2) The *turnover* of assets that occur with the buying and selling of securities in a mutual fund, thereby adding to transaction and tax costs that the investor must assume

3) A failure to be positioned within the correct market sector at the correct time

4) The necessary amount of cash reserves that are to be kept by the traditional mutual fund manager to fulfill investor redemptions

Index funds also possess several disadvantages, however. First, the investor cannot diversify away the same market risk that bedevils all publicly traded securities. This risk is, of course, magnified if the index fund attempts to track a benchmark index that is currently out of favor with investors. Second, some of the newer market entries into the index fund market are misleading in that some active management techniques are followed. Third, and probably most important, the investor in a mutual fund sacrifices all potential for a return *in excess* of the benchmark index that an excellent professional money manager may be able to achieve.

Mutual Funds vs. Variable Annuities

A long-running controversy among investment professionals' attempts to answer the question: Which are preferable, mutual funds or variable annuities?

A *variable annuity* (VA) is an insurance product that permits the owner to invest in a family of mutual funds with the purpose of accumulating (usually) tax-deferred savings, typically for retirement. The amount available for distribution is, in turn, contingent on the performance of the mutual funds selected. Normally, variable annuities, as an insurance product, guarantee that the owner's beneficiary will never receive less than the sum of the periodic contributions, should the owner die before the annuity starting date. In addition, variable annuities may exhibit lower levels of stock market and total risk than the market as a whole, given the minimum guarantee.

Specifically, let us compare variable annuities (VAs) to mutual funds (MF) with respect to a number of important issues:

1) Fees: VAs normally charge higher maintenance fees than a mutual fund. This is in part because VAs must provide for the risk of the owner's death in the form of mortality charges.

2) Liquidity: The VA is usually less liquid than the MF since it includes surrender expenses that are charged in the first few years of the contract. These surrender charges are presumably there to encourage the owner of the VA to treat the annuity as a longer term investment and to recover the initial costs of marketing the investment (similar to the *load* sales charge that exists with some mutual funds).

3) Death Benefit: As mentioned, as an insurance product, the VA usually offers a guaranteed death benefit, although, of course, the beneficiary of the contract and not its owner benefits from this provision.

4) Annuitization Option: Only the VA can offer this distribution option, which essentially guarantees that the owner cannot outlive his or her invested funds. A mutual fund does not offer this contract advantage.

5) Income Taxes: The VA features, in most instances, tax-deferred earnings. However, once these earnings are withdrawn, they are taxable at ordinary income tax rates and, if taken before the owner attains age 59.5, a 10% penalty is also imposed. In contrast, the MF does not afford a deferral of taxes on earnings (taxes on dividends are imposed annually), but when the MF shares are sold, any profits are taxable as capital gains. In addition, since passage of the 2003 Tax Act (JGTRRA), dividends from MFs are likely to be *qualified*, thus enjoying a taxable rate preference.

6) Estate Implications: Finally, MF shares are permitted in a *step up* in basis at the shareholder's death. This means that the estate's heirs will receive the MF shares as if they had been purchased on the date of death of the deceased shareholder, a fact that can substantially reduce any income tax bill on the subsequent sale of any appreciated shares. VAs do *not* provide a basis step up and, rather, constitute *income in respect of a decedent* (IRD) resulting in a lower inherited basis and, potentially, more income taxes to be paid by the heirs of the estate.

In summary, variable annuities likely provide a more favorable investment opportunity for an investor who definitely intends to use the investment vehicle for retirement and who expects to be in a *lower* marginal income tax bracket during the distribution phase than when accumulating the savings. In contrast, mutual funds provide an effective savings and diversification vehicle for the small investor and particularly one who anticipates part-time employment during retirement and/or the same or *higher* tax bracket at retirement. Mutual funds may also be preferable for someone who is not interested in providing a death benefit to heirs or for someone who wants to provide his or her heirs with potentially significant income tax benefits.

CLOSED-END INVESTMENT COMPANIES

Closed-end investment companies stand in marked contrast to open-end mutual funds. Closed-end funds do not buy and sell (or redeem) their own shares. Rather, these funds have a one-time stock issuance and then close their books. No new shares are issued. The stock that is the subject of the initial capitalization then trades on the secondary market at a discount or premium to net asset value (NAV) similar to any other negotiable security. The funds may be listed on the organized stock exchanges (such as the New York Stock Exchange) or traded in the over-the-counter market among broker-dealers. The assets are professionally managed in accordance with the fund's investment objectives and policies.

Closed-end fund structures are often used for portfolios of *illiquid* securities (for example, bonds). If these illiquid securities were purchased by an open-end mutual fund, and if investors sought to redeem those shares, then the mutual fund would be forced to liquidate the holdings of the portfolio, possibly at an unfavorable time. This is avoided with a closed-end fund, which can much more easily structure when the illiquid securities are to be sold, since the request for investor redemption is not an issue. In addition, if the investor in a closed-end fund wishes to liquidate his or her shares, they may be sold in the open market, just like any other stock, at the prevailing price.

The market value of closed-end company shares is closely related to the potential return on the investment. However, as noted, this market value typically is *not* the net asset value (NAV) per share, but may be above or below this value, depending on the demand and the supply of stock in the secondary market. If the market price is *below* the net asset value of the shares, the shares are selling at a *discount* (similar to the market price of a bond that is selling below par), whereas if the market price is *above* the net asset value, the shares are selling at a *premium.*

UNIT INVESTMENT TRUSTS (UITs)

A variation on the closed-end investment company is the fixed unit investment trust, also known as a *unit investment trust* (UIT). These trusts are unmanaged and are funded with fixed income securities (such as bonds) put together by a broker-dealer and titled in the name (usually) of an independent trustee. An example of such a trust is Merrill Lynch's Government Securities Income Fund, which invests solely in U.S. Treasury securities that are a direct guarantee of the federal government.

A unit investment trust is a *passive* investment, since its assets are not traded but are frozen. Like a closed-end fund, no new securities are purchased and the securities that are originally bought are rarely sold. The trust collects income (for example, interest income on its bond portfolio) and, eventually, the repayment of principal. The trust is self-liquidating because as the income and principal is received from the trust's investments, they are *not* reinvested but are distributed to the unit holders. Such trust is particularly attractive to retiree investors who seek a steady, predictable flow of income. Further, if the investor needs additional monies, the units may be sold back to (redeemed by) the trust at their current net asset value (NAV). It is also possible to find a secondary market for UITs among other broker-dealers.

UITs do have several disadvantages, however. First, the investor must pay a rather sizeable up-front fee of 3 to 5 percent when the trust is formed and then pay for trustee fees out of trust earnings. In addition, while the trust may acquire high-quality securities (such as investment grade bonds), these securities are not without default risk. Finally, there is also the risk that the realized return on the fixed income security may be less than anticipated.

Participating UITs

A *participating unit investment trust* (PUIT) invests in the shares of a management company--specifically mutual fund shares. This is in contrast to the normal form of UIT that invests only in fixed income assets. Participating trust structures are frequently used when investors buy variable annuity contracts.

EXCHANGE TRADED FUNDS (ETFs)

As a preliminary note, *exchange traded funds* (ETFs) should be distinguished from *exchange funds* that are used in managing concentrated stock portfolios. Exchange funds allow investors to achieve greater diversification and lower the risk of holding a significant investment in a single security, often employer stock. As a result, if investors own securities with a low tax basis, exchange funds permit an exchange of these securities for shares in a limited partnership or limited liability company (LLC) *without* causing a taxable event. In an exchange fund, the minimum investment is usually $1.0 million and investors must be *accredited* (see previous discussion on private placements).

In contrast to an exchange fund, an *exchange traded fund* (ETF) is simply a security representing a basket of stocks or bonds and is more like a mutual fund. However, unlike a mutual fund and like an individual stock, ETFs are priced and traded throughout the day using market or limit orders. Further, like an index fund, ETFs also attempt to track a broad group of stocks from different industries and market sectors. They bear brand names such as SPDRs (*spiders*), HOLDRs, Ishares, and VIPERs. *All* of them are *passively managed,* correlating to a wide variety of sector-specific and broad-market indexes. Finally, unlike mutual funds, stocks may be distributed to ETF shareholders for redemption (instead of selling the securities), thus minimizing any taxable gains. This benefit also applies when stocks are removed from the particular index.

Another advantage of ETFs is their lower expense ratios and lack of an up-front sales load. They generally do not have a manager or analyst actively managing the portfolio; thus, their management fees are less. According to Morningstar, Inc., the average ETF has an expense ratio of 0.42% of assets annually, compared with an average expense ratio of 0.86% for index funds and 1.41% for actively managed mutual funds. However, as with stocks, investors must pay a commission to buy and sell ETF shares, which may be a disadvantage for those with small sums of monies to invest. In such cases, the savings on ETF's management costs may quickly be erased by the trading costs, making mutual funds a better option.

So who should use ETFs as part of their investment portfolio? Specifically, those investors who want to invest in an industry sector or index and not have to manage a multitude of stocks or mutual funds. ETFs will also be of interest to investors who want a low cost, tax-efficient portfolio or fund since they have greater control over when a taxable event will be recognized. Finally, investors in, for example, self-directed 401(k) plans may find ETFs attractive because of their low cost. However, this last advantage does need to be balanced against the possibility of *dollar cost averaging* that is used by many investors (see chapter 15). Such investors who make periodic regular investments are likely to favor plain vanilla mutual funds over ETFs since they avoid the commissions that add up quickly with ETF purchases. For example, if a broker charges $10 per transaction in an ETF and an investor is periodically purchasing $300 of shares per month, the commissions alone will cost the investor 3% of the investment. This is much greater than the cost of investing periodically in a mutual fund.

HEDGE FUNDS

The academic textbook definition of *hedge* is "a trading strategy in which derivative securities are used to reduce or completely offset an investor's risk exposure to an underlying asset." As such, most hedge fund strategies tend to "hedge" against a downturn in the markets traded. They do this through a variety of investment vehicles, some of which are largely unregulated or loosely regulated by the SEC and/or state securities commissioners. Among these vehicles are short selling, leverage, concentrated investing and derivatives such as options and futures. Since these strategies are not highly correlated to equity markets generally, they may be able to deliver consistent returns with a lower risk of long-term loss.

Hedge funds are also unique in how they reward their portfolio managers. Specifically, they significantly weight fund managers compensation towards performance incentives, whereas mutual fund managers are typically remunerated according to the volume of assets managed, regardless of performance. In addition, unlike many mutual fund managers, hedge fund managers are also usually heavily invested in a substantial portion of the funds that they run and share the rewards as well as the risks with the investors. As a result, hedge funds tend to attract highly skilled and experienced portfolio managers and investors of some experience and considerable net worth. For example, many endowments and pension funds (*institutions*) allocate considerable assets to hedge funds.

In recent years, the number of hedge funds has risen considerably as has the number of dollars invested in such funds. As the number of funds has risen, so have the investment strategies that are used. Some hedge funds today use considerable leverage and derivatives, while others are more conservative and employ little or no leverage. The performance of many hedge fund strategies is not dependent at all on the direction of the stock (equity) or bond markets, but rather only on the result of the investment strategy that is pursued. This, of course, is unlike conventional mutual funds or even exchange traded funds (ETFs), which are generally 100% exposed to market risk. However, some hedge fund strategies are limited as to how much investor's capital they can successfully employ before the rates of return diminish. As a result, many successful hedge fund managers *limit* the amount of capital (invested dollars) that they will accept.

An investor of considerable means who is most interested in managing the risk of possible loss from his or her (its) investment is the most likely type of investor in a hedge fund. In addition, an investor who is very concerned about the skill and expertise of the portfolio manager should strongly consider contributing to a hedge fund. Conversely, such a fund is usually beyond the financial means of the smaller investor who is looking for capital growth or current income, the two primary investment objectives of mutual fund shareholders.

PRIVATELY MANAGED ACCOUNTS

A privately managed account is an account comprised of a diversified portfolio of individual securities managed by an institutional portfolio manager. In such an account, however, the investor owns 100% of the securities in the portfolio, rather than only a small percentage of the total as in a mutual fund. Investment restrictions may be added to avoid duplicating securities held in other managed accounts or to avoid certain stocks or industries for so-called *socially conscious investors* (for example, tobacco or gambling stocks). Certain large amount, investment minimums have also historically applied.

There are both tax and management advantages associated with a privately managed account. From a tax standpoint, tax-sensitive investors (normally higher income tax bracket taxpayers) benefit from a portfolio manager who utilizes strategies designed for maximum after-tax performance. In addition, since the investor determines when the securities in the portfolio are sold, he or she controls when a taxable event will be incurred. In the typical mutual fund, since all capital gain distributions are passed through to the shareholders, the portfolio manager makes the taxable event determination.

There is also no so-called "herd effect" with a privately managed account. That is, a longer term investor (sometimes referred to as a *buy and hold* investor) will *not* be affected by the redemptions of shorter term investors during a volatile market period. Thus, the portfolio manager in a private account does not have to maintain or "hold back" any cash in reserve to meet these short term redemptions, which reserve, by definition, will not generate a higher rate of investment return.

Privately managed accounts are also used in transitioning an investor with large concentrated stock holdings in one company or industry to a better-rounded, diversified portfolio.

SEPARATELY MANAGED ACCOUNTS

In many respects, the term *separately managed account* has the same characteristics as a *privately managed account*. Indeed, both are types of fee-based, managed accounts where the investor owns 100% of the securities in the account and the investment decisions are made by a professional money manager. Different broker-dealers may have their own names for their products-though the products themselves are very similar. However, both separately managed and privately managed accounts differ from mutual funds, in that the professional manager is purchasing the securities in the portfolio on behalf of the private investor and not on behalf of the fund. Finally, both types of accounts provide for popular *taxable gain/loss harvesting,* which is a technique for minimizing the investor's tax liability through the selective realization of gains and losses in the individual account.

Let us look at an example of how a separately managed account is structured.

Example 4-1: ABC Mutual Fund holds shares of two companies: Company X and Company Y. You purchase 100 shares of ABC Mutual Fund. Therefore, in the traditional *mutual fund purchase*, you own 100 shares of ABC Mutual Fund; you do *not* own any shares of either Company X or Company Y. However, if you invest in a *separate account*, the private money (portfolio) manager for that account purchases shares of *each* of those companies on your behalf. Your account is separate and distinct from that of any other investor.

The ability to maintain an *individual* cost basis in a separate account is key to the management of one's income tax liability. This can be a significant benefit for high net income investors. Consider, for example, a separate account where the investor has purchased two securities over time at similar prices. Over time, one of the securities has doubled in value (100 %) while the other has fallen by 50%. By instructing the portfolio manager to sell both securities, the gains generated by the security that has increased in value may be offset by the losses from the security that has declined, thereby totally eliminating any capital gains tax liability. Of course, this advantage is not available to the mutual fund shareholder.

LIMITED PARTNERSHIPS

A *limited partnership* is a type of partnership that limits the liability of the partner to only the amount of capital that he or she has contributed to the partnership. In the typical limited partnership, one general partner manages the business (and assumes all liability for the acts of the business), while the limited partners only contribute capital and share in the partnership's profits and losses. In other words, the general partner most often contributes services to the partnership and the limited partner (or partners) provides the money. As such, the form of business organization lends itself quite easily as a capital-raising device and opportunity for outside investors to participate in a potentially profitable business opportunity.

There are several different forms of limited partnerships, some of which (because of their taxable implications and interrelationship with the so-called *passive loss* rules) are discussed again in Kaplan University's *Individual Income Tax Planning* textbook by Mershon and Fevurly. The different forms of limited partnerships include:

1) Public Limited Partnership (also known as a *Public Reporting Limited Partnership*): A limited partnership that is registered with the SEC and offered to the general public through broker-dealers; such partnership does not trade on an exchange and therefore has both limited marketability and limited liquidity.

2) Master Limited Partnership (MLP): A limited partnership that is registered with the SEC and trades on an exchange; an investment that combines the tax benefits of a limited partnership with the marketability of publicly traded companies.

3) Private Limited Partnership: A limited partnership that has *not* registered with the SEC and is *not* traded on an exchange; by law, such form of partnership is limited to no more than 35 limited partners.

4) Venture Capital Limited Partnership: A limited partnership that is formed by a venture capital firm to invest in small beginning or *start-up* businesses.

Typically, two types of investment activities-- commercial real estate development or rental activities and oil and gas companies-- lend themselves to the limited partnership form. Specifically, therefore, the form is most suitable for an investor that wants to invest in those types of businesses, but lacks the knowledge or experience to take an active role in the management of the business. Further, the form permits a pooling of investor resources whereby investors can combine capital and obtain a level of diversification and risk reduction that they could not achieve individually. For example, a limited partnership may be able to invest in numerous commercial development properties that the individual may either not know about because of geographical limitations or not be comfortable with if assuming the investment risk alone.

The major disadvantage to the limited partnership form is (with the exception of an MLP) the *lack* of inherent marketability and liquidity of the underlying investment. Some partnerships have arrangements whereby investors may offer their interest for sale to the other limited partners, or general partner, but there is no guarantee that they will buy it. Also, if the investment activity has not developed as anticipated (for example, a commercial office building is built and it is not fully occupied), the other partners may purchase the interest, but at a reduced price. Finally, in most instances, a limited partnership is usually highly *leveraged*, meaning that it is using borrowed funds to finance its investment activities. While this leverage will magnify any capital gains if the partnership's investments have done well, it also magnifies the potential for significant losses of the limited or general partner.

In summary, limited partnership investments tend to be relatively risky and generally unsuitable for the average investor. Mutual funds or exchange traded funds (ETFs) offer investors many of the same advantages of limited partnerships, including diversification and professional management, but without as much marketability or liquidity risk.

IMPORTANT CONCEPTS

Open-end investment company (mutual fund)

Net asset value (NAV)

Growth fund

Income fund

Growth and income fund

Balanced fund

Tax exempt fund

Money market fund

Global equity fund

International equity fund

Hedge fund

Index fund

Passive management

Variable annuity

Closed-end investment company

Unit investment trust (UIT)

Participating UIT

Exchange traded fund (ETF)

Exchange fund

Privately managed account

Separately managed account

Limited partnership

Master limited partnership (MLP)

QUESTIONS FOR REVIEW

1. Why is the proper name of a *mutual fund* referred to as an open-end investment company?

2. What is the primary difference between a *no load* and a load mutual fund?

3. What is a *wrap account* and how does a broker-dealer (or investment advisor) normally charge for assets under management (AUM) in such an account?

4. How (at what price) does a mutual fund trade on the secondary market?

5. If a small investor is interested in a mutual fund that primarily offers the chance for significant capital appreciation, in what type of mutual fund should he or she invest?

6. What is a *balanced fund*?

7. What is the primary use of a money market mutual fund for many investors?

8. What is a notable advantage of investing in a bond fund instead of investing directly in corporate bonds?

9. What is the difference between a *global equity fund* and an *international equity fund*?

10. What is an *index fund*? What types of investors are primarily interested in such a fund?

11. Define what is meant by the term *turnover of assets* within a mutual fund. Why should a potential investor be interested in this?

12. Contrast a variable annuity (VA) to a mutual fund (MF) regarding each of the six factors noted in the chapter. In summary, when is each of these investment vehicles most likely suitable?

13. Contrast a closed-end investment company to that of an open-end investment company.

14. What types of securities are normally offered by a closed-end investment company? Why?

15. How (at what price) does a closed-end fund trade on the secondary market?

16. What is a *unit investment trust* (UIT)? What types of investors are usually interested in this form of managed asset?

17. Contrast an exchange fund with an exchange traded fund (ETF). When (in what situation) is an exchange fund used?

18. What is an exchange traded fund (ETF) and how does it compare to a traditional mutual fund? Who should use an ETF as part of their investment portfolio? Why?

19. What is the textbook definition of a *hedge*? How is this concept applied in a *hedge fund*?

20. What types of investment strategies do most hedge fund managers use?

21. List one tax advantage and one management advantage associated with a privately managed account.

22. Define the term *tax harvesting*. What type(s) of investment accounts provide for this?

23. What are four types of limited partnerships? Which of these is publicly traded?

24. What two types of investment activities have historically lent themselves to being operated in the limited partnership form?

25. Is a limited partnership generally suitable for the average investor and why or why not?

SUGGESTIONS FOR ADDITIONAL READING

Tools and Techniques of Investment Planning, Stephen R. Leimberg, Robert T. LeClair, Robert J. Doyle, Jr., and Thomas R. Robinson, The National Underwriter Company, 2004.

Investments: An Introduction, 7th edition, Herbert B. Mayo, Thomson/ South-Western, 2002.

Investment Analysis and Portfolio Management, 7th edition, Frank K. Reilly and Keith C. Brown, Thomson/South-Western, 2003.

The Wall Street Journal Guide to Money and Investing, 3rd edition, Kenneth M. Morris and Virginia B. Morris, Fireside Publishing, 2004.

CHAPTER FIVE

Insurance Based Investments

• • •

In recent years, the insurance industry has also offered products that include enhanced investment features. Among these are variable products, such as variable life insurance and variable annuities that invest in the securities market. These products go beyond the traditional or standard *whole life* form of life insurance policy that has dominated the insurance market for many years.

Upon completing this chapter, you should be able to:

- Explain issues that bear on the life insurance versus investment determination and why this is important
- Describe the characteristics and uses of variable life insurance products
- Analyze when the use of an annuity may be appropriate in investment planning
- Define a *guaranteed investment contract* (GIC)

LIFE INSURANCE VS. INVESTMENTS

An ongoing question for regulators, particularly the IRS, is: When is an asset purchase considered to be an insurance contract and when is it considered to be an investment? This is important primarily because the taxation of life insurance, notably the income tax free nature of the life insurance death benefit, *differs* from that of an investment. Unfortunately, a clear answer to this question may not be gleaned from the intent of the individual when purchasing an asset or contract. Many individuals are interested in a cash value type of life insurance contract as an investment, specifically because it also provides for a tax-deferred accumulation of lifetime earnings. These earnings may subsequently be used to assist in meeting a financial planning and/or investment goal of the individual, such as retirement.

An asset purchase must satisfy a technical definition in Internal Revenue Code (IRC) Section 7702 (a) if it is to be treated, for income tax purposes, as *life insurance.* Specifically, the contract must meet either a cash *accumulation test* (normally applied to traditional whole life policies) or a *guideline premium and cash value corridor test* (normally applied to universal life contracts). A variable life insurance contract must meet either of these previous tests *plus* meet the definition of a variable life contract, including diversification requirements under IRC Section 817 (h).While the particulars of any of these tests are beyond the scope of this book, it is worth noting that if they are *not* met, the policy will instead be taxed as an *investment.* What does this mean? Primarily, it means that:

1) The periodic increase in the cash value of the contract (the cash value *inside build up*), if any, is taxable *annually* at ordinary income rates

2) Any distributions made from the contract in the form of dividends to the policyholder are taxable *annually* at ordinary income rates (similar to that of a dividend from a stock or mutual fund but *without* being considered as *qualified* for preferential rates)

3) The income tax free nature of the death benefit or face amount to the policy beneficiary (or beneficiaries) is *lost*

Let us look at each of these taxable consequences in a bit more detail.

Cash Value Inside Build Up

If a contract is treated as life insurance and not as an investment, the general rule is that the annual cash value increase is *not* subject to current income tax. Further, a life insurance policy holder may withdraw amounts from the contract up to his or basis (generally premiums paid minus any dividends paid) *tax-free* before any gain is realized. This, of course, means that loans from a life insurance policy are typically *not* subject to immediate taxation (the notable exception to this being a policy that is considered to be a *modified endowment contract* or MEC).

In contrast, an investment enjoys no such preferential method of taxation. Specifically, capital appreciation in the invested asset is *realized* each year. However, whether this appreciation is *recognized* for income tax purposes depends on whether the investor sells or otherwise disposes of the asset; in addition, whether this appreciation or capital gain is taxable as a short term or as a long term gain depends on how long the investor has owned (or *held*) the asset. If the invested asset has been held for one year or less, the gain is taxable at ordinary income tax rates whereas, if held for more than one year, the gain enjoys a lower *long-term capital gains* rate of no more than (currently) 15 percent.

Dividends

The general rule is that dividends paid on a participating life insurance contract are a return of capital and *not includible* in gross income. (Note that a participating contract is one that has historically been underwritten by a mutual life insurance company-versus a stock life insurance company.) There are usually several different dividend options available with any whole life insurance policy, but all result in the general exclusion of life insurance dividends from current income taxation (again, the notable exception to this rule is dividends payable from a *MEC*, which are taxable once received).

In contrast, the dividends from an investment (notably a stock) are currently taxable as ordinary income. Under the Tax Act of 2003 (JGTRRA), *qualified dividend income* (generally, dividends paid by domestic corporations and certain foreign corporations) is treated as net capital gain and is, therefore, subject to lower tax rates. However, such dividends, representing corporate earnings, are not only still taxable to the shareholder, but the payor corporation also does not receive an income tax deduction for the same. This, in turn, leads to the concept of *double taxation* of earnings that is so frequently noted as a disadvantage of the regular corporate form of business organization.

Death Benefit

Of course, the payment of a death benefit to the beneficiaries of the insured is the essence of a life insurance policy. Under IRC Section 101 (a) (1), this benefit is generally excludible from the taxable income of the beneficiary (or beneficiaries). Like most provisions in the income tax law, there is also an exception to this result (referred to as the *transfer for value* rule), but so long as the life insurance policy is not sold to another for more than the premiums already paid by the contract owner, the insurance proceeds are non-taxable. Finally, income taxes are never due if the life insurance policy actually matures as a death benefit and the proceeds are used to repay any lifetime loans made from the policy.

There is nothing similar in the taxation of investments. Indeed, in most cases, the tax attributes of an investment die with the owner. That is, if the beneficiaries of the investor are to receive any benefit, an investment must typically first be liquidated (converted to cash) and then subsequently reinvested by the new owner/beneficiary. There is some advantage provided to the beneficiary in the form of an investment basis that is *stepped up* at the decedent/owner's death, but this is not the same consequence as the complete exclusion of life insurance proceeds from income taxation at the death of the insured. Accordingly, unlike life insurance that is primarily purchased for *death motivated reasons*, an investment is purchased first and foremost because of its potential for significant growth during an individual's *lifetime*.

VARIABLE AND VARIABLE UNIVERSAL LIFE (VUL)

While there are several different types of cash value (or *permanent*) life insurance policies, only variable and variable universal life (VUL) require that the *producer* (life insurance professional) must also maintain a securities license. Variable life insurance combines traditional permanent insurance with mutual-fund type investments and allows the policy owner to direct the investment of cash values among a variety of different investments. Many companies that market variable life insurance policies offer a broad choice of investment options such as growth mutual funds, bond funds, real estate funds, and sector funds. Variable universal life (VUL) insurance takes this concept one step further and also offers owners the advantage of flexible lifetime premiums and a greater certainty of a minimum death benefit payable from the policy.

Variable life has a guaranteed minimum face amount and a fixed, level premium like traditional whole life insurance, but differs from whole life in the following ways:

1) The policy owner's funds are placed in a separate account that is segregated from that of the company's general investment fund; in turn, this means that, in the event of financial instability of the underwriting company, the policy owner achieves some level of individual creditor protection not possible in a whole life policy.

2) There is no minimum guaranteed cash value; at any point in time, the cash value in a variable policy is based on the market value of the assets in the separate account; accordingly, variable life policy owners bear *all* of the investment risk associated with the policy.

3) The death benefit is *variable*, meaning that it may increase or decrease, but not below the guaranteed minimum, based on a specified formula relating the investment performance of the separate account to the policy's face value.

A variable life insurance policy is most suitable for those individuals who desire control over the amount of cash value that is accumulated in their policy and who want the possibility of increasing life insurance protection. However, these individuals should have a basic understanding of investments and believe that they are capable of making good investment decisions. They also should be aware that the growth of the death benefit in the policy (since it is tied to a formula reflecting the performance of the underlying cash value) is by no means assured and, therefore, a temporarily depressed death benefit level when the insured dies is a distinct possibility. Variable universal life (VUL) is a combination of a universal and variable life insurance policy. Specifically, it is possible for VUL policy owners to:

1) Determine the amount and timing of premium payments

2) Adjust the amount of the policy's death benefit in response to changing needs

3) Withdraw money from the policy without an interest charge if there is sufficient cash value to cover already-assumed mortality and expense charges

The death benefit of a VUL policy is not variable in the same sense as the death benefit of a variable life policy. Rather, the policy owner may typically choose between two death benefit options. Under Option A, the death benefit of the policy remains *level*, similar to a traditional whole life policy. Under Option B, the death benefit is equal to a level pure insurance (or mortality) amount *plus* a cash value portion that is determined by formula. Therefore, the death benefit *increases* as the cash value grows. Usually, the policy also permits the policy owner to increase the face value (death benefit) even further by providing subsequent evidence of insurability.

A VUL policy is especially suitable as a supplement to an existing life insurance plan that assures a minimum required base level of coverage. It is less suitable, however, as a means of providing such base level coverage. Rather, term or whole life may be a better alternative as a first policy. In addition, VUL is particularly attractive where an individual is a self directed investor and believes that he or she can generate a cash value in excess of that possible by the issuing company and its portfolio managers. Finally, the investor should be willing to consider accessing that cash value for the satisfaction of certain lifetime financial goals, such as retirement or the providing of higher education for the investor's children or spouse.

ANNUITIES

There are almost as many ways to classify annuities as there are annuity products. For example, annuities may be classified on the basis of number of lives covered (single or joint); when the benefit payments commence (immediate or deferred); the method of premium payment (single payment or multiple payment); settlement options (pure life, pure life with a period certain, pure life with a refund provision, or joint and survivor); or the type of annuity payment (fixed or variable). However, as an insurance-based investment product, we will concentrate on how the earnings within an annuity are accumulated, that is either in a specified or *fixed* amount or in a fluctuating or *variable* amount.

Annuities are the *only* investment vehicles that can guarantee investors that they will *not* outlive their income. It is a contract offered by an insurance company where the investor makes an up front cash payment--either single or multiple--in return for the company agreeing to pay the owner a specified amount periodically on a specified date. The money that is paid up front to the insurance company is invested by them and is periodically credited with some type of interest or growth factor--this is known as the *accumulation phase* of the annuity. So long as the owner of the annuity is an individual (and not a non-natural person, such as a corporation), the growth or earnings portion of the annuity grows on a tax-deferred basis. Indeed, no income tax is payable on the earnings until the earlier of: a) the surrender of the contract; b) withdrawal from the contract; or c) the time that payments under the annuity begin (commonly referred to as *annuitization*). Classification as a fixed or variable annuity refers to the underlying investments during the annuity's accumulation phase; a fixed annuity is invested in the general fixed account of the insurance company, whereas a variable annuity is invested in separately managed sub-accounts selected by the annuity owner.

Annuities grow tax-deferred during their accumulation phase, although withdrawals of invested funds by the owner during this phase are taxed on a LIFO (last in, first out) basis. This means that withdrawals are considered to come first from any growth of or earnings generated by the annuity (and are thus fully taxable), and subsequently from any non-taxable principal. Payments made from the annuity during the *distribution* or *payout phase* are considered to be split. That is, a portion of each payment is considered to be paid from non-taxable principal and another portion represents interest or growth on this principal and is income taxable. The proportion of each is determined by an income tax concept known as *the exclusion ratio,* with amounts distributed that are considered as interest or growth, taxable as ordinary income (not capital gains). In addition, certain withdrawals before the annuitant age of 59.5 may be subject to an additional 10% penalty. (You should note that the tax treatment just described applies to all annuities purchased from an insurance company that are not part of a qualified retirement plan or a so-called *non qualified annuity*; the tax treatment of annuities purchased by an employer/sponsor of a qualified retirement plan--a so-called *qualified annuity*-- is separately discussed in Kaplan University's *Planning for Retirement* textbook by Jeffrey B. Mershon.)

Fixed Annuities

A combination insurance-and-investment product, the fixed annuity offers a guaranteed rate of return, tax-deferred growth, and a steady stream of income during the distribution phase of the annuity. The rate of return paid on current contributions to the annuity may be guaranteed for one year to as many as ten years, but depends on the performance of the insurance company's general investment portfolio, which is usually invested in fixed income types of investments (for example, bonds). Similar to a savings account in a bank, once interest is credited to the contributions made to the annuity, the cash value will not decrease even if the market value of the insurance company's general investment portfolio decreases. In summary, in the fixed type of annuity, the insurance company (rather than the investor) bears the investment risk.

There are two basic kinds of fixed annuities--immediate and deferred. Approximately 90% of all outstanding annuities contracts are one of these two kinds. With an *immediate* fixed annuity, the investor makes a single up-front payment, in return for which he or she receives a regular monthly check for the remainder of his or her life. With a *deferred* fixed annuity, the investor either pays a big up-front premium or spreads payments over time; withdrawals then occur at a later date. In both kinds of fixed annuities, however, the investor usually earns a somewhat higher return than on traditional cash investments and also is provided with a guarantee that he or she will be paid not less than a specified, guaranteed minimum rate. Then, depending on the payout option that is chosen by the investor, the monthly checks typically last as long as the *annuitant* is alive, and sometimes longer, if the contract permits the naming of a designated beneficiary.

The primary disadvantage of the fixed annuity is just that: it provides for a *fixed, unchanging* rate of return. Therefore, the annuitant assumes the risk that the inflation rate will exceed the rate of return credited to the cash value of the contract. Current purchasers may also worry that they are locking themselves into lifetime payments while interest rates are at historic lows. Accordingly, prudent financial planning likely suggests that only a portion of an investor's total portfolio consists of a fixed annuity ($100,000 of a $500,000 portfolio, for example) with the rest divided among a diversified mix of stock and bond mutual (or exchange traded) funds. In this manner, the overall purchasing power of the investor/annuitant is likely to be preserved once he or she begins making distributions from the annuity contract.

A specialized type of fixed annuity is a *single premium deferred annuity* (SPDA), which provides, as the name implies, a promise that a payment will begin in the future in return for a single premium. The principal feature of such annuity is that earnings accumulate tax-free until distributed. In addition, so-called "bailout provisions" permit the owner to withdraw all of his or her money without the imposition of a contract surrender charge if the interest rate that is credited falls below a certain minimum amount (referred to as the bailout rate).

Variable Annuities

A variable annuity is based on a different method of investing the accumulated cash value. The investor/contract owner may select from a number of separate accounts that are similar to mutual fund investments with options including diversified stock, bond, and specialized (such as sector) funds. The funds in these accounts are invested separately from the other assets of the insurance company. Each year some money is taken out of the contact owner's premium (or deducted from the account value) to cover the expenses of the company, including the mortality expense that is charged on the owner's lifetime expectancy. The remaining balance is then applied to purchase so-called *units of credit* in the separate accounts. In contrast with fixed annuities, the accumulated cash value in a variable annuity depends on the market value of the underlying assets in the selected separate accounts, with the investor assuming the investment risk. If the separate accounts are invested poorly, the annuitant may receive fewer dollars than would have been paid under a fixed annuity.

Conceptually, variable annuities are simply mutual funds in an "insurance wrapper." They permit the tax on all income, whether ordinary or capital gain, to be deferred until any monies are actually distributed. Like any annuity, distributions from a variable annuity, if annuitized, are taxed according to the exclusion ratio concept, although this ratio is computed differently in the case of a variable annuity than in a fixed annuity. Also, and more importantly as compared to the underlying mutual funds, variable annuities offer a number of contractual guarantees to the contract owner. However, the owner may pay a heavy price for these guarantees, notably the imposition of both contract and tax surrender charges.

Most variable annuities impose contract surrender charges if any money is withdrawn within the first five to nine years of initial investment. Therefore, such annuities are really suitable only as *long term investments*, such as in saving for an investor's retirement. As a general rule, variable annuities are less attractive than mutual funds if there is any possibility that the money used to fund the annuity may be needed relatively soon. (Note: A comparison of mutual funds to variable annuities is included as part of chapter 4 of this textbook.) This is, in part, because the period of tax deferral will usually be insufficient to overcome the additional fees and surrender charges associated with the annuity. In addition, as previously noted, most distributions from an annuity--whether fixed or variable--made *prior* to the annuitant attaining age 59.5 are subject to a 10% penalty tax on the taxable amount withdrawn (plus ordinary income tax). A notable exception, however, to the imposition of this penalty is a distribution that is made as part of a *substantially equal periodic payment for the life of the annuitant* (otherwise known as a Section 72 (q) payment after the Internal Revenue Code Section of the same number and subsection).

Equity-Indexed Annuities (EIAs)

An equity-indexed annuity (EIA) is a relatively recent insurance-based investment product. It is essentially a hybrid of the fixed and variable product and may appeal to an investor who wishes to participate in the equity (stock) market without bearing the full investment risk of a variable annuity.

The rate of return credited to the cash value of an EIA is linked to a stock market index, such as the Standard& Poor's 500 Index. However, the annuity is *not* actually invested in the stocks making up the index. Rather, like a fixed annuity, the return on an EIA is paid from the insurance company's general account. Further, the amount allocated to the EIA is based on a percentage of the appreciation in the referenced index (for example, 80%), which is then also often subject to an annual limitation or *cap*. If the equity index that is used as a benchmark declines in value, a minimum guaranteed amount is credited to the annuity, thereby providing investors with some of the upside potential of stocks but the downside protection of an amount below which the investment cannot fall. Nonetheless, as the price to be paid for the benefit of eliminating these periodic market losses, investors in an EIA also need to be aware that the aforementioned cap placed on credited capital gains will, in turn, likely *limit* how much contract appreciation may be achieved.

GUARANTEED INVESTMENT CONTRACTS (GICs)

Guaranteed Investment Contracts (GICs) are similar to certificates of deposit (CDs) issued by commercial banks issued by commercial banks, but instead the issuer is an insurance company. In general, a GIC will pay a rate of interest about 1% greater than a comparable maturity CD. However, unlike a CD, GICs are *not* federally insured and, therefore, despite the inclusion of the word *guaranteed* in its title, they carry more risk than a federally insured CD.

The major purchasers of GICs are institutions, specifically companies who find such an investment vehicle attractive as an option in a 401(k) or pension plan for employees. Companies typically choose between either a participating or nonparticipating contract. A *participating* GIC provides the company with a variable rate of return based on interest rate changes. Alternatively, a *nonparticipating* GIC earns a fixed rate of return. The choice of whether the company purchases a participating or a nonparticipating GIC depends on its expectation of interest rates over the term of the contract (usually 2 to 5 years). If the company believes that interest rates are likely to *increase*, the purchase of a participating GIC is likely prudent, whereas a nonparticipating GIC is a better choice if interest rates are expected to *decline*.

The insurance company offering the GIC is contractually obligated to repay the principal and guaranteed interest on the instrument to the purchaser's 401(k) or other benefit plan. Since the purchaser knows when this principal and interest will be paid (that is, at the maturity date of the contract), a GIC can serve as a very effective funding vehicle for a benefit plan where the participant's normal retirement age is also known. In addition, the provisions of the benefit plan may permit the participant to withdraw funds as part of an *in service withdrawal* (see Kaplan University's separate text on *Planning for Retirement* by Mershon). Accordingly, the proceeds of the GIC may be accessed at the same time, often times without penalty as would be the case with a traditional CD. The deposits paid to the insurance company used to fund the GIC are held in the insurer's general account, therefore the benefit plan does incur some default risk that the payment may not, in fact, be made. However, generally, only insurance companies of the highest quality rating issue GICs, so the risk of default is relatively minimal.

IMPORTANT CONCEPTS

Definition of life insurance

Taxation as investment

Cash value inside build up

Life insurance dividend

Death benefit

Variable life insurance

Variable universal life (VUL) insurance

Annuitization

Exclusion ratio

Last in, first out (LIFO) taxation

Fixed annuity

Immediate fixed annuity

Deferred fixed annuity

Single premium deferred annuity (SPDA)

Variable annuity

Equity-indexed annuity (EIA)

Guaranteed investment contract (GIC)

Participating GIC

Nonparticipating GIC

QUESTIONS FOR REVIEW

1. Why is it important to determine if an asset purchase is an investment or life insurance contract?

2. What is the taxable consequence is a life insurance contract does not meet the statutory definition of *life* insurance?

3. What is meant by the term cash value *inside build up*? Contrast this to how the annual earnings on an *investment* are taxed.

4. What is the general rule regarding the taxability of dividends from a life insurance contract? Contrast this to the taxation of dividends payable from a stock.

5. Are death benefits from a life insurance income taxable to the beneficiary? Explain.

6. How does a variable life insurance contract differ from that of traditional whole life?

7. Which individuals are most likely to consider variable life insurance as a potential investment?

8. What are three characteristics of variable universal life (VUL) insurance?

9. What is the *only* investment vehicle that can guarantee investors that they will *not* out-live their income?

10. When are the earnings generated from an annuity taxable? (Assume that the owner is an individual.)

11. Contrast the provisions of a fixed annuity to that of a variable annuity.

12. When does the *exclusion ratio* apply in the taxation of distributions from a *non qualified annuity*?

13. What is the difference between an immediate fixed annuity and a deferred fixed annuity?

14. What is a *single premium deferred annuity* (SPDA)?

15. What is the "price paid" for the contractual guarantees provided in a variable annuity?

16. Describe the characteristics of an *equity indexed annuity* (EIA).

17. Who typically purchases a *guaranteed insurance contract* (GIC) and for what purpose?

18. What is the difference between a participating and a nonparticipating GIC?

SUGGESTIONS FOR ADDITIONAL READING

Tools and Techniques of Investment Planning, Stephen R. Leimberg, Robert T. LeClair, Robert J. Doyle, Jr., and Thomas R. Robinson, The National Underwriter Company, 2004.

Investments: An Introduction, 7th edition, Herbert B. Mayo, Thomson/ South-Western, 2002.

Investment Analysis and Portfolio Management, 7th edition, Frank K. Reilly and Keith C. Brown, Thomson/South-Western, 2003.

The Wall Street Journal Guide to Money and Investing, 3rd edition, Kenneth M. Morris and Virginia B. Morris, Fireside Publishing, 2004.

Real Estate and Real Estate Investment Trusts (REITs)

• • •

With the "sideways movement" of securities markets in recent years, many investors have turned to real property to keep pace with inflation and provide a positive real rate of return. The focus of this chapter is on real estate as a potential investment and how an investor may take advantage of real property ownership beyond its use as a primary residence.

Upon completing this chapter, you should be able to:

- Describe the use of real estate as an investment
- Contrast and compare an investment in unimproved land to that of commercial and/or rental property and describe what attributes of each may be important to a potential investor
- Identify characteristics of real estate limited partnerships (RELPs)
- Explain the types of real estate investment trusts (REITs)
- Discuss features of a real estate mortgage investment conduit (REMIC) and its close cousin, the collateralized mortgage obligation (CMO)

REAL ESTATE AS AN INVESTMENT

Very broadly, some analysts categorize investments as consisting of *financial* and *real* assets. *Financial assets* include stocks and bonds and all assets that cannot be reduced to the direct or indirect ownership of real estate. Real assets include real estate, which may be further defined as land and the improvements (buildings) on that land. Real estate also includes natural resources, such as oil or natural gas, which are under that land. Sometimes these resources are referred to as *mineral rights* and are sold or conveyed separately from that of the land or improvements.

The distinction between financial and real assets is important because there is some evidence that the respective assets are *negatively correlated*. That is, as financial assets *decrease* in value (for example, the Dow Jones Industrial Average is down for the trading period that is analyzed), real assets may *increase* in value. Therefore, real assets may in some cases be an effective diversifier and inflation hedge when positioned within an investor's portfolio. However, the *location* of the subject real estate will be the single most important factor in determining both the direction and amount of any price movement; this is not the case with financial assets as they do not generally suffer from this same limitation. In addition, due to typical financing constraints, real estate purchases are usually much more highly leveraged than those of financial assets; accordingly, the value of real estate in any given location is *highly sensitive* to interest rate changes, particularly those of longer term obligations (mortgage notes).

Finally, some degree of management is necessary with *all* real estate investments (that is, a real estate purchase that is made other than for use as a primary residence). This manager may be either the investor or, more often than not, a professional property manager or management firm. As a practical matter, this makes small real estate investments impractical because of the associated reduction in the cash flow generated from the operation of the property.

USE AS A PRIMARY RESIDENCE

Most individuals, if they own real estate at all, purchase real property (land and any buildings thereon) for use as a primary residence or home for themselves and their family. As such, while they may think of their home as an investment (opportunity for profit), that is *not* the primary reason that they make the purchase. As a use asset, this is also the reason that a home is shown as such on the statement of personal financial position. (Alternatively, if the residence is converted to a rental property, the asset would now be shown as an investment on the statement of personal financial position.) Of course, the exception to this motivation is those individuals who purchase residential real estate for rental purposes and to generate future cash flow. Rental income is reported on an individual's IRS Form 1040 on Schedule E and, in this case, the investor is entitled to claim operating expenses as well as tax depreciation over the useful life of the residence. An individual who purchases real estate for use as a primary residence is entitled only to a deduction for mortgage interest incurred (within limits) on IRS Form 1040 Schedule A, as well as real estate property taxes. In addition, that individual must also elect to *itemize* his or her income tax deductions. Finally, an individual may *not* generally claim a loss for income tax purposes if real property is used as a primary residence (even if the owner of that residence anticipated that his or her property would in fact appreciate and an offsetting gain would result).

UNIMPROVED LAND

Unimproved (or *raw*) land is truly a *passive* investment. As such, it cannot generate income or tax depreciation (land is never depreciable since it is not considered to ever *wear out*). Its primary source of return is the potential for price or capital appreciation. The investment is suitable mainly for high income and net worth investors who are able to bear the associated investment risk without realizing any immediate return. In fact, unimproved land may result in a short term *negative* cash flow for the investor due to the insurance cost and other expenses (such as property taxes) incurred in maintaining the investment.

When unimproved land is sold, it is subject to capital gains tax treatment so long as the owner is *not* considered to be a *dealer* in such land (so called *dealer tax treatment*). Dealer tax treatment will result in the gain being taxable at ordinary income tax rates to the investor. There are a number of factors that courts (and the IRS) use to distinguish between an investor and a dealer in unimproved land, but generally this determination depends on the extent of the active participation of the individual (or his or her agents) in future transactions involving the subject land. For example, if an individual buys and sells a number of different tracts of unimproved land, and subsequently subdivides that land, dealer tax treatment may apply.

Tax on the gain of unimproved land (or for that matter, any type of real estate that is held for investment purposes) may be deferred by using the installment sale method of tax accounting. These rules, as provided for in Internal Revenue Code (IRC) Section 453, permit an investor to delay reporting any gain until cash is received in a given year. Installment sales are often used as financing vehicles (particularly among family members) rather than obtaining a loan from a bank. However, just as a bank would charge interest if a loan were obtained, so also is there an expectation among the seller and purchaser in an installment sale that some amount of the agreed-upon payment is categorized as interest. Indeed, if interest is not charged (or if the rate charged is insufficient under tax law), IRC Section 483 will *impute* interest on a portion of the sale price. In addition, as long as at least one payment will be received after the close of the taxable year in which the sale is made, installment sale treatment is *automatic* and must be *elected out of* by the seller if he or she does not wish for such tax treatment to occur.

For more on the income tax consequences of property that is sold under the installment sale method of tax accounting, you are referred to Kaplan University's *Individual Income Tax Planning* textbook by Mershon and Fevurly.

COMMERCIAL AND RESIDENTIAL RENTAL PROPERTY

Real property with associated buildings (so-called *improved land*) that is held for rental purposes is the most common type of real estate purchased as an investment. The rental income generated may be derived from real property that is held for either commercial or residential purposes. The rental income is taxable as ordinary income, although the property itself is a capital asset qualifying for capital gain treatment upon sale or disposition. An individual will typically purchase either type of real property directly from the seller or through a real estate broker. This is referred to as the *outright* or *direct* ownership of real property. However, the investor may also hold such property *indirectly* by purchasing an interest in a *real estate investment trust* (REIT) or *real estate limited partnership* (RELP). Both of these indirect forms of real estate ownership will be subsequently discussed in this chapter.

The direct ownership of real estate does *not* limit the personal liability of the investor for acts associated with the operation of the property. For this reason, among others, a liability insurance policy is a must for the investor. A direct owner also has absolute management responsibility over the property, although an agent (property manager) may be hired to perform the daily management tasks, such as maintenance of the property and collection of rent. However, under agency law, a direct owner of real property is responsible for the negligent acts of his or her property manager if acting on the owner's behalf. This, of course, underscores the need for the property owner to evaluate the capabilities of any agent carefully before choosing him or her (or it) to manage the subject property.

Like the valuation of securities generally, arriving at a proper value to pay for an investment in commercial or residential income producing real property is an important determination. This proper value is sometimes referred to as the *intrinsic value* since it represents the discounted present value of the property's future cash flows. The intrinsic value of a real estate rental property may be computed using a *net operating income (NOI)* concept incorporating the following steps:

Gross rental receipts from the property

+ Nonrental or other income (for example, laundry receipts)
= Potential gross income (PGI)

- Vacancy and collection losses
= Effective gross income (EGI)

- Operating expenses (excluding interest and depreciation)
= Net Operating Income (NOI)

As this is a cash flow type of computation, you must be careful to exclude depreciation and amortization expenses from the total of operating expenses. Depreciation (used to expense tangible property) and amortization (intangible property) are only reductions associated with computing the tax basis of property and are *not* a factor when performing a cash flow analysis. Also not included in the NOI computation is debt service (interest expense) on mortgages on income producing real property. Property financing is a financing decision and not an operating decision. The focus of operating expenses in the NOI computation is the *property's* cash flow and *not* that of the *investor's* cash flow.

Example 6-1: Assume that a 20-unit apartment building project is listed for a sales price of $1.0 million. It is financed by the investor by securing an $800,000 mortgage at 10% interest for 30 years ($84,246 this year). The apartment building is depreciated using the straight-line depreciation method over 27.5 years ($18,182 this year). It has 15 one-bedroom and 5 two-bedroom apartments renting for $600 and $750 per month, respectively. Other income is $2,000 per year from the washing machines situated in the building. Vacancy and collection losses equal 5% of potential gross income. Operating expenses are $55,000 for this year. Accordingly, the annual net operating income (NOI) for the apartment building project is $92,250 computed as follows:

Gross rental receipts: $153,000 [($9,000 x 12) + ($3,750 x 12)]

+ Other Income: $ 2,000

= PGI: $155,000 (PGI stands for "Potential Gross Income")

- Vacancy/Collection: $ 7,750 ($155,000 x .05)

= EGI: $147,250 (EGI stands for "Effective Gross Income")

- Operating Expenses: $ 55,000

= NOI: $ 92,250 (NOI stands for "Net Operating Income")

(Note that the mortgage interest expense and depreciation expenses are *not* included in the operating expenses computation.)

Finally, once the net operating income (NOI) from the income producing property is computed, we can then determine the intrinsic value of the property. We do this by dividing the NOI from the property by an estimated *capitalization rate* (or *cap rate*) for the market and location in which the property is situated. The appropriate cap rate to be used is a function of many factors, but it essentially represents the *required rate of return* that an investor must have to purchase the property. The *higher* the cap rate, the *greater* is the perceived risk of the purchase or property to the investor/buyer.

Example 6-2: Continuing with the facts and results of Example 6-1, assume that the investor applied a cap rate of 10% to the property. This means the investor (probably with the assistance of a qualified appraiser) computed the intrinsic value of the apartment building project to be $922,500 or $92,250 NOI divided by .10. Since the project is listed for a sales price of $1.0 million, and considering no other extraneous factors, this means that it is *overvalued* from the perspective of the investor/buyer. However, if the investor applied a cap rate of only 9% to the project, he would be willing to pay an intrinsic value of $1,025,000 ($92,250 divided by .09) for the property and, therefore, he would consider it to be *undervalued*. Notice that with a lower cap rate, the investor/buyer assumes there to be less risk associated with the project and his prospective investment.

In summary, when discussing the advantages and disadvantages of a potential investment in income producing real estate, it should be kept in mind that real property of any kind is almost always *illiquid*. That is, it cannot be converted to cash quickly without the possibility of a significant loss. There is also no organized market on the national or local level in the same way that this market exists for securities or financial assets. Real estate is, thus, also substantially less *marketable* than securities. Finally, the investment return on real estate is also significantly impacted by the available tax benefits, therefore adding to the risk of a challenge by the IRS. Practically, the expected return on a real estate purchase is difficult to evaluate since there are so many local factors, some of them unanticipated, that may lead to a reduction in the future cash flow actually realized from the investment.

REAL ESTATE LIMITED PARTNERSHIPS (RELPs)

A popular form of indirect ownership in real estate is to invest as a limited partner, usually through an investment vehicle known as a *syndication*. A *syndicated limited partnership* consists of two owners--one is the syndicator or promoter of the partnership, who usually also serves as the general partner, and the second is the investor or limited partner. The syndicator will typically acquire a tract (or tracts) of real property and then attempt to sell it (or them) to the limited partner investors. In addition to charging fees for the management of the property tracts, the syndicator will retain an ownership interest in the tracts. An *offering brochure* (the equivalent of a *prospectus* in a mutual fund) is then provided to potential investors. These investors have only legal liability limited to the amount of their investment in the syndication (hence, the term *limited partner*).

Real estate syndications are usually adopted as a so-called *tax shelter*. That is, historically, anticipated losses from the sale and operation of the limited partnership could be used to offset earned (and otherwise) taxable income. Since the 1986 Tax Reform Act, however, losses incurred on the sale of real estate are categorized as a *passive loss* and are subject to the so-called *passive activity tax rules*. In general, the term *passive activity* means any activity that involves the conduct of any trade or business where the investor has an interest but does *not* materially participate. Further, this term also specifically includes *any* rental activity of either real or tangible personal property *regardless of whether* the investor materially participates. As a result, losses attributable (or *passed through*) to a limited partner in a real estate syndication may only generally be 1) offset against a corresponding type of income, known as *passive income*, in the year within which the loss is generated or 2) deducted when the passive activity is sold or otherwise disposed of (that is, the passive losses are *suspended* until the activity generating the loss is no longer operational). There are exceptions to these rules, whereby a limited portion of losses from a residential real estate activity (so long as the investor is not a limited partner) may be used against earned or *active* income, but that exception is best reserved for a discussion in an income tax text (see for example, Kaplan University's *Individual Income Tax Planning* by Mershon and Fevurly). Of course, limited partners, by definition, are *passive investors* and, indeed, do not want to become active investors for fear of incurring personal liability for their activities.

Many, if not most, real estate limited partnerships (RELPs) are heavily leveraged. This means that only the partnership entity (and specifically, the general partner) is *at risk* (incurs personal liability) if any bank loans are not repaid by the partnership. Limited partners are typically *not* at risk to pay a proportionate amount of the loan in the event that the partnership's real estate activities cannot generate enough cash to pay off the debt. Therefore, the *at risk rules* provide that losses are deductible *only* to the extent that the investor is personally liable. In turn, the investor is not able to create tax *basis* in the real property once it is sold and recover this amount in a tax-free manner. Accordingly, not only is a limited partner in a RELP restricted by the *passive activity loss rules* from taking tax losses, but even if this tax hurdle can be overcome, he or she is also not usually considered to be *at risk* so that any income tax deductions for leveraging the investment are permitted.

As consistent with the business form generally, a limited partner's right to transfer his or her interest in real estate is restricted by the terms of the partnership agreement. Typically, this interest may not be transferred without the consent of the general partner or syndicator. In addition, unlike the general partnership form, the death of a limited partner will not cause the termination of the partnership. Alternatively, if the sole general partner in a real estate syndication were to die, the partnership would likely dissolve (unless the written partnership agreement provided for a successor general partner). To ensure that this does not happen, often times the general partner in a RELP is a regular C corporation.

Blind Pools

A *blind pool* is a type of real estate limited partnership where the partnership is formed, but the properties in which the partnership will invest have yet to be identified. Accordingly, the limited partner puts even greater trust in the skills and judgment of the general partner. These pools are also sometimes used for other investments (such as an oil and gas working or royalty interest), but in all blind pools, the reputation of the general partner must precede him or her (or it) to attract future investors who do not have the quality of the investment on which to rely.

REAL ESTATE INVESTMENT TRUSTS (REITs)

A real estate investment trust (REIT) is similar to a closed-end investment company (see Chapter 4 of this text) except that instead of in investing in securities, it invests in a managed, diversified portfolio of real estate or real estate mortgages and construction loans. The investor achieves diversification and, more importantly, marketability in a publicly traded REIT. The shares of the REIT are either listed on an exchange (the more common situation) or traded over-the-counter among broker/dealers. Although REITs are taxed like a corporation, they are not subject to tax at the corporate level *if* they distribute at least 90% of their net annual earnings to shareholders. (Note that this is in contrast to mutual funds that must distribute 98% of their net earnings so as to avoid tax at the entity level.) Therefore, REIT shareholders enjoy limited liability and higher dividend payouts while avoiding the double taxation of corporate ownership. Finally, REITs must be registered with the SEC pursuant to the provisions of the Securities Act of 1933.

As income producing investments, REITs do not react substantially to daily changes in the stock market. Rather, they are more sensitive to interest rate fluctuations. Generally, the movement of REITs is *opposite* to that of interest rates; as interest rates rise, the market value of REITs decline and, as interest rates fall, the value of REITs will increase. In addition, studies have shown that returns on REITs have become less correlated with that of bonds. For example, Ibbotson & Associates have shown that the correlation of REITs investment returns with those of long-term U.S. government bonds has declined in recent years, leading to the conclusion that an investor may effectively diversify a portfolio with a REIT if willing to assume the associated interest rate risk. As a result, by investing a portion of their portfolio in a REIT, in addition to stocks and bonds, an investor may experience greater returns with less systematic risk.

Shareholders pay taxes on distributions (i.e., dividends) from the earnings of a REIT. This distributed income is taxable as ordinary income (not capital gains) to the shareholder. However, because REITs do not generally pay corporate taxes (recall the *90% of earnings distribution rule*), most dividends that are payable by a REIT do *not* qualify for the favorable tax treatment (a 5% or 15% rate depending on the individual's marginal income tax bracket) brought about by the JGTRRA legislation of 2003. A small portion of dividends paid by REITs may constitute *qualified dividend income* (for example, if the REIT fails to distribute at least 90% of earnings and is therefore subject to corporate income tax), but this is the rare exception and not the general rule.

REITs are available to investors in three types- equity REITs, mortgage REITs, and hybrid REITs- the characteristics of each of which are now discussed.

Equity REITs

Equity REITs invest mainly in established income-producing properties such as office buildings and shopping centers, who then lease the property to others. Such REITs also typically use a moderate amount of leverage to finance the property purchases. Due to their portfolio of investments, equity REITs generally provide moderate income to their shareholders and opportunities for increasing cash flows and capital appreciation. Some equity REITs focus on new construction and recently completed properties that have not yet been fully rented. Accordingly, there may be low initial cash flows from proven rents, but considerable growth potential and significant capital gains when the investments are sold.

As mentioned, equity REITs also frequently take on a modest amount of leverage. Indeed, equity REIT income is derived from the difference between the net rental income generated from properties that are purchased and interest that is paid on any loans. If equity REITs take on too much leverage, and then also experience a higher than expected vacancy rate from actual rentals, their cash flow may be negatively impacted, resulting in decreased dividend payments to shareholders and a decline in the net asset value of the REIT shares. This is also why, as a group, equity REITs are considered to be a *riskier* investment than that of their close cousin, the mortgage REIT.

Mortgage REITs

Mortgage REITs make loans to develop property and/or finance construction. As such, they essentially invest in real estate *indirectly* (that is, only by lending funds that are used to build properties). In contrast to equity REITs, mortgage REITs generally provide for *higher income*, but also offer *less opportunity for growth* in the net asset value of their shares. In some instances, mortgage REITs also invest in mortgage-backed securities such as *Ginnie Mae* or *Freddie Mac* obligations (see chapter 2 of this textbook). Therefore, the question arises, why might an investor purchase a mortgage REIT rather than investing in the mortgage-backed security directly? The answer is primarily one of security. An investor directly purchasing a mortgage-backed security must be concerned about reinvestment rate risk and the possibility that, as mortgages are refinanced, the pools of mortgages from which their investment income is derived may be liquidated (never to be seen again). Alternatively, most mortgage REITs have indeterminate lives and continue to acquire additional mortgages as the older mortgages in the pool are paid off. Therefore, mortgage REITs offer a higher certainty of steady income (and associated yield) than mortgage backed securities.

Mortgage REITs have investment characteristics similar to long term corporate bonds and are, therefore, not likely to be good inflation hedges. Indeed, the major type of investment risk that a mortgage REIT shareholder assumes is that of purchasing power risk. If inflation accelerates, thus causing interest rates to rise, the value of the REITs underlying mortgages and loans will typically *fall*. Accordingly, in inflationary times, share values in mortgage REITs are likely to decline. This is particularly the case if the REIT has invested in fixed rate types of mortgages. If the mortgage REIT has instead invested in adjustable rate mortgages (ARMs), or other types of variable rate loans, purchasing power risk is minimized since interest rates will tend to move in concert with the direction and amount of inflation.

Finally, mortgage REITs may purchase a limited amount of investments other than real estate properties. Specifically, only 75% of such REITs income must come from real estate investments; the remainder may come from securities, such as mortgage-backed securities.

Hybrid REITs

Hybrid REITs combine the features of both equity and mortgage REITs. This means that they invest in established income-producing properties as well as mortgages and securities. Thus, a hybrid REIT provides for capital appreciation growth as well as the possibility for higher income (although not with the same expected return as either of its separately structured cousins).

REITs vs. RELPs

As we have previously discussed, real estate limited partnerships (RELPs) offer a real estate investment alternative to a real estate investment trust (REIT). Both are indirect forms of investing in real estate without the burden of personal management by the investor. However, there are differences. The primary differences are as follows:

1) **Liquidity:** REITs are relatively liquid (at least in recent years given the strength of most local real estate markets) and actively traded on national and regional stock exchanges, as well as over the counter. RELPs, with the exception of a small number of publicly traded partnerships, are generally not readily marketable and illiquid. In addition, a REIT shareholder may sell as few or as many shares as he or she deems appropriate whereas a RELP investor must generally sell his or her entire interest (if there is a market for the same).

2) **Tax Treatment:** A REIT is a portfolio investment and is subject to taxation like a stock (that is, income dividends are generally taxable as ordinary income and dispositions are taxable as capital gains or losses). A RELP, on the other hand, is strictly a passive activity investment and generates passive losses, which may only generally be used when an investor also has passive income. Because a REIT generates so-called *portfolio* income (see *Individual Income Tax Planning* by Mershon and Fevurly), losses from a RELP may not be used to offset taxable income from a REIT.

3) **Organizational Structure:** A REIT (as a corporation) is managed by a Board of Directors whereas a RELP is managed by a general partner. Further, upon the death of a REIT shareholder, the organizational structure does not automatically terminate.

4) **Investor Risk:** The major risk associated with a REIT is usually the loss of potential purchasing power over time, although this may be mitigated with certain underlying investments. A RELP (as a limited partnership) suffers from extreme liquidity and marketability risk.

REAL ESTATE MORTGAGE INVESTMENT CONDUITS (REMICs)

A *real estate mortgage investment conduit (REMIC)* is a self-liquidating, flow through entity (similar to a partnership) that invests exclusively in real estate mortgages or in mortgage-backed securities. Typically, the REMIC issues debt securities that are known as *REMIC bonds.* They may be issued either as *regular interests* that are publicly traded or as *residual interests,* which currently are privately placed and not available to the general public. Investors who hold those securities receive a specified cash flow from the underlying pool of mortgages. In this respect, REMIC bonds are very similar to *collateralized mortgage obligations* (CMOs). However, REMICs are intended to be the exclusive means for issuing multiple-class real estate mortgage-backed securities in the future (thereby replacing CMOs). CMOs are subsequently discussed. Most newly issued CMOs and REMICs provide for monthly payments to the investor and are offered in denominations ranging from $1,000 to $25,000, depending on the issuer of the security.

As evident from the word *conduit* in its name, a REMIC is a pass through entity that is wholly exempt from federal income tax. Thus, it acts as a conduit and holders of REMIC bonds (not the entity itself) must report any taxable income from the underlying mortgages. However, like original issue discount (OID) bonds, the holders of REMIC bonds must use the accrual accounting method to report income on their bonds, even if they are cash-basis taxpayers. Thus, *phantom income* accrues, meaning that REMIC bonds are best positioned in a tax-deferred account (like a retirement plan). Further, a special rule requires that a part of the gain on the sale of a REMIC bond is taxable as ordinary income (contrast this to the normal rule of corporate bond taxation where any gain is taxable as capital gain). The portion of the gain on the sale of a REMIC bond that is treated as ordinary income is equal to the excess of the amount that would have been includible on the bond if its yield were 110% of the Applicable Federal Rate (AFR) in effect when the holder's holding began, over the amount actually included by the holder in gross income during the time that the bond was owned.

> **Example 6-3:** Assume that a REMIC bond with a coupon rate of 6% per year is acquired for its par value of $1,000. The AFR at the time of acquisition is 8%. In three years the bond is sold for $1,150; therefore, the gain on the bond is $150 ($1,150 less $1,000). The amount of interest that is actually included in income is $180 ($60 times three). The amount that would have been included in income if its yield were 110% of the 8% AFR is $290.40 (8.8 x 1.10 divided by 100 = .0968; .0968 x $1,000 x 3). Therefore, $110.40 ($290.40 less $180) of the $150 gain on the sale is taxable as ordinary income and the remaining $39.60 is taxable as long term capital gain.

The price sensitivity of REMIC bonds tends to be *less* than that of corporate bonds of similar quality and maturity. This is because the velocity of the change in the price is mitigated by changes in the rates of prepayments on the underlying mortgage pools. Specifically, prepayments on the existing mortgages tend to pick up when the overall market interest rates decline and homeowners begin to refinance their debt obligations. As prepayments *increase*, the average maturity of the pool of mortgages *decreases*. As a result, the price of the REMIC bonds will not tend to rise as much as its corporate counterpart. Prepayments may also slow down when interest rates increase because there will be fewer refinancings of existing mortgages (the opposite result than when the economy is expanding). Nonetheless, however, homeowners must still make mortgage payments of interest and principal. Therefore, even as interest rates rise, the price of the REMIC bonds will tend to fall less since mortgage principal is still being repaid.

Accordingly, for what type of investor is a REMIC bond most suitable? An investor who desires both increased liquidity and more predictability of mortgage principal repayment may find such a bond attractive. Further, since REMICs may be structured to offer *classes* of bonds that mature over a time frame of, generally, anywhere between three and 30 years, investors may invest in classes that match their investment time horizon and avoid some uncertainty regarding when bond principal will be repaid. The price of this assurance is an assumption of interest rate risk by the investor as with any type of fixed-income investment. In addition, the investor must assume the reinvestment rate risk of the prepayment of existing mortgages pooled by the REMIC.

Collateralized Mortgage Obligations (CMOs)

Like a REMIC, collateralized mortgage obligations (CMOs) do not view mortgage pools as a means of passing through payments to investors in exactly the same form as received. This is also a distinction that REMICs and CMOs possess from those of mortgage pass through participation certificates, which represent a direct ownership interest in the pool. Rather, CMOs package mortgage payments received on the basis of cash flow expected over the life of the pool. They do this by issuing separate classes of securities known as *tranches* (French for *slices*). The typical CMO has A to Z tranches, representing the most accelerated form of repayment, a medium or intermediate form of repayment, and the slowest or least accelerated form of repayment, respectively. The Z tranche bears no coupon (similar to a *zero coupon bond*), but receives the cash flow from the mortgage pool *after* the other tranches are satisfied. It thus carries the highest yield but, consequently, also carries the most amount of interest rate risk.

CMOs and REMICs are often used interchangeably in the marketplace, but technically real estate mortgage investment conduit (REMIC) bond is the proper term. The Tax Reform Act of 1986 allowed mortgage securities pools to elect the tax status of a REMIC (that is, a tax-exempt entity). Beginning January 1, 1987, most new CMOs have been issued in REMIC form to create tax and accounting advantages for the issuers. Issuers include government and quasi-governmental organizations, such as the Government National Mortgage Association (Ginnie Mae) and the Federal Home Loan Mortgage Company (Freddie Mac), as well as other private label, third party guarantee financial institutions. Investors include institutions of all sizes but, in recent years, individual investors have also become increasingly active in the real estate mortgage securities market.

IMPORTANT CONCEPTS

Financial assets

Real assets

Use asset (real estate as primary residence)

Unimproved land

Dealer tax treatment

Commercial rental property

Net operating income (NOI)

Capitalization rate (cap rate)

Intrinsic value of real estate

Real estate limited partnership (RELP)

Passive activity tax rules

At risk rules

Blind pool

Real estate investment trust (REIT)

Equity REIT

Mortgage REIT

Hybrid REIT

Real estate mortgage investment conduit (REMIC) bond

Collateralized mortgage obligation (CMO)

QUESTIONS FOR REVIEW

1. What have past studies suggested may be the correlation between *financial* and *real assets*? Why is this important?

2. What use do most individuals make of a real estate purchase?

3. Why would an investor typically invest in unimproved or *raw* land? How may tax on any gain from the sale of such land be deferred?

4. Contrast the direct purchase of improved land to that of indirect ownership. What is the primary form of indirect ownership of real estate in the secondary marketplace today?

5. In computing *net operating income* (NOI), what should be *excluded* when analyzing the applicable amount of operating expenses? Why is this the proper way to proceed?

6. How is the *intrinsic value* of real estate improved land derived? What is meant by the term cap rate in deriving this value?

7. "Real estate is, by its very nature, an illiquid investment." Explain this statement.

8. What is a real estate *syndication* and in what form of business entity is such investment vehicle normally offered to the investing public?

9. There are two basic income tax implications if a loss from the sale of real estate held as an investment occurs. What are these implications?

10. Often times the general partner in a *RELP* is operated as a regular C corporation. Why is this?

11. What is a *blind pool*?

12. What requirement must be satisfied before a real estate investment trust (REIT) is *not* separately taxed?

13. What are two major advantages that an investor in REIT enjoys that are not possible with the direct ownership of real estate?

14. Are the market values of REITs generally sensitive to daily changes in the stock market? Explain.

15. Why are most dividends payable from a REIT *not* considered to be *qualified* for favorable income tax treatment?

16. What are the three types of REITS available to investors? Which one is generally considered to have the most investor risk and why is this the case?

17. Contrast a mortgage REIT to that of an equity REIT in terms of a) potential income payout and b) opportunity for capital growth.

18. What are four primary differences between a REIT and a RELP?

19. What is a real estate mortgage investment conduit (REMIC)? Who issues such securities?

20. Where should a REMIC bond best be positioned within an investor's portfolio? Explain.

21. For what type of investor is a REMIC bond most suitable?

22. Is there any difference between a REMIC and a collateralized mortgage obligation (CMO)? Explain.

23. What is a CMO *tranche*? Which one of these tranches carries the highest yield (and corresponding investor risk)?

SUGGESTIONS FOR ADDITIONAL READING

Tools and Techniques of Investment Planning, Stephen R. Leimberg, Robert T. LeClair, Robert J. Doyle, Jr., and Thomas R. Robinson, The National Underwriter Company, 2004.

Investments: An Introduction, 7th edition, Herbert B. Mayo, Thomson/ South-Western, 2002.

Investment Analysis and Portfolio Management, 7th edition, Frank K. Reilly and Keith C. Brown, Thomson/South-Western, 2003.

The Wall Street Journal Guide to Money and Investing, 3rd edition, Kenneth M. Morris and Virginia B. Morris, Fireside Publishing, 2004.

CHAPTER SEVEN

Alternative Investments

• • •

This chapter considers so-called *alternative investments* among these derivatives, tangible assets (such as collectibles), and natural resources. A derivative is an investment alternative that derives its value from that of another investment (usually, securities). Tangible assets are characterized by their lack of marketability, as compared with other investment assets. Finally, many natural resource investments are sometimes referred to as *wasting assets,* since their supply is, by definition, limited and will eventually be exhausted. Of course, this is not the case with so-called *renewable* natural resources, such as lumber and water.

Upon completing this chapter, you should be able to:

- Explain the use of derivatives, including options and futures as an alternative investment
- Describe the characteristics of stock options as investments and their use as a hedging technique
- Identify attributes of an investment in tangible assets (collectibles) and/or natural resources (oil and gas wells)
- Compare alternative investments to more traditional investments

DERIVATIVES AS AN INVESTMENT

A *derivative* is an investment vehicle which has a value that is based on another security's value (such as a listed stock). Likely the most common of these alternative investments are stock options, futures contracts, and forward agreements. For each of these three general derivative positions, an investor may enter into a transaction as either the *long position* (i.e., the buyer) or the *short position* (i.e., the seller). Institutional investors have historically used derivatives to increase overall portfolio return or to hedge portfolio risk. However, in recent years, individual investors (particularly those of higher net worth and discretionary income) have made derivatives a fundamental part of privately-managed *hedge funds*. By way of review, a *hedge*, in the financial world, means an investment that is made to reduce the risk of adverse price movements in a security.

The use of derivatives is not for the faint of heart. In essence, the investor who uses derivatives not only has to be concerned about the price movement of the underlying security, but also that of the derivative vehicle. Therefore, he or she needs to be correct *twice* to generate a superior rate of return. However, derivatives may be used to *leverage* an individual's potential percentage return by generating significant dollar gains from a much smaller initial investment. Investment professionals refer to individuals who are interested in a sizeable gain over a short period of time as *speculators* or *traders*. In contrast, an individual who owns the underlying security (and intends to own it for some period of time) is referred to as an *investor*. The prudent way to invest in derivatives is as an investor that takes an offsetting market position (for example, being in the *short* or sell position in the event that the market declines) as a method of controlling or minimizing total market risk. This is known as *hedging* or using *hedging techniques*.

STOCK OPTIONS AS AN INVESTMENT

An option is a contract between a buyer and seller with specified terms. The most common of option contracts involve stocks, but there are also options written on indexes, interest rates, and foreign currencies. Two parties are involved in each contact (the buyer and seller); however, these parties are also referred to by other names as follows:

> Buyer = Long = Holder = Owner
> Seller = Short = Writer

The *buyer* in an option contract pays a premium for the cost of the contract to the seller. In turn, this gives him or her (or it, if an institution) the *right* to exercise the option (i.e., buy or sell the underlying stock). The *seller* in an option contract receives the premium from the buyer and, subsequently, has the *obligation* to buy or sell if the option is exercised by the buyer or holder.

Every option contract has at least three specifications:

1) **The underlying instrument:** Usually, this is a stock. However, as mentioned, it may also be anything with fluctuating value such as the overall market index.

2) **The contract price:** The contract specifies an option *premium* that the buyer must pay for the right to implement the contract. A *strike* or *exercise* price at which the purchase or sale of the underlying instrument will occur is also included.

3) **The expiration date:** All contracts expire on a specified date (usually, the Saturday following the third Friday of the month). In addition, new contracts (with the exception of a special type of option called a LEAP or Long-term Equity AnticiPation Security, subsequently discussed) are issued with 9-month expirations. Typically, the option may be bought or sold at any time during this specified life cycle.

Finally, each contract includes *100 shares* when issued, otherwise referred to as a *round lot*.

Options are generally available only on stocks that are widely held or that are actively traded. The five options exchanges trade options only on about 1,500 issues or only a portion of the thousands of stocks that are listed on a national or regional exchange. If an investor owns the underlying stock on which the option is written, he or she is *covered* and needs to *close out* his or her position by delivering the stock to the buyer or holder of the option. However, an investor may trade options *without* actual ownership of the underlying stock. This is referred to as trading *naked* and not only involves the obligation to *close out* the option with the buyer, but also requires the writer to buy the stock for delivery if the option is exercised. This can be particularly expensive since the writer must also pay double commissions to the broker-dealer through whom the transaction is processed.

As noted earlier, the price of an option contract is known as the *premium*. This premium is quoted on a per-share basis and, because the option contract is issued in 100-share lots, the total premium is then calculated by multiplying by 100. There is no tax due at the time the option is written and the premium is paid to the seller or writer (it is a nondeductible capital expenditure to the buyer). Rather, the premium is considered to be *deferred* until the transaction is completed. If the option is exercised, the seller adds the premium to the exercise price to determine the total amount received. If the option expires and is not exercised, the premium is recognized as a short term capital gain (remember new contracts are typically issued with a 9-month expiration date) and is included in the seller's income for the calendar tax year in which the option expired. An option's premium reflects both the *intrinsic value* and *time value* of the option, both of which will be subsequently discussed.

Option buyers may usually exercise a contract at any time between the issue and expiration date of the option. This is known as an *American-style option* and is typical of most stock options traded on the exchange. A *European-style option* may only be exercised on the day before its expiration. These are occasionally used with some forms of index options and foreign currency options. Although there may be limitations on when they may be exercised, European-style options (like their American-style counterpart) can still be traded at any time prior to their expiration to close out an investor position.

The Options Market

Options trade on all the major U.S. exchanges, most notably the Chicago Board of Options Exchange (CBOE) and over-the-counter (OTC). Exchange traded options are known as *listed options* and have standardized exercise prices and expiration dates. OTC options are *not* standardized with terms that are individually negotiated between buyer and seller. Only minimal secondary market activity for OTC options exists because these contracts are not standardized. Position limits are established for the most heavily-traded listed options and apply to individuals, married couples, and registered broker-dealer representatives acting in a discretionary account. Such limits are currently 75,000 contracts "on the same side of the market" (that is, either in a long or short position) that may be exercised within a five business-day period.

The Options Clearing Corporation (OCC) issues all option contracts. It is owned by the exchanges that trade options and guarantees that the obligations of both parties to the trade are fulfilled. In addition, the OCC designates the exercise prices and expiration months for new contracts within market standards to maintain uniformity and marketability. (The market determines the premium for the contract.) If the holder of an option wishes to exercise the option, his or her broker-dealer notifies the OCC, who then notifies on a random basis the "short" side of the option, namely the broker-dealer of the seller. The short broker-dealer then assigns the option to a short customer. Options contracts are traded without a certificate or formal writing. Indeed, an investor's only proof of subsequent ownership is his or her trade confirmation.

Calls and Puts

Call Options

A *call* is an option contract giving the holder the right to *buy* the underlying stock at a specified exercise (or strike) price. An investor may buy calls (*go long*) or sell calls (*go short*). If an investor buys a call option, he or she has the *right to buy* 100 shares of a specific stock at the exercise price before the expiration date of the option *if* he or she chooses to exercise. If the investor sells a call option, he or she has the *obligation to sell* 100 shares of a specific stock at the exercise price *if* the buyer chooses to exercise. Accordingly, it should be evident that the buyer of any option controls the ultimate result by choosing to exercise the option or not; alternatively, the seller or writer of any option is the victim of the buyer's decision. Sellers are only exercised *against* and do not have the opportunity to exercise. Or, said another way, the buyer wants the option contract to be *exercised*; the seller wants the option contract to expire (unexercised). The seller wins at expiration because he or she gets to keep the option premium.

A call is *in-the-money* when the market price of the underlying stock exceeds the exercise price of the option. Accordingly, buyers want options to be in-the-money and sellers do not. A call is *out-of-the-money* when the market price of the underlying stock is less than the strike price. Accordingly, sellers want options to be out-of-the-money and buyers do not. The *intrinsic value* of an option is the minimum price it will command as an option and is the difference between the market price of the underlying stock and the exercise price of the option. It is represented by the in-the-money amount. A call has intrinsic value when the market price is above the exercise price.

Example 7-1: Assume that the market price of ABC stock is $50 per share and that the investor has previously purchased a call option on ABC stock with an exercise price of $30 per share. Therefore, the option is $20 in-the-money ($50 less $30) and the call will be exercised. Its intrinsic value is also $20. Alternatively, if the market price of ABC stock has declined to $20 per share (and the investor is still holding the same call option), the option is $10 out-of-the-money. Thus, the option will be allowed to expire unexercised and has an intrinsic value of zero (unless the stock price increases to more than the option's $30 exercise price before the option's expiration date).

Options *never* have negative intrinsic value; intrinsic value is only a positive amount or an amount of zero. A call that has intrinsic value at its expiration date will be exercised.

The *time premium* for any option is the amount that the market price of the option exceeds its intrinsic value. An option carries such a premium precisely because the option investor knows that, *with time*, the underlying stock price may well push past the exercise price of the option, therefore putting the option in-the-money.

Example 7-2: Continuing with the facts of Example 7-1, where ABC stock is $50 per share and the intrinsic value of the call option is $20. Now assume that the investor must pay $28 to purchase the ABC stock call option. Since its intrinsic value is $20 in the first set of facts, the time premium is $8 ($28 less $20). Alternatively, in the second set of facts (where the option is out-of-the-money and has an intrinsic value of zero), the time premium would be $28 ($28 less zero).

As a result, it is easy to see that an option that is out-of-the-money has a greater time premium since it has *no* intrinsic value. Indeed, time is the *only* value that an out-of-the-money option possesses. However, time premium is *not* the same amount as time value, which is one of the two components of the option premium charged to the buyer for the right to exercise the option. *Time value* is computed by subtracting the intrinsic value of the option from its total premium.

Example 7-3: Assume that the stated premium for a call option on KRF stock is $5.00 and that the intrinsic value is $3.00 (as computed by subtracting the exercise price of the call option from the current market price of KRF stock). Accordingly, the time value of the option is $2.00 (or the $5.00 stated premium less the $3.00 intrinsic value).

No taxable gain or loss is recognized upon the exercise of a call option. A capital gain or loss is recognized only when the stock acquired through the exercise of the call is sold. At that time, the cost of the call (or the premium charged) is added to the purchase price of the stock to compute any taxable gain or loss. The holding period is measured from the date *after* the call is purchased, *not* from the date that the call is purchased. If the call option is not exercised (that is, it is allowed to expire), then the option is considered sold as of the expiration date and the buyer recognizes a short term capital loss equal to the premium amount.

Put Options

A *put* is an option contract giving the holder the right to *sell* the underlying stock at a specified exercise price. Like calls, an investor may also buy puts (go long) or sell puts (go short). If an investor *buys* a put option, he or she has the *right to sell* 100 shares of a specific stock at the exercise price before the expiration date of the option *if* he or she chooses to exercise. If the investor *sells* a put option, he or she has the *obligation to buy* 100 shares of a specific stock at the exercise price *if* the buyer chooses to exercise. Puts are like looking in the mirror from calls; all transactions are the *opposite* of the call since the investor is taking the opposite position in the market.

A put is *in-the-money* when the market price of the underlying stock is less than the exercise price of the option. Like a call, buyers want a put that is in-the-money and sellers do not. A put is *out-of-the-money* when the market price of the underlying stock exceeds the exercise price. Like a call, sellers want a put that is out-of-the-money and buyers do not. A put has intrinsic value when the market price of the underlying stock is *below* the exercise price of the option. Like a call, the intrinsic value of a put is represented by its in-the-money amount.

> **Example 7-4:** Assume that the market price of DEF stock is $25 per share and that the investor has previously purchased a put option on DEF stock with an exercise price of $30 per share. Therefore, the option is $5 in-the-money ($25 less $30) and the put will be exercised. Its intrinsic value is also $5. Alternatively, if the market price of DEF stock has increased to $45 per share (and the investor is holding the same put option), the option is $15 out-of-the-money. Thus, the option will be allowed to expire unexercised (unless the stock price falls to no more than the option's $30 exercise price before the option's expiration date) and has an intrinsic value of zero.

Like a call, a put that has intrinsic value at its expiration date will be exercised.

The *breakeven point* for any option is the point at which the investor neither makes nor loses money. For *calls*, the breakeven point is found by adding the exercise price of the option and the premium paid for the option. For the call buyer, the contract is profitable above the breakeven; for the call seller, the contract is profitable below the breakeven. For *puts*, the breakeven point is found by subtracting the premium paid for the option from the exercise price of the option. For the put buyer, the contract is profitable below the breakeven; for the put seller, the contract is profitable above the breakeven.

> **Example 7-5:** Assume that the following quote in the *Wall Street Journal* appears for a call option written on XYZ common stock:
>
> XYZ Jan 2006 65 call at 7
>
> Since the "65" in the quote represents the exercise price of the call option (it expires in January of 2006) and the "7" represents the premium, the "breakeven point" for an investor who has purchased such option is $72 ($65 + $7). If the market price of XYZ common stock increases to above $72, the option contract is profitable for the buyer.

Exercising a put option constitutes a sale of the stock and is recognized as a taxable event. The cost of the put (or premium paid) is subtracted from the selling price of the stock in computing capital gain or loss for tax purposes. The date of exercise of the put option is treated as the sale date of the stock. If the put option is not exercised (allowed to expire), then the option is considered sold as of the expiration date and the buyer recognizes a short term capital loss equal to the premium amount.

Long-Term Equity AnticiPation Securities (LEAPS)

Long-term Equity AnticiPation Securities or LEAPS are long-term options that generally have expiration dates up to as much as 39 months (3 years and 3 months). These types of options allow investors to position themselves for market movements that are expected beyond the normal nine-month timeframe of the standard option. LEAPS that are currently traded expire in 24 months (two years) and, like a regular option, may be bought or sold at any time during this life cycle. LEAPS are only available on a limited number of securities (around 500) and indexes (around 10). Fundamentally, they operate like any other written option, but their tax treatment is unique. Although investors may have held the contract for more than 12 months (and, therefore, theoretically qualifying the contract for long term gain or loss treatment), LEAP sellers or writers must report *short term capital gains* at expiration. However, LEAP buyers or holders may report a *long term loss* at this same date.

Combinations

Investors can simultaneously buy or sell more than one option contract on opposite sides (buy and sell) of the market. The most common of these positions, known as either a *spread* or a *straddle,* may be used to limit position costs and risks (in other words, as a *hedging technique*). They will be further addressed in chapter 16 of this text when discussing *hedging and option strategies*. An investor will engage in a combination because he feels certain that there will be some future movement in the price of the underlying security. However, he or she does not know in which direction the movement will occur, so they buy on both sides of the market (or classes of options) and will profit, as long as either side (or class) reaches an in-the-money amount greater than his or her combined premium.

A *spread* is the simultaneous purchase of one option and sale of another option of the same class (call or put). For example, a *call spread* is the purchase of a call option (being *long*) and the sale of a call option (going *short*). A *put spread* is the combination of the purchase of put option (being long) and the sale of a put option (going short). Investors can buy or sell three types of basic spreads as follows:

1) A *price spread* is one that has different exercise prices but the same expiration date:

   Long XYZ Nov *50* call at 6
   Short XYZ Nov *60* call at 4

2) A *time spread* is one that has different expiration dates but the same exercise prices:

> Long XYZ *Nov* 60 call at 4
> Short XYZ *Jan* 60 call at 6

3) A *diagonal spread* is one in which the options differ in both time and price; on an options report, a line connecting these two positions would appear as diagonal:

> Long XYZ *Nov 50* call at 6
> Short XYZ *Jan 60* call at 6

A *straddle* is composed of a call option and a put option (that is, different classes) with the same exercise price and expiration month. Investors can engage in two basic types of straddles as follows:

1) A *long straddle* is the purchase of a call and put with the same exercise price and expiration date:

> Buy 1 ABC *Jan 50* call at 3
> Buy 1 ABC *Jan 50* put at 5

2) A *short straddle* is the sale of a call and put with the same exercise price and expiration date:

> Sell 1 ABC *Jan 45* call at 4
> Sell 1 ABC *Jan 45* put at 6

FUTURES AND FORWARD CONTRACTS

To many investors, the *forward contract* is the most basic derivative product that is available. Generally, such a contract provides its holder with both the right and obligation to conduct a transaction involving an underlying asset (usually a security or commodity) at a predetermined future date and price. There must always be two parties to the contract: the eventual *buyer* (said to be in the *long position*), who pays the contract price and receives the underlying asset, and the eventual seller (said to be in the *short position*), who delivers the security for the fixed price. The settlement date for such contract is purposely set to be in the future. However, at times, this date is established to be executed immediately (known as a *spot market* transaction).

Forward contracts are negotiated in the over-the-counter (OTC) market. This means that such contracts are agreements between two private parties--one of which is usually a commercial or investment bank--rather than being traded through a formal security or commodity exchange. An advantage of this private arrangement is that the terms of the contract are completely flexible between the parties; however, a distinct disadvantage is that the contract is often *not marketable*, meaning here that it is extremely difficult for one of the parties to exit the contract before it matures. This lack of marketability is really a by-product of the contract's flexibility since the more customized the forward contract becomes, the less marketable it will be to someone else. *Futures contracts (futures)* solve this problem by standardizing the terms of the agreement to the extent that it can be traded on an exchange. In contrast to the forward market, both parties in a futures contract trade through a centralized market, known as a *futures exchange*. As a result, either party may always unwind its previous commitment, prior to expiration of the contract, simply by trading back (redeeming) its existing position back to the exchange at the prevailing market price.

The futures price is analogous to the forward contract price and, at any time during the life of the contract, is established at a level so that a new long or short position does *not* have to pay a premium to enter into the market. However, the exchange will require both parties in a futures contract to post collateral, or *margin*, to protect itself against the possibility of default. These margin accounts are held by the exchange's clearinghouse and are *marked to market*, meaning that they are adjusted on a daily basis for contract price movements in order to ensure that both parties always maintain sufficient collateral to guarantee their future participation. All contracts are financially guaranteed by the clearinghouse that processes the transaction, thereby improving market performance by eliminating such worries as the credit-worthiness of either party. The underlying subject of the futures contract is usually either financial securities, such as foreign currencies, or physical commodities, such as agricultural products, oil, coffee, or cattle. Regardless, all of these underlying assets have two common characteristics: *extremely volatile price movements* and *strong participation* from both buyers and sellers.

Financial Futures

The financial futures market is composed of both *exchange-traded* futures and *over-the-counter* (OTC) futures. Exchange-traded futures are contracts listed on organized exchanges, such as the Chicago Mercantile Exchange and many other exchanges. These contracts are quite standardized and are valued according to the *marked to market* rule just discussed. In contrast, the OTC futures market is essentially a negotiated private placement market, loosely regulated and involving contracts on millions of dollars of financial investment vehicles. Here, the contracts are much less standardized and are generally *not* marked-to-market. Typically, only large financial institutions and international corporations participate in the OTC futures market.

The financial futures market includes:

1) *Currency futures:* Contracts on foreign currencies
2) *Interest rate futures:* Contracts on U.S. Treasury securities and other interest related financial instruments or benchmark rates, such as the London Inter-Bank Offered Rate (LIBOR)
3) *Index futures:* Contracts on domestic or foreign stock indexes (for example, the S&P 500 or the EAFE index)
4) *Single stock futures:* Contracts on individual stocks
5) *Narrow-based or sector futures:* Contracts based on a small number of stocks from a narrow sector of the market (such as health care or energy).

Financial futures are generally considered to be executory contracts or ones that mandate performance at some future date. Broadly (along with commodity futures), financial futures are known as *regulated futures contracts* for tax purposes. Accordingly, gains and losses thereon are *capital* in nature, regardless of the nature of the underlying financial instrument. Any gain or loss on the contract is to be reported and treated by an investor as if 40% of the gain or loss is short-term and 60% is long-term. Any excess of long-term capital gains over short-term capital losses are generally taxable at the regular long-term capital gains rate of 5% or 15%, depending on the investor's marginal income tax bracket. The combination of these rates results in a maximum effective rate of 23% on all futures transactions [(35% x 40%) + (15% x 60%)].

Most investors will hold financial futures in order to *hedge* the current holdings of a particular position in one financial instrument against the risk of an adverse price change. Therefore, they take an opposite position (either long or short) in this same instrument and *close out* (also known as *offsetting* or *unwinding*) the transaction at the agreed-upon future maturity date. Note that all futures transactions must be carried out through a margin account with a broker-dealer that remits orders to the trading floors of the various futures exchanges dealing in the underlying asset.

> **Example 7-6:** George calls his broker-dealer and tells him "Buy a Japanese Yen futures contract for my margin account at 80." This means that his broker will buy for George a standardized amount of Japanese Yen denominated in U.S. dollars, say $100,000 for a price paid of 80 or $80,000. In addition, George will have to post collateral (or deposit of money) in his margin account with the broker. Once the trade has been made, George is *long* or in the position of a buyer. He will then *close out* the transaction by *going short* or selling another contract on this same amount of Japanese Yen. Therefore, George may decide to *close out* his buyer's position by selling another contract on Japanese Yen when the price of another contract reaches $83,000 (thereby recognizing a gain of $3,000). Of course, it is likely that George will not *net* the total of $3,000 since brokerage fees (including any margin loan interest) and commissions for executing the trades will be charged.

While it is possible to enter into a financial futures contract that spans two to three years, most contracts are written to require settlement (mature) within one year. Therefore, investors who are regularly engaged in the futures market may enter into a series of contracts with new contracts designed to take effect when the old ones are settled or *closed out*. It is also possible to take *delivery* of the underlying asset at the settlement date. However, closing out (or offsetting) the contract with the opposite position is the much more common practice.

Commodity Futures

Unlike financial futures where only a paper ownership right is involved, in commodity futures a purchase of the actual item occurs. Specifically, a commodity purchase represents ownership of a definite physical product, such as agricultural products or crude oil. Most investors purchasing commodities buy a contract to either make or accept delivery of the specified commodity on a given future date. If the contract runs to its termination, the investor must complete the contract either by making a delivery of the commodity or by paying cash in acceptance of the commodity. However, the vast majority of commodity futures contracts are closed out before their termination or maturity date.

Like financial futures, most investors (in this case, typically farmers) hedge the risk that commodity prices will be lower in the future by taking an offsetting position. For example, assume that a farmer plants corn (is long) and wants to get today's price for delivery in the future (of course, he is concerned that corn prices will be lower in the future than they are today; his willingness to enter into the contract also suggests that the current futures price must be providing him a reasonable return on his labor). Therefore, he sells (goes short) a futures contract guaranteeing today's price upon delivery of the corn at some time in the future. If the cash market price is *below* the price guaranteed in the futures contract, the farmer will exercise the contract, deliver the corn, and realize his profit. Alternatively, if the cash market price is *above* the futures contract price, the farmer is obligated to deliver his corn at the futures price. He may, of course, prior to the delivery date, choose to close out his position and *ride the market* to a more favorable price for his corn. If he does this, however, the farmer is essentially *speculating* and not *hedging* his investment risk.

An investor may also take part in a *managed futures* program with a particular commodities broker or full-service broker-dealer. Under this arrangement, the commodities broker has the discretionary power to trade for the investor's account. Given the rapid price movements and low margin positions that are characteristic of commodities, it is likely critical that an investor deal only with a broker that is a specialist in the field. It is not likely that an average broker-dealer whose expertise is securities transactions only (stocks and bonds) will also be knowledgeable in the areas of commodities.

Finally, the Commodity Futures Trading Commission (CFTC), an agency of the federal government, regulates the trading of commodities. This agency establishes price fluctuation limits (before it will intervene), prohibits excessive market positions, and oversees the disbursement of investor funds by commodities brokers and full-service broker-dealers.

TANGIBLE ASSETS AND NATURAL RESOURCES

Tangible assets (collectibles) as an investment are generally distinguished by their *lack of marketability*. In contrast, natural resources (particularly oil and gas investments) are characterized by their *inelasticity of demand*. Inelastic demand means that the quantity demanded of the natural resource will change by less, in percentage terms, than a given percentage in price. That is, if the resource exhibits inelasticity, a sharp increase in its price has little impact on the demand for it. This occurs primarily because there are not ready substitutes for the natural resource.

Collectibles

Collectibles are rare objects accumulated by investors. Examples are stamps, coins, oriental rugs, paintings (art), and baseball cards (among others). An activity of accumulating collectibles ceases to be a hobby and turns into an investment when the collector has a profit motive for continuing. This profit motive is not as important for investment reasons as it is for the income tax implications associated with conducting a business in the buying and selling of collectibles.

Collectibles generally provide no current income to the investor, but they do have the potential for significant long-term capital appreciation. Furthermore, they tend to vary sharply in underlying value during inflationary periods, when people are attempting to move their assets from paper currency into something more tangible. In this respect, collectibles share, with gold, the characteristic of serving as an *inflation hedge*. Finally, the returns on collectibles have historically exhibited a *negative correlation* with that of financial assets (stocks and bonds), therefore suggesting that these assets may effectively diversify an investor portfolio and reduce overall investor risk.

A significant disadvantage of collectible investing is that most individuals are not expert enough to really be able to effectively value the item that they are collecting. Therefore, there are additional costs associated with the investment to pay independent dealers and appraisers to assist them in making a prudent choice of assets. In addition, collectibles are subject to considerable swings in popularity within the limited market. What is "hot" one calendar year may be extremely "cold" the next year. Indeed, the absence of an organized and relatively unregulated market puts *both* buyers and sellers at considerable risk; neither is likely to have adequate knowledge of all factors that may impact the supply of the collectible at any given point in time to be able to pinpoint a true and "fair" price for the same.

An individual who is investing in collectibles is usually purchasing a capital asset. Accordingly, any gain on the sale of a collectible is long-term capital gain, presuming it is held for the requisite period of time (more than a year from the date it is first acquired). However, the tax rate on the gain from a collectible is *not* the same as that for other capital assets. Under current law, the long-term capital gain on a collectible is taxed at a *maximum flat rate of 28%* and does *not*, therefore, qualify for the preferential 5 or 15% long-term capital gain rate applicable to other investments. Like other investments, the investor may control the timing of any gain or loss on the collectible (for example, he or she simply holds onto the tangible asset for the given year and does not sell it), but this may be even more important in light of the higher tax rate applied when a taxable event does in fact occur.

Gold and Gold Mutual Funds

Gold (and other precious metals) are believed to be an *inflation hedge* in the investment marketplace. That is to say that when the investor anticipates that higher-than-average domestic inflation rates are likely to occur (or when the investor's dollars are being eroded because of international currency fluctuations), the price of gold will therefore tend to increase. In addition, if there is political or economic tension here or elsewhere in the world, gold is viewed as an extremely stable and secure investment. Still, for these very same reasons, gold is also considered to be a highly *speculative* investment since it is not as readily influenced as other investments by the normal economic factors of supply and demand.

There are various ways of participating in the market for gold, which includes gold bullion, gold coins, gold mining stocks and gold mutual funds. Bullion and coins are a direct investment in the metal, with its price fixed at various times in one of three major exchanges: London, New York, and Hong Kong. At certain points in time (for example, when inflation is high or anticipated to be high), gold-mining stocks have been very profitable. Nonetheless, these stocks also tend to follow the price of gold itself and offer primarily the convenience of not housing the metal directly. A gold mutual fund offers the investor a way of participating in the metal without the risks incurred by an unsophisticated investor dealing directly in gold or even gold-mining stocks. As with other mutual funds, the gold mutual fund provides the opportunity for diversification as well as investment management expertise not available to the typical unsophisticated investor who may be attracted to gold only for cosmetic or non-economic reasons.

Taxable gain or loss on a gold (or other precious metals) transaction is a capital gain or loss as long as the investor is not a dealer in metals. Taxable gain is realized and recognized to the extent that an investor receives more on disposition than he or she originally paid for the metal. A loss is allowable to the extent that the disposition amount is less than the original acquisition price. Similar to other capital assets, the length of time that the metal was held prior to disposition determines whether the gain or loss is short or long term in nature. However, unlike, for example, securities generally, it is possible to accomplish a non-taxable (*like kind*) exchange with gold or other precious metals. Specifically, if the metal received is of the same nature and character as the metal surrendered in the exchange, there is no immediate tax. Accordingly, if one investor trades gold coins for the gold bullion of another investor, no gain or loss is recognized on the transaction.

Natural Resources/Oil and Gas

While, of course, an investment in natural resources encompasses more than solely oil or gas wells, for many investors they are the one and the same. Therefore, oil and gas wells will be the focus of this discussion.

There are three basic types of oil and gas investments:

    1) Exploratory drilling (also known by the popular term of *wildcatting*)

    2) Development (or the search for oil or gas close to proven wells or after finding a proven field)

    3) Income (investment in the production of proven reserves or an existing well)

Of these three basic types, the investor incurs the greatest risk with exploratory drilling. This is because, historically, only 10% of exploratory wells are successful. However, as should be expected by the risk and return relationship, if a wildcat well does "hit," the potential return is considerable. Alternatively, by participating only in proven development or income properties, investor risk is reduced considerably.

Few investors buy a direct interest in oil and gas wells. Rather, most prefer the limited partnership vehicle (see chapter 4) as the means by which to invest in natural resources. They generally perceive that the advantage of limiting their liability to the extent of their investment outweighs the disadvantage of not making operating decisions with respect to the wells. Accordingly, most invest as limited partners that are entitled only to an income or *royalty interest* in the wells that are the subject of the general partner's investments. Nevertheless, those who do invest directly do so by acquiring what is known as a *working interest* in a co-owned oil or gas well. These investors participate in every item of income and expense attributable to the operation. As a result, they are accorded certain income tax advantages, notably an exception to the passive activity rules that limit the amount of losses that a limited partner (or *passive investor)* may deduct against income.

There are several major tax advantages associated with an investment in oil or gas wells. Specifically, a deduction is permitted for the *depletion* of the remaining oil and gas reserves left in the ground once drilling has occurred and proven successful. There are two types of depletion and, to the extent permitted (as mentioned, generally only a direct working interest investment qualifies for tax benefits), an investor will typically use the method that generates the *largest* deduction. *Cost depletion* essentially prorates the investor's contribution in the property between the number of oil or gas units sold during the taxable year and the number of estimated units remaining. It is the theoretical equivalent of *straight line depreciation* that is applicable to direct real property investments (see chapter 6). Alternatively, *percentage depletion* allows for a deduction of a specified percentage of the gross income derived from the property and is the functional equivalent of the *modified accelerated cost recovery* (MACRS) system used to depreciate commercial or rental real estate (see chapter 6). Of the two types of depletion, percentage depletion is preferred by many investors since it yields the greater amount of up-front tax benefits. Thus, percentage depletion is also included as a *preference item* when computing an investor's potential alternative minimum tax (AMT) liability.

Intangible drilling costs (IDCs) incurred in exploratory and development oil or gas programs are also potentially income tax deductible. Accordingly, an investor may either: 1) capitalize these costs over the projected *useful life* (production period) of the well, or 2) deduct (or *expense*) them currently in the taxable year in which the expense is paid or incurred. However, as a practical matter, this choice may already be made for the investor in the limited partnership form of oil or gas investment. This is because the election to capitalize or expense IDCs is normally pre-selected by the general partner of the partnership with the decision to expense these costs immediately as the prevailing standard.

There are numerous fees that a limited partner in an oil and gas *syndication* (see chapter 6) are likely to pay. Among these are management fees, sales commissions, and broker-dealer fees. In total, these fees will generally range from 15% to 20% of the equity invested in the limited partnership. In exchange for his or her investment as a limited partner (and payment of all these fees), the investor receives the possibility of considerable income and the potential for significant capital appreciation of his or her proportionate partnership interest. In addition, an investor who desires additional diversification of his or her portfolio into an asset class that is negatively correlated with that of the securities markets will likely find an oil or gas investment attractive.

IMPORTANT CONCEPTS

Derivative	Spread
Hedge	Straddle
Stock option	Forward contract
Long	Futures contract
Short	Financial futures
Option exercise price	Commodity futures
Option premium	Price inelasticity
Intrinsic value of an option	Collectible
Time value of an option	Gold
Chicago Board of Options Exchange	Gold mutual funds
Options Clearing Corporation (OCC)	Exploratory drilling
Call	Development oil or gas
Put	Income oil or gas
In-the-money	Royalty interest
Out-of-the-money	Working interest
Time premium	Cost depletion
Breakeven point of an option	Percentage depletion
Long-term equity anticipation security (LEAPs)	Intangible drilling costs (IDCs)

QUESTIONS FOR REVIEW

1. What is a *derivative* investment? Give an example.

2. In a stock option contract, who is long and who is *short*? Explain.

3. What are the three specifications that are included in any stock option contract?

4. In options trading, what is the difference between being in a *covered* position and being in a *naked* position? Which of these two positions involves the most risk for the investor?

5. At what time is the option on a premium taxed to the seller or writer? Explain.

6. What is the difference between an *American-style* and a *European-style* option?

7. Where are stock options traded? Which body issues all stock options?

8. If an investor *buys* a call option, what does this entitle him or her to do? What happens if the investor *sells* this same type of option?

9. When is a call option *in-the-money?* When is it *out-of-the-money?*

10. What is meant by the term intrinsic value of an option and how is this computed?

11. How is the *time premium* of an option computed?

12. When is a put option *in-the-money?* When is it *out-of-the money?*

13. Assume that you read the following in the *Wall Street Journal:*

     ABC Sept 2006 45 Call at 6.

     What is the *breakeven point* of this call option? When is it likely that the option will be exercised?

14. How is the capital gain or loss of a put option computed for income tax purposes?

15. What is a LEAP? How does it differ from the standard form of stock option?

16. What is a *spread* as it is used in options trading? What is a *straddle* used for this same purpose?

17. Contrast a *forward contract* to that of a *futures contract.* Which one of these is predominant in the secondary marketplace and why?

18. If a futures contract is *marked to market,* what does this mean?

19. What are the five types of financial futures in which an individual can invest? Why is an investor likely to hold any of these types of futures?

20. What is the meaning of the term *hedge* as it is practiced in the futures market?

21. What is meant by the term *closing out* a future contract?

22. If a farmer plants wheat (and then participates in the commodity futures market), he is said to be what? If he wants to *hedge* his risk, what does he do?

23. What is meant by the term *price inelasticity* and what type of asset normally exhibits this characteristic?

24. What is the major risk associated with investing in collectibles?

25. What is the income tax rate that applies at the time of disposition or sale of a collectible?

26. Why does an investor usually make an investment in gold bullion or gold coins?

27. If gold coins are traded for gold bullion, is this a taxable transaction? Explain why or why not.

28. What are the three basic types of oil and gas investments? In which type does a potential investor incur the most risk?

29. Contrast *cost depletion* to *percentage depletion.* Which one normally provides the largest immediate income tax benefit?

30. How (in what form) do most investors make an oil or gas investment? Why?

SUGGESTIONS FOR ADDITIONAL READING

Tools and Techniques of Investment Planning, Stephen R. Leimberg, Robert T. LeClair, Robert J. Doyle, Jr., and Thomas R. Robinson, The National Underwriter Company, 2004.

Investments: An Introduction, 7th edition, Herbert B. Mayo, Thomson/ South-Western, 2002.

Investment Analysis and Portfolio Management, 7th edition, Frank K. Reilly and Keith C. Brown, Thomson/South-Western, 2003.

The Wall Street Journal Guide to Money and Investing, 3rd edition, Kenneth M. Morris and Virginia B. Morris, Fireside Publishing, 2004.

CHAPTER EIGHT

Sources of Investment Risk

• • •

The previous seven chapters of this textbook discussed the types of investment vehicles that are available in the present day primary and secondary marketplace. The remainder of this text (specifically chapters 8-18) will look at the factors that a financial planner should consider in making an investment decision, including investment strategies and asset allocation principles. The text will conclude with an analysis of certain income tax considerations that bear on the making of the proper investment decision.

Upon completing this chapter, you should be able to:

- Define investment risk
- Discuss the importance of diversification and asset allocation in minimizing investment risk
- Identify the components of total risk, including the appropriate measurement of each component
- Describe the sources of systematic risk

DEFINITION OF INVESTMENT RISK

Investment risk is the uncertainty that an investment's actual or *realized* return will not equal its *expected* return. Of course, an investment's realized return may be tracked through an enumeration of its actual annual historical returns. But how does one compute an investment's *expected return*?, This return is specifically computed by adding up all of the possible annual returns and then multiplying them by the probability that they will occur. The probability of a given return occurring is usually based on historic returns, which, of course, may or may not be relevant to actual future returns.

> **Example 8-1:** Assume that an investment has a 20% probability of experiencing a negative 10% annual return and that it also has this same 20% probability of encountering a negative 5% annual return. Further, assume that the investment has a 20% chance of attaining a positive 5% return and a 40% chance of achieving a positive 10% return annually. Therefore, we would *expect* an actual or realized return of a positive 2% for this investment or $[(.20)(-.10) + (.20)(-.05) + (.20)(.05) + (.40)(.10)]$.

Of course, the *greater* the probability of an actual positive return, the *higher* the possible overall total return. However, to achieve this higher overall total return, the more *investment risk* that an investor must assume (the classic risk/reward principle). If an investor is unwilling to take any investment risk, his or her likely total return will be smaller.

Importance of Diversification and Asset Allocation

There are several strategies that will assist the investor in managing any investment risk that is assumed. Among these are portfolio diversification and asset allocation. While each of these is discussed much more fully in chapter 17 of this text, they are mentioned here because of their importance in helping the investor to achieve what should be his or her fundamental investment goal: *obtaining the highest possible return while assuming the lowest amount of possible investment risk.*

Diversification is structuring an individual's investment *portfolio* (mix of investment assets) with an appropriate combination of aggressive, moderate, and conservative investments. Of course, what is aggressive versus what is moderate and/or conservative also depends on the investor's time horizon. For example, an individual under age 40 who is saving for a retirement investment goal may purchase an *aggressive investment* (defined as an investment that exhibits a wide variation of actual returns) much more safely than an individual age 65 or over. Why? Because the younger individual has a much longer time to experience the probability of significant positive returns to offset the likelihood of several negative returns. Further, as we shall see, since each asset class may not move either in the same direction as another (known as *correlation*), or in the same amount, it is possible to combine asset classes to reduce an investor's overall risk.

Asset allocation has been shown to be a very predictive determinant of a portfolio's overall realized return (for example, the Brinson academic studies investigating the same issue). As such, before an individual selects his or her individual investments, it may be prudent to determine how much money should be allocated to each of the three traditional asset classes: 1) cash and cash equivalents; 2) stocks (*equities*); and 3) bonds (*debt*). As each of these asset classes exhibits a different risk/return tradeoff, an effective blending is likely critical to the achievement of an investor's financial goals. In addition, some investors will want to invest in additional asset classes, such as real estate or precious metals, which have historically proven to be relatively uncorrelated to financial assets, making them particularly useful in reducing a portfolio's risk.

TOTAL RISK

The total (absolute) risk associated with any investment has two components: 1) *unsystematic*, also known as *diversifiable* risk and 2) *systematic*, also known as *nondiversifiable* risk. This relationship may also be reduced to the equation:

Total Risk = Unsystematic Risk + Systematic Risk

As we will discuss in the subsequent chapter, total risk is measured by the *standard deviation of an asset*.

Total risk is defined as the combination of all systematic and unsystematic risk that the investor bears. In turn, as we shall learn, the investor can only *manage* systematic risk, whereas he or she can greatly *reduce* unsystematic risk through the proper diversification of assets. Unsystematic risk may be reduced significantly through diversification by owning securities of companies in different industries or sectors of the market. For example, it is possible to reduce (some would say eliminate) unsystematic risk by owning 10-15 different stocks of companies involved in the different industries of energy, health care, financial services, etc. In contrast, systematic risk cannot be reduced since all investment assets are subject to this type of risk; it can only be managed.

Unsystematic Risk

Unsystematic risk is risk that affects only a *particular company* and its securities. Examples are the *business or financial risk* associated with how a company operates. Broadly, the liquidity risk that affects certain types of assets is also a type of unsystematic risk. All these types of risk are characterized by the fact that diversification (simply not investing in that stock or asset) may be used to protect the investor. If investing in a particular stock or asset, its risk may be offset by counter-movements in the other assets within the investor's portfolio.

Business or company risk is the economic or operating risk reflected in the fluctuation of the company's earnings. In turn, the variation in a company's earnings directly impacts the valuation of its stock through the price/earnings relative valuation measure that is widely adopted by financial analysts. The best defense against business risk is to invest in more than one company and in companies that are engaged in different lines of business or market sectors.

Closely related to business risk is the *financial risk* that a company incurs with respect to how it finances its business operations and/or expansion. Specifically, the more debt (or *leverage*) used by a firm to raise business capital, the greater its financial risk. This is because debt (particularly that which is secured or collateralized) must eventually be repaid to its holder (in the investment world, this is a bond owner) or the company will eventually become insolvent. An insolvency can lead to the liquidation of the business and investors in the company may lose their entire investment. Financial risk is effectively monitored by ratings services, such as Standard & Poor's or Moody's Investment Services.

Finally, *liquidity* risk is the possibility of not being able to sell an asset without a significant loss of principal. Generally, most cash equivalents (such as a checking or passbook savings account) are considered highly *liquid* since they can be quickly converted into cash without any loss to principal. In contrast, collectibles and real estate are characterized by their *lack* of liquidity. As we have discussed, however, the lack of liquidity of an asset should not be confused with a potential lack of marketability of that same asset. As an example, publicly traded stocks may be relatively illiquid (they may experience a decline in value from the investor's original invested amount at the time of sale), but they are certainly still marketable. A number of ready buyers may likely be found to purchase a publicly traded stock, although perhaps *not* at the same price that the investor originally paid for the asset.

Investors holding illiquid assets should be mindful of liquidity risk and are well advised to have sufficient liquid assets available to offset any financial emergencies. This is also one of the main reasons that financial planners recommend maintaining three to six months of living expenses in liquid assets (an "emergency" or "contingency fund") prior to investing in securities generally.

Systematic Risk

Also known as *nondiversifiable risk*, systematic risk reflects the widespread or economy-wide uncertainty associated with an investment in *any* type of asset. This part of total risk is inescapable because no matter how effectively an investor diversifies, the risk of the overall economy cannot be avoided. The most prominent example of systematic risk is the business cycle experienced by all businesses (and, by extension, its equity or debt) in the constant ebb and flow of economic supply and demand. As long as a business is a *going concern* and contributes to the supply and demand paradigm, it cannot protect itself from systematic risk. It can only attempt to effectively manage this risk.

There are five basic components of systematic risk as follows:

1) Purchasing power (*inflation*) risk
2) Reinvestment rate risk
3) Interest rate risk
4) Market risk
5) Exchange rate (*currency*) risk

It is easy to remember these components of systematic risk by the pneumonic *PRIME*, using the first letters of each risk category.

Systematic risk is measured by the *beta coefficient (beta)* of an asset, which will be described more fully later.

Purchasing Power Risk

Purchasing power risk, or *inflation risk*, is the potential loss of purchasing power of an investment due to inflation. An example is the rising price of economic goods and services over time. Historically (at least since 1926), the rate of annual inflation has averaged 3%. This means that, using the so-called *Rule of 72*, the price of these goods and services has doubled every 24 years (72 divided by 3). As a result, any investment asset that generates a specified annual income return (such as an immediate fixed annuity) is subject to a loss of real purchasing power as inflation erodes the value of the dollars received. Nonetheless, the actual risk associated with inflation is not so much with the current level of inflation (since an *inflation premium* is normally built into the purchase price of any investment asset), but with levels of *unanticipated* inflationary pressures. Indeed, some theoretical valuation models (such as the *multi-factor model* or *arbitrage pricing theory*) attempt to account for this unanticipated or unexpected rate of inflation, but it remains, at best, still a very inexact science.

Reinvestment Rate Risk

Reinvestment rate risk primarily impacts fixed-income securities, particularly those that are sensitive to refinancing, such as mortgage-backed securities, like GNMA (Ginnie Mae) certificates. Specifically, reinvestment rate risk is the risk that proceeds available for reinvestment must be reinvested at a lower interest rate than the original investment vehicle that generated the proceeds. As an example, when mortgage interest rates fall, existing mortgage holders will rush to refinance their mortgages. Holders of these mortgage certificates will, therefore, experience, a sudden flurry of principal repayments, which puts them in the undesirable financial position of having to reinvest these repayments at now lower yields.

Interest Rate Risk

Some commentators include reinvestment rate risk as one of the two components of *interest rate risk* (the other component being the risk to the value of the principal of a fixed income asset such as a bond). However, interest rate risk is a very broad type of systematic risk stating that a change in market interest rates will cause the market value of a fixed income security to fall. In other words, interest rates and bond prices move in *opposite directions*. When interest rates decline, bond prices increase; when interest rates increase, the price of a bond will fall. A *discount bond* is one that is selling in the secondary market at a price *less* than its par value. This happens whenever the prevailing market interest rate (as reflected in any new issues of debt securities) *exceeds* the existing bond's coupon rate. Conversely, a *premium bond* is one that is selling in the secondary market at a price *more* than its par value. Bonds sell at a premium whenever interest rates fall *below* the existing bond's coupon rate.

Interest rate risk has nothing to do with the quality of the issuer of the bond. Rather, it simply reflects the fact that (new) bonds may now be issued at a higher rate of interest than that being paid by existing bonds. Given the inverse relationship between market interest rates and bond prices, as the bond price falls, the current yield to an investor will *rise*. Accordingly, the price of the existing bond will have to decline sufficiently to make it more attractive to potential buyers that can now purchase a newly issued bond paying a higher interest rate. Therefore, as an investment strategy, shorter term securities are more attractive in rising interest rate environments since holders of such securities will receive their principal repayments much sooner than if investing longer term. The price of a bond in the secondary market is a function of its coupon rate, its maturity date, and in what direction market interest rates move before it matures. As we shall see in chapter 13 of this text, all of these factors are succinctly captured in the concept of *bond duration*.

Market Risk

Market risk is the most fundamental type of systematic risk. In fact, CFP Board, in its latest edition of CFP ® Certification Examination topics, equates market risk with systematic risk. However, more properly, market risk is a *component* of systematic risk.

Market risk is the risk of the overall securities marketplace and is sometimes simply referred to as *volatility*. It applies mainly to stocks and stock options and cannot generally be avoided by an investor in the stock market, no matter which exchange lists the stock he or she is purchasing. Volatility describes market risk because it refers to the movement of the investment rather than the reason for this movement. Such a word also implies that some reference point or benchmark is being used to track this movement; in this case, that benchmark is the stock market itself. The *more volatile* the movement of a stock (as represented by the term beta coefficient or beta), the *greater* its risk in comparison with other stocks included within the market index.

As is commonly understood, stocks tend to perform most favorably when economic conditions are favorable and there is an absence of unanticipated factors affecting the future growth of a company's earnings. This is commonly referred to by the popular term *bull market*. Alternatively, if economic conditions are unfavorable or deteriorating, the term *bear market* is applied to encapsulate the existence of market risk. Of course, what moves markets (or the *cause* of the resulting volatility) has been the subject of many books and articles and will not be dealt with here. Rather, it is sufficient to state that if an investor purchases any security (most notably, stocks) for his or her portfolio, market risk *cannot* be avoided. It can only be *managed* (which, of course, is what professional money managers are paid to do).

Exchange Rate Risk

The final component of systematic risk is *exchange rate* (or *currency*) *risk*. Such risk is the uncertainty associated with changes in the value of currencies and affects primarily those individuals who invest in foreign securities. As an example, assume that an American investor invests in a German stock and pays for the purchase with the newly adopted Euro. Even if the share value appreciates, the American investor may still lose money if the Euro depreciates (or weakens) relative to the American dollar. Conversely, however, the American investor may reap a double benefit (including the appreciation of the German stock) if the Euro appreciates (or strengthens) with respect to the American dollar.

When a country intentionally changes the value of its currency relative to another country's currency (usually the American dollar), this process is known as *devaluation* or *revaluation* depending on the directional change in the value of the currency. If a country's currency value *declines* with respect to another currency's value (in other words, it now takes more of the adjusted currency to exchange for the benchmark currency), it is referred to as *devaluing* the adjusted currency. If a country's currency value *increases* with respect to the referenced currency, it is referred to as *revaluing* the adjusted currency.

> **Example 8-2:** Jay invests $10,000 U.S. in Mitsubishi stock (a Japanese company) when the exchange rate is 80 Japanese yen to the U.S. dollar. The stock of Mitsubishi then increases in value by 50% relative to the yen. However, during this same time, the U.S. dollar has strengthened against the yen to 100 yen per dollar, meaning that the dollar will now purchase 20 more yen than when Jay bought the Mitsubishi stock. Jay then sells the stock and receives 1.2 million yen ($10,000 x 80 x 1.50), which he must then convert back into U.S. dollars. Accordingly, Jay receives $12,000 when he converts the yen back into U.S. dollars (1.2 million yen divided by the 100 yen to the dollar exchange rate) for an actual return of 20% ($2,000 divided by $10,000). Alternatively, if the exchange rate had remained at 80 yen per dollar, his actual return would have been 50% ($5,000 divided by $10,000).

As we discussed in chapter 3 of this textbook, a popular method of investing in foreign securities while minimizing exchange rate risk is to purchase American Depository Receipts (ADRs) for those shares. An American Depository Receipt is a receipt issued by a U.S. bank on foreign securities purchased by the bank through a foreign representative and held in trust for the benefit of the ADR owner. Such a receipt is priced in American dollars and traded on all U.S. exchanges in the same manner as stocks. Further, while dividends on these foreign shares are declared in the local currency, they are paid in American dollars, subsequent to the U.S. bank withholding for any foreign taxes that are due (and for which the American investor receives an income tax credit).

Finally, a closely related risk to that of exchange rate risk is that of *political* (or *country*) *risk*. Political risk refers to the risk that a foreign country will not be able to honor its financial commitments, or that it is pursuing policies that are likely to be problematic for foreign investors. Often it is caused by a major change in the political governance or economic system of a country. Investors or financial planners wishing to invest internationally should analyze such risk carefully as it could potentially impact the amount of future investment return.

Other Investment Risk

Two other often-overlooked types of risk that an investor should consider are *tax risk* (sometimes referred to as *tax-rate risk)* and the *risk of investment manager change* relating to his or her professionally managed assets (see chapter 4).

Tax Risk

Tax risk is the ever-present uncertainty associated with the tax laws that potentially impact the ownership and/or disposition of investment assets. For example, income and transfer tax laws in effect today may not be the same in the future. As such, it is becoming more and more difficult to effectively evaluate how long an investment asset should be held and, perhaps, when it should be sold.

Since the Tax Reform Act of 1986 (which itself was so massive as to require a renaming of the Tax Code to the *Internal Revenue Code of 1986*), there have been at least seven additional major tax bills. Further, as of this writing, the Bush administration is considering the results of an independent commission that has suggested even more fundamental changes in our tax system. In addition, major changes have occurred in the regulatory arena that have essentially deregulated the financial services industry (witness the Gramm/Leach/Bliley legislation in 1999 that repealed the long-standing Glass Steagall Act). Therefore, the only statement that may really be definitively made about tax law and regulation is that it never stays the same.

That being said, an investor does need to be aware that a fundamental tool of income tax planning and management is that of income conversion. Specifically, this means that an investor should attempt to convert or re-characterize income from that of ordinary income (such as salary or wages) into that of capital gains. Generally, any asset purchased for investment purposes will constitute a capital asset and, thus, qualify for a preferential rate if held for a sufficient period. This preferential rate is currently 5% or 15%, depending on the investor's regular marginal income tax bracket and holding period of the asset. In turn, this compares to a top marginal ordinary income tax bracket of 35% (a potential 30% spread in applicable taxable rates). Multiplied over many years and many investment dollars, this 30% spread may result in sizeable income tax savings and, ultimately, considerably more after-tax compounded dollars.

Indeed, tax management is a valuable tool in controlling investment tax risk, with the importance of effective management increasing the higher the individual's marginal income tax bracket and tax rate.

Investment Manager Risk

As is generally well known, the majority of actively managed funds under the management of a professional money manager *under-perform* compared to the broader market indexes. Accordingly, passively managed funds, such as an index fund, have recently increased in popularity. In addition, even if an actively managed fund does out-perform the overall market in one year, there is no guarantee that it will do so the next year. In part this is because a professionally managed fund may lose its portfolio manager. This is particularly true if such manager is considered to be outstanding from the viewpoint of his or her peers, so that he or she is recruited away from one fund to manage another. This is what is collectively referred to as *investment manager* risk.

There is really no effective way to learn about what may be happening internally at a mutual fund or mutual fund family to effectively avoid investment manager risk. However, the risk may be minimized by researching the historical performance of the fund or fund family. If the annual return achieved by the manager exceeds the average, it is unlikely that the manager will leave the fund in the immediate future as the fund family will likely fairly compensate him or her for their efforts. Additionally, some managers will speak openly about what is fundamental to their investment philosophy. For example, the well-respected Peter Lynch, while running the Fidelity Magellan Fund, spoke openly about his aversion to large size mutual funds. Thus, it should have been of little surprise to the investors of the fund that he ultimately chose to pursue other business endeavors.

IMPORTANT CONCEPTS

Investment risk

Expected return

Total or absolute risk

Diversification

Asset allocation

Unsystematic or diversifiable risk

Systematic or nondiversifiable risk

Standard deviation

Beta coefficient

Business risk

Financial risk

Liquidity risk

Purchasing power risk

Reinvestment rate risk

Interest rate risk

Market risk

Volatility

Exchange rate risk

Devaluation

Revaluation

Political risk

Tax or tax rate risk

Investment manager risk

QUESTIONS FOR REVIEW

1. Define what is meant by the term *investment risk*.

2. What should be the fundamental investment goal of any client?

3. What have academic studies shown to be the single most important determinant of an investor's overall realized return and an effective tool in minimizing investor risk?

4. What are the two components that make up the total or absolute risk of an investment?

   Which one of these two components can be *diversified away*?

5. What is the unsystematic risk of an investment?

6. How does an investor go about effectively reducing unsystematic risk?

7. Assume that a company finances its business operations with an excessive amount of bank loans. What type of risk is experienced by an investor who invests in the stock of this company?

8. List two types of investments that are characterized by their lack of liquidity. What does this mean to a potential investor in these types of investments?

9. What is the systematic risk of an investment?

10. What are the five generally accepted components of systematic risk? Give an example of the type of investment asset most affected by each of these components.

11. What is the relationship of market interest rates and bond prices?

12. Assume that a bond is selling in the secondary market currently at a price more than its par value. Why does this occur?

13. "Market risk is sometimes simply referred to as the volatility of an investment." Explain what is meant by this statement.

14. What is an effective method of managing the exchange rate risk that is associated with the purchase of a foreign security?

15. Contrast *devaluing* a foreign currency to that of *revaluing* that same currency.

16. What is an effective tool that may be used to minimize the tax rate risk associated with an investment?

17. Explain *investment manager* risk. Where is it most commonly experienced in an investor's portfolio?

SUGGESTIONS FOR ADDITIONAL READING

Tools and Techniques of Investment Planning, Stephen R. Leimberg, Robert T. LeClair, Robert J. Doyle, Jr., and Thomas R. Robinson, The National Underwriter Company, 2004.

Investments: An Introduction, 7th edition, Herbert B. Mayo, Thomson/ South-Western, 2002.

Investment Analysis and Portfolio Management, 7th edition, Frank K. Reilly and Keith C. Brown, Thomson/South-Western, 2003.

The Wall Street Journal Guide to Money and Investing, 3rd edition, Kenneth M. Morris and Virginia B. Morris, Fireside Publishing, 2004.

CHAPTER NINE

Measurements of Investment Risk

• • •

As a logical progression from the previous chapter wherein the types and sources of investment risk were discussed, this chapter considers how to quantitatively compute that risk. Accordingly, a proper understanding of certain formulas used to measure investment risk and the ability to compute the appropriate measure using a financial function calculator (notably the Hewlett Packard, or HP, 10 B II) is very important.

Upon completing this chapter, you should be able to:

- Identify types of probability distributions and the role that such distributions play in quantifying investment risk
- Explain and compute the standard deviation of an asset or portfolio
- Explain the concept of semi-variance and its use in quantitative analysis
- Apply and compute covariance and/or correlation coefficient as a measurement of investment risk
- Explain and compute the beta coefficient of an asset or portfolio
- Apply and compute coefficients of determination as a measurement of investment risk
- Use and interpret coefficients of determination in portfolio evaluation

RISK LEVEL QUANTIFICATION

As noted in the previous chapter, the measurement of total (unsystematic and systematic) risk is the *standard deviation* of an investment asset. Standard deviation incorporates the following measurements and concepts:

1) It measures the asset's *variability* of returns (around an average or mean rate of return).

2) It is generally used to measure the investment risk of a *non-diversified* portfolio of assets (Note: It is possible to compute the standard deviation of a diversified portfolio, however, standard deviation is commonly used as a measure of risk for only a non-diversified portfolio.)

3) It is a measure of the *total risk* of an investment asset or portfolio.

Alternatively, the measurement of systematic risk is the *beta coefficient* of an investment asset. Beta coefficient (beta) incorporates the following measurements and concepts:

1) It is a measurement of the asset's *volatility* of returns to a benchmark or index, notably the broader secondary market (usually as represented by the Standard & Poor's index of 500 stocks).

2) It is used to measure the investment risk of a *diversified* portfolio of assets.

3) It is a measure of the *systematic risk* of an investment asset or portfolio.

However, both of these measurements (to be reliable and valid) depend on the statistical theory of probability distributions.

PROBABILITY DISTRIBUTIONS

As discussed in the previous chapter, investment risk is most easily defined as the *uncertainty of a future result;* in this case, the risk is the uncertainty that an investment's realized return will not equal its expected return. To deal with the uncertainty of returns, investors need to understand the statistical likelihood of achieving a desired return. Accordingly, the science of probability distributions may be very helpful in promoting this understanding.

Probabilities represent the likelihood of various results and are typically expressed as a decimal or fraction. The sum of the probability of all possible results must be 1.0 (or 100%) so as to encompass and describe all the likely occurrences. These probabilities are obtained using one of two methods: either, 1) spreadsheet models or 2) simulation. Spreadsheet models are *deterministic* in nature, meaning that the inputs are fixed and may only accommodate *one* value or possible result to one cell at a time. Further, if you want to view alternative solutions using a spreadsheet, you need to manually change the inputs in the model. Spreadsheet models provide classical *what if* scenarios, but with the significant restriction of permitting the potential investor to only see a *single result,* typically the most likely or average outcome. In contrast, simulation uses a computer software program to automatically and constantly analyze the effect of *many* varying inputs (for example, the expected return) on a desired output (for example, an ending or future value). In essence, simulation couples or marries "what if" scenarios with the science of probability distribution.

A well known type of computer simulation is Monte Carlo simulation, which randomly generates values for uncertain variables over and over again (continuously) to simulate a model. For each uncertain variable (one that has a range of possible values), the investor defines the possible values with a probability distribution. The type of distribution that is selected depends on the conditions surrounding that variable, but there are fundamentally only two types of probability distributions that need to be analyzed (at least for purposes of this discussion). The first of these is a *normal* probability distribution, popularly referred to as a *bell curve,* wherein the mean value is the most probable over time and each outcome (or result) is more likely to be close to the mean value rather than far away. The second type of these distributions is a *lognormal* probability distribution where the mean is typically to the right of the highest point on the curve. In turn, this also means that the overall distribution is positively skewed, with most outcomes occurring at or near the lower limit. Finally, if a lognormal distribution appears, the upper limit of outcomes is unlimited, but a single outcome may not fall below zero. Both of these types of distribution are graphically represented at Figure 9-1 below.

In applying each fundamental type of probability distribution, it is important to understand what types of occurrences are likely to result using each model. If an investor is analyzing the possible range of annual percentage (or other periodic) returns for a portfolio, a *normal* distribution would be used since the actual portfolio percentage return may be either negative or positive at a given point in time. Conversely, if an investor is analyzing the ending future value of the portfolio, a *lognormal* distribution would be the standard model. This is because an un-leveraged portfolio (that is, one where borrowed money or margin is not used to make subsequent purchases) may not go below zero. Stated more simply, the ending value of portfolio may go to zero, but not below it, since once reaching zero, the investor has lost all of his or her money. Therefore, in most instances, the normal or bell curve type of probability distribution will be of most utility to a prospective investor since he or she is most interested in the probability (likelihood) of actually obtaining the expected percentage return necessary to accumulate wealth.

Figure 9-1

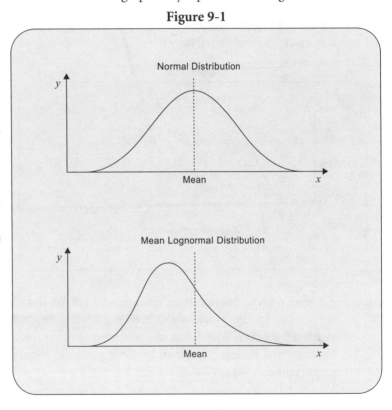

Skewness

Skewness measures how far the actual outcomes of a probability distribution deviate from the mean or average outcome. In other words, in the lognormal distribution of Figure 9-1, skewness quantifies in decimal terms how far the *median* outcome (that is, the single outcome where there is an equal number of occurrences above and below that outcome) is away from the *mean* outcome (that is, the arithmetical average of all the occurrences that are observed). In positively skewed distributions, the median is *below* the mean; in negatively skewed distributions, the median is above the mean. In practical terms, this means that an investor has *less* than a 50% chance of actually earning the mean outcome or percentage return in a positively skewed investment, but *more than a 50%* chance of actually earning the mean percentage return in a negatively skewed investment. However, as we shall discuss below, comparing the probability of achieving the mean return in a positively skewed versus negatively skewed investment is *not* a fundamental precept of investor behavior. Rather, the probability of realizing a *negative* return is a greater motivation.

Figure 9-2 below graphically represents and contrasts a positively skewed distribution with a negatively skewed distribution.

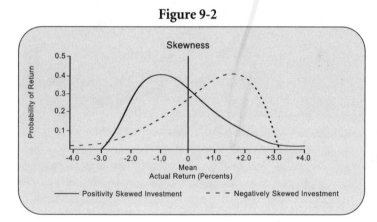

Figure 9-2

As one may easily observe from the negatively skewed distribution representation, the negative *tail* of distribution is considerably *longer than* that of the positively skewed representation. Accordingly, an investment reflecting a negative skewness exposes the investor to a low or negative percentage return *below* the worst potential returns of an investment with a positive skew. In addition, the investment reflecting positive skewness offers the investor the opportunity for a greater number of positive returns (notice that the positive tail of distribution is longer than that of the negative skewness). In summary, *a risk-averse investor would prefer the positively skewed investment to the negatively skewed one.* Since the assumption that most investors are inherently risk averse is a fundamental building block of modern portfolio theory (see chapter 10 of this text), this is a very important conclusion indeed.

Kurtosis

Kurtosis is another measurement that is sometimes used in probability distribution theory and its implications for investor behavior. Kurtosis measures the degree of variation or *fatness* in the tails of the distribution. The greater the fatness, the further away from the mean return and the more the assumed investment risk as measured by standard deviation. The kurtosis of a normal probability distribution is zero. A distribution with the same kurtosis is known as mesokurtic.

Like Figure 9-2 representing skewness, it is easily observed that risk-averse investors prefer a probability distribution with *low* or minimal kurtosis (that is, where the respective tails are less fat). However, let us carefully compare the two distributions: the one reflecting a kurtosis of zero with the second exhibiting a kurtosis of a negative three. It is true that in the distribution with a kurtosis of zero that the possibility for a negative

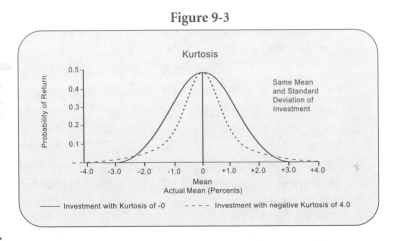

Figure 9-3

return is exactly offset by the opportunity for a positive return (note that the respective tails are equally fat). This is also the case with the negative kurtosis representation. However, in the negative kurtosis representation, if a negative return results, it will be *greater than* that of the kurtosis with zero. Therefore, according to investment theory, a risk-averse investor will *always* weight the possibility of a greater investment loss more heavily than that of the opportunity for a positive return. Further, if an investor analyzes only the mean return and the standard deviation of the investment, while ignoring positive or negative excess kurtosis, an important consideration is neglected.

Both skewness and kurtosis are used to improve upon the measurement of investment risk accounting for only mean and standard deviation. For example, when both skewness and kurtosis turn negative, what will be the likely investor behavior? Essentially, kurtosis increases the magnitude of the negative return for the risk-averse investor, thereby adding to his or her discomfort in holding on to the investment.

Finally, once quantitatively computing both a skewness and kurtosis decimal for an investment, it is possible to determine with greater accuracy what the percentage possibility of a negative return will be and over what time period. (Note: The actual computation of skewness and kurtosis is beyond the scope of this textbook.)

STANDARD DEVIATION

Standard Deviation of a Single Asset

Standard deviation is an absolute measure of the variability of the actual investment returns around the average or mean of those returns (otherwise known as *the expected return* of the investment). It is the single most accepted measurement of total or absolute risk in investment theory and tells an investor how far from the mean the investment's actual return is likely to vary. In a *normal probability* distribution, 68% of all actual or observed returns will fall within one negative or positive standard deviation from the mean.

Example 9-1: Assume that ABC stock has generated the following actual rates of return for the last four years:

Year 1: 15%

Year 2: 8%

Year 3: 2%

Year 4: 18%

Accordingly, it reflects an average or mean return of 10.75% and a standard deviation of 7.18 computed as follows on the HP 10 B II financial function calculator:

15 Σ+

8 Σ+

2 Σ+

18 Σ+

Shift, x,y (above the 7 key) (Note: This is the average or mean return of the distribution.)

Shift, S_x, S_y (above the 8 Key) (Note: This is the standard deviation of the distribution or what is called the *sample* standard deviation.)

Therefore, given the assumption of a normal probability distribution, an investor who purchases ABC stock would expect, based on ABC's historical returns, to achieve an actual return of a +3.57% and a + 17.93 approximately 68% of the time (that is, one negative and one positive standard deviation of 7.18 from the mean return of 10.75%). Alternatively, we could say that we have a 68% "confidence" that the expected return for ABC stock will fall within that range. He or she should also expect an actual return of a minus 3.61% and a +25.11% approximately 95% of the time (that is, two negative and two positive standard deviations from the mean return of 10.75%). Finally, if we go out three negative or standard deviations from the mean (a -10.79% and a +32.29), we would have approximately 99% confidence that the future return of ABC stock will fall within this range. It is very important to understand, however, that these expected returns are based on *historical* results. There is no guarantee, of course, that the future is so strongly linked to the past. Still, short of a crystal ball, investors have little else on which to base their expectations. All of these results are graphically represented in Figure 9-4 below.

Figure 9-4

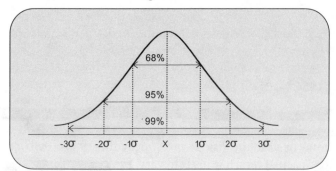

The standard deviation of a single asset may also be represented in formula terms by the following formula:

Formula 9-1: Sample for Standard Deviation of a Single Asset

$$S_r = \sqrt{\frac{\sum_{t=1}^{n} (r_t - \bar{r})^2}{n-1}}$$

In taking this analysis further, it should be easy to understand that the *greater the variability of actual returns* as reflected by standard deviation, the *greater the total risk of the investment*. However, like our comparison of negative and positive skewness above, standard deviation is not the only consideration that an investor should take into account when comparing the total risk of two possible investment assets. This brings us to our next topic of discussion, the *coefficient of variation* between two assets.

Coefficient of Variation (CV)

The *coefficient of variation* (CV) is a measure of the *relative* measure of total risk per unit of expected return. It is used to compare investments with varying rates of return and standard deviations and is computed by dividing the standard deviation of an asset by its average or mean return. For example, the CV of ABC stock in Example 9-1 above would be 0.6679 or 7.18% (its standard deviation) divided by 10.75% (its average or mean return). That is, it exhibits approximately 0.67 units of risk per unit (1.0) of expected return.

Now let us compare another potential investment, XYZ stock, with ABC stock to see which one should, perhaps, be purchased considering only the level of risk per unit of expected return (the coefficient of variation) between the two stocks.

> **Example 9-2:** XYZ stock has an average or mean return over the past four years of 20% and a standard deviation of 12%. Therefore, it has a coefficient of variation of .60 (or its standard deviation of 12% divided by its mean return of 20%). Accordingly, XYZ stock exhibits 0.60 units of risk per unit of expected return.

Note carefully that a consideration of the coefficient of variation between ABC stock and XYZ stock has led you to a possible *different* investment decision. While XYZ stock appears to be riskier given its standard deviation of 12 (compared to ABC stock that reflects a standard deviation of 7.18), the level of risk per unit of expected return for XYZ is more favorable than that of ABC stock. That is, an investor purchasing XYZ stock incurs only 0.60 units of total risk per unit of expected return whereas a purchaser of ABC stock assumes 0.67 units of total risk per unit of expected return. Therefore, all other investment factors being equal, a purchase of XYZ stock may indeed be more preferable, even though it exhibits a *higher* standard deviation (or measure of total risk).

Standard Deviation of a Two or More Asset Portfolio

The formula for computing the standard deviation of a two-asset portfolio is as follows:

Formula 9-2: Standard Deviation of a Two-Asset Portfolio

$$\sigma_p = \sqrt{W_i^2 \sigma_i^2 + W_j^2 \sigma_j^2 + 2W_i W_j COV_{ij}}$$

In the formula, the letter W represents the weighting or percentage of the assets within the portfolio and the Greek symbol for omega (σ) represents the standard deviation of those respective assets. σ_p represents the standard deviation of the two-asset portfolio we are attempting to compute. (Also note that if more than two assets in the portfolio are present, the formula would be changed slightly with the replacement of the number 2 by the Greek letter for Sigma or). It is likely that for CFP® examination purposes, the student will not be asked to compute the standard deviation of a portfolio with more than two assets.

There is now only one input missing in the above formula that we have not yet discussed: that of the *covariance* between the two assets in the portfolio. We will discuss the meaning of this term later, but covariance measures the extent to which two assets (typically, stocks) are related to each other. In other words, how the price movements of one of the assets is related to the other asset. As we shall see, and preferably for diversification purposes, we would like these price movements to be exactly opposite one another (or to be *negatively correlated*). However, in the real world, this is extremely rare. Therefore, the best that we can usually hope for is a *low positive correlation* between the assets. For illustration purposes, in the following example, we will assume that the correlation between our two assets, ABC stock and XYZ stock (also known as their *correlation coefficient* or R), is 0.25. Accordingly, this makes the covariance between the assets 21.54 or the standard deviation of asset #1 (here, ABC stock with a standard deviation of 7.18) multiplied by the standard deviation of asset #2 (here, XYZ stock with a standard deviation of 12) times their correlation coefficient of 0.25. In full presentation, this is COV= 7.18 (R) x 12(σ_i) x 0.25(σ_j) = 21.54.

Example 9-3: Continuing with the assets and risk measurements used in Examples 9-1 and 9-2, ABC stock has an expected mean return of 10.75% and a standard deviation of 7.18. In addition, XYZ stock has an expected mean return of 20% and a standard deviation of 12. Assume that these two stocks are combined in a portfolio and are weighted in the proportions of 40% for ABC stock and 60% for XYZ stock. They also exhibit a covariance of 21.54. Therefore, the standard deviation of the portfolio when we include ABC stock with XYZ in the specified proportions is 8.39

computed as follows:

$$\sigma_p = [(0.4)^2 (7.18)^2 + (0.6)^2 (12)^2 + 2 (0.4)(0.6)(21.54)]^{0..5} = [8.25 + 51.84 + 10.34]^{0..5} = [70.43]^{0..5} = 8.39$$

You should note that the 0.5 in the above computation represents the same algebraic function as that of the square root symbol in Formula 9-2.

Also, the expected return of the portfolio when combining assets ABC stock and XYZ stock is now 16.30% computed as follows:

ABC stock (0.40 x 0.1075) + XYZ stock (0.60 x 0.20) = 0.0430 + 0.12 = 0.1630

Therefore, in summary, the following represents the combination of ABC stock and XYZ stock in the same portfolio:

	ABC stock	XYZ stock	Portfolio
Weighting	.40	.60	1.00
Expected return	.1075	.20	.1630
Standard deviation	7.18	12	8.39

You should observe closely what has occurred here. Specifically, we have *increased* the expected return of ABC stock by combining it in a portfolio with XYZ stock (from 10.75% to 16.3%) while *decreasing* XYZ stock's standard deviation or total risk (from 12 to 8.39). At the same time, the CV (coefficient of variation) of the portfolio is only 0.52, compared to 0.67 for ABC stock alone and 0.60 for XYZ stock separately. We have, thus, discovered the magic of portfolio diversification.

SEMI-VARIANCE

Before we can discuss the key to portfolio diversification, covariance, we first need to mention a variation of standard deviation sometimes used as measurement of total risk. This is a concept and measurement known as *semi-variance.*

The use of standard deviation as a measure of total risk has been criticized by some finance experts because it considers the possibility of returns in *excess of* the expected or mean return in addition to those returns below the mean. However, the typical risk-averse investor does not view an excess return as unfavorable; indeed, his or her real concern is only with those percentage returns *not* equaling the mean (in other words, *downside risk*). As a result, another measure of risk, known as semi-variance, has been developed to compute only those returns that are below the mean or expected return (with no consideration given to those exceeding the mean).

Unlike standard deviation, the actual computation of semi-variance is beyond the scope of this textbook. However, as noted, only those deviations from the mean or expected return with a *negative result* are used; those with a positive percentage return are not used. In addition, because semi-variance is cumbersome to compute in practice without using a spreadsheet, most stock analysts and/or portfolio managers use standard deviation as the preferred measure. Finally, because stock-return distributions do tend to be *symmetrical* around the mean (that is, because the same shape of the curve exists both above and below the mean, therefore suggesting reasonably similar variability or total risk), the standard deviation computation will effectively generate the same measurement in the context of portfolio management as does the semi-variance.

COVARIANCE (COV) AND CORRELATION COEFFICIENT (R)

The covariance and correlation coefficient between assets are discussed together here because there is a direct relationship between the two concepts. That is, if you are given one (for example, covariance), you can compute the other (for example, correlation coefficient).

Covariance is a measure of the extent to which two variables (here, investment assets) move in a predictable manner to one another, either positively or negatively. If two assets move in exact and perfect predictability, in whatever direction (up or down), they are said to have *perfect positive covariance*. Conversely, if the assets move exactly opposite of one another, that is, one always goes up when the other goes down, they are said to have *perfect negative covariance*. Finally, if the assets move in completely independent directions (in other words, they show *no* predictability either up or down), their covariance is *zero*.

The problem with covariance, as we have seen in the previous Example 9-3, is that it yields only a number, either positive or negative. There are no boundaries on this number such that it is not easy to interpret by investment professionals. Rather, analysts and portfolio managers use a concept known as the *correlation coefficient* that standardizes covariance and puts the relationship between the movement of two assets within a range of -1.0 and a +1.0. The formula for correlation coefficient (also signified by the capital letter R or, sometimes, p_{ij}) is the algebraic inverse of covariance as follows:

Formula 9-3: Correlation Coefficient

$$R = \frac{COV_{ij}}{\sigma_i \sigma_j}$$

For example, let us look back to our computation of covariance as used in Example 9-3 or 21.54. In using those same numbers to compute the stipulated correlation coefficient of 0.25, we divide the covariance of 21.54 by the product of the standard deviation of ABC stock (7.18) times the standard deviation of XYZ stock (12), resulting in a denominator of 86.16. Then, when we divide 21.54 by 86.16, we derive the stipulated correlation coefficient of 0.25.

Covariance is critical, however, because it does tell us in which direction the two assets move-- either together (positively) or opposite (negatively). Therefore, we also know that if the covariance of an asset is negative, *so is its correlation coefficient.* As a result, we can derive some general rules regarding the appropriate assets to select in diversifying an investor's portfolio and, therefore, reducing his or her total risk. These are as follows:

1) *Perfectly positively correlated assets* have a value of +1.0. In this case, the assets move exactly together and there is no reduction in the total risk of the portfolio. For diversification purposes, we should not utilize assets that exhibit this relationship.

2) *Perfectly negatively correlated assets* have a value of -1.0. In this case, the total risk of the portfolio is *completely eliminated.* For diversification purposes, we should strive to use only those assets that exhibit this relationship.

3) More practically, since all investment assets are subject to systematic risk, we should attempt to combine assets in a portfolio that exhibit a *low positive correlation coefficient.* Accordingly, we proved in Example 9-3 that by combining an asset (XYZ stock) having a low correlation coefficient of 0.25 with another (ABC stock), we *reduced* the total portfolio risk.

4) Finally, unless the assets are all perfectly positively correlated, the *standard deviation* (or total risk) of the portfolio will be *less* than the *weighted average* standard deviation of each asset. We also proved the truth of this assertion in combining XYZ stock in a 60% proportion with ABC stock's 40% proportion to generate an actual standard deviation of 8.39 as compared to their weighted average standard deviation of 10.05 [(0.40) (7.12) + (0.60) (12)= 10.05].

All that we need now to complete our discussion of the measures of investment risk is to include some measure not only of how the investment assets move in relation to one another, but also how they move in relation to the overall market!

BETA COEFFICIENT (BETA)

The beta coefficient (*beta*) is a statistical measure of the volatility or risk of a *specific security's* rate of return or price *relative to the market as a whole.* It is calculated on the basis of the historical record of the security and is compared against the movement of the market, which is defined as having a beta of 1.0. As noted, unlike standard deviation that generally measures the variability of returns in a non-diversified portfolio (unsystematic risk) beta measures the volatility of returns assuming a diversified portfolio (systematic risk). Therefore, *the greater the beta of the security, the greater the systematic risk associated with the individual security.*

The formula for Beta involves using the standard deviations of both the specific or individual security and that of the market as a whole. That result is then multiplied by the correlation coefficient between the individual security and the market. In formula terms, this is expressed as follows:

Formula 9-4: Beta Coefficient of a Sample Asset

$$\beta_i = \frac{COV_{im}}{\sigma_m^{\,2}} = \frac{\rho_{im}\,\sigma_i}{\sigma_m}$$

Example 9-4: Assume that the standard deviation of Stock X is 16 and the standard deviation of the market is 10. Further assume that the correlation coefficient between Stock X and the market is 0.40. Accordingly, the Beta of Stock A is 0.64 (or {16 x 0.40} ÷10).

So what does the number of 0.64 mean in practical terms? Specifically, it means that the movement of Stock X is only 64% as volatile as that of the market as a whole. As a result, if the market (usually as measured by the S&P 500 index) increases 14% over the course of a year, Stock X would be expected to increase only 8.96%. However, if the market decreased by this same percentage (14%), Stock X would only be expected to go down in the same proportion (8.96%). Therefore, all other investor considerations remaining equal, Stock X is "less risky" (on a relative basis) than the market as a whole. Further, since the overall market consists, in part, of stocks, Stock X is only 64% as volatile as the average stock.

Finally, when a portfolio of securities is assembled, it is said to have a *weighted beta*. Of course, ultimately, this portfolio has to have a weighting of 1.0 (or 100%), but to achieve this total, several securities are combined (all with their own individual Beta) and then included in the portfolio according to the desired percentage. The resulting weighted Beta, therefore, represents the volatility of the portfolio to the market as a whole.

Example 9-5: Continuing with facts of Example 9-4, we now combine Stock X with Stock Y and Stock Z to make up the investor portfolio. 30% of the portfolio consists of Stock X with its Beta of 0.64. Stock Y has a Beta of 1.24 and is included in a 40% ratio. Finally, Stock Z has a Beta of 0.85 and makes up the remaining 30% of the portfolio. Therefore, the weighted Beta of the portfolio is 0.943 broken down as follows:

	Weight	x	Beta	=	Weighted Beta
Stock X	0.30	x	0.64	=	0.192
Stock Y	0.40	x	1.24	=	0.496
Stock Z	0.30	x	0.85	=	0.255
Total Weighted Beta				=	0.943

The above investor is likely attempting to protect him or herself no matter the direction of the overall market (up or down). An investor expecting the market to be bullish will select a stock (or mutual fund) with a beta higher than 1.0, such as Stock Y. Conversely, if the investor expects the market to be bearish, he or she would likely purchase stocks (or funds) with betas less than 1, such as Stocks X and Z above. The noted portfolio is a bit less volatile than that of the market, since it exhibits a total weighted Beta of 0.94.

COEFFICIENT OF DETERMINATION (R^2)

The coefficient of determination (R^2) or the square of the correlation coefficient (R) measures the proportion of the variation in one variable (a security or mutual fund) explained by the movement of the other variable (the overall market). It also measures the extent to which a portfolio is diversified. For example, index funds based on the S &P 500 will have an R^2 of close to 100%, meaning that they are fully diversified (and have little unsystematic risk). In contrast, a sector fund will have a very low R^2 of 5% to 25%, meaning it is relatively non-diversified in relation to the overall market (or exhibits considerable unsystematic risk). Therefore, *the higher the R^2 of the security or fund, the more its beta coefficient or beta may be "trusted" (that is, the more the overall market is an appropriate benchmark for the measurement of investor risk).*

> **Example 9-6:** Assume that KRF mutual fund and the overall market have a correlation coefficient (R) of 0.60. Therefore, the coefficient of determination (R^2) for the fund is 0.36 (or 0.60 x 0.60). This means that 36% of the investment risk of KRF is systematic--or attributable to the movement of the benchmark market index (usually the S&P 500 Index) -- and 64% is unsystematic-or movement that is independent of the market index. Accordingly, in this case, the Beta coefficient of the KRF mutual fund would *not* be the most preferable measure of risk. Alternatively, however, KRF mutual fund may be an effective diversifier of a portfolio since its systematic risk is relatively low.

R-squared values range between 0 and 100%, where 0 represents the least amount of correlation with the overall market and 100% represents perfectly positive correlation. Measuring the correlation of the security or fund's movement to that of the market describes the extent to which the investment asset's volatility is a result of the daily fluctuations of the market, or, stated otherwise, the *percentage of the asset's systematic risk, relative to the market index used.*

Use in Portfolio Evaluation (Jensen, Treynor, and Sharpe)

The common measures of portfolio risk and risk-adjusted performance will be discussed in greater detail in the next chapter on portfolio management theory. However, the Jensen method (which computes a concept known as *alpha*) and the Treynor method use Beta as the relevant risk measure for the portfolio and incorporate this measure in their formulas. Therefore, by definition, each of the methods implies a diversified portfolio and is appropriate for portfolios with a high degree of systematic risk or, stated differently, is appropriate for portfolios that are strongly correlated to the market index used. (Conversely, of course, Jensen and Treynor are inappropriate measures for non-diversified portfolios or those exhibiting significant unsystematic risk.) The key to using either method as the relevant measure of portfolio evaluation is an R^2 of approximately 0.75 or more, indicating relative diversification to the overall market and greater systematic risk.

In contrast to Jensen and Treynor, the Sharpe method of portfolio evaluation, utilizes standard deviation as the relevant risk measure for the portfolio and incorporates this measure in the denominator of its formula. Therefore, by definition, the Sharpe method implies a non-diversified portfolio and is appropriate only for those portfolios exhibiting a great amount of unsystematic risk. The key to using Sharpe as the relevant measure of portfolio evaluation is an R^2 of less than 0.75, indicating a lack of diversification to the broader market and greater unsystematic risk.

IMPORTANT CONCEPTS

Standard deviation

Variability

Total risk

Beta coefficient

Volatility

Systematic risk

Probability distribution

Spreadsheet Model

Simulation

Monte Carlo Simulation

Normal distribution (bell curve)

Lognormal distribution

Skewness

Kurtosis

Standard deviation of single asset

Standard deviation of a two asset portfolio

Coefficient of variation

Semi-variance

Covariance

Correlation coefficient (R)

Coefficient of determination (R^2)

Weighted beta

Jensen Method (*alpha*) of portfolio evaluation

Treynor Method of portfolio evaluation

Sharpe Method of portfolio evaluation

QUESTIONS FOR REVIEW

1. What is the relevant measure of the *total* risk of an asset or portfolio? Is such portfolio assumed to be diversified or non-diversified in this instance? Explain.

2. What is the relevant measure of *systematic* risk of an asset or portfolio? Is such portfolio assumed to be diversified or non-diversified in this instance? Explain.

3. There are two methods used in developing a probability distribution to assist in the measurement of investment risk. What are these methods? Contrast one to the other.

4. What is Monte Carlo Simulation and when might it be used in the financial planning process?

5. If a lognormal probability distribution, in which direction (left or right) does the mean fall with respect to the highest point of the curve? Practically, what is the implication of the mean positioned in this manner?

6. In investment planning, when would you typically expect a normal probability distribution to occur?

7. What does *skewness* measure? If a probability distribution is negatively skewed, what does this portend for the likely behavior of a risk-averse investor?

8. What does *kurtosis* measure and how does it interact with skewness in influencing the behavior of a risk-averse investor?

9. Assume that the standard deviation of a single asset is 15 and that its annual expected return is 10%. Assuming a normal probability distribution, what does this imply for the actual future investment return of the asset?

10. What does the *coefficient of variation* measure? Why might it be a more preferable method of analyzing total risk than that of standard deviation?

11. There is one additional measurement of risk that is critical in computing the standard deviation of a two or more asset portfolio. What is it and why is this measurement so important?

12. Unless the securities within a portfolio are all perfectly positively correlated, the standard deviation of the portfolio will be _____ than the weighted average standard deviation of the individual securities. Fill in the blank and explain why this occurs.

13. What is *semi-variance*? Why is it sometimes preferred instead of standard deviation in measuring the total risk of an asset or portfolio?

14. What characteristic of the *correlation coefficient* between two assets is an improvement upon that of merely finding their *covariance*? Asked another way, what aspect of covariance makes it particularly difficult to analyze and use in practice?

15. What types of correlated assets (low or high) are more useful in properly diversifying a portfolio to minimize total risk? Why?

16. What does the *beta coefficient* (beta) of an asset measure? How is beta computed (using what factors)?

17. Assume that a stock has a beta coefficient of 1.50. If the market increases by 10%, is this stock likely to increase or decrease and in what percentage?

18. Why might an investor wish to know the *weighted beta* of a portfolio?

19. What does the *coefficient of determination* (R^2) of an asset or mutual fund measure? If a fund has a relatively high R^2, what does this imply for the use of its beta coefficient as a reliable (or non-reliable) measure?

20. What risk measurement do each of the following formulas use in evaluating the performance of a portfolio and what does each therefore imply about the nature of the portfolio?

    a) Jensen method (*alpha*)

    b) Treynor method

    c) Sharpe method

21. If a portfolio exhibits an R^2 of 0.75, which portfolio evaluation measure should likely be used and why?

SUGGESTIONS FOR ADDITIONAL READING

Tools and Techniques of Investment Planning, Stephen R. Leimberg, Robert T. LeClair, Robert J. Doyle, Jr., and Thomas R. Robinson, The National Underwriter Company, 2004.

Investments: An Introduction, 7th edition, Herbert B. Mayo, Thomson/ South-Western, 2002.

Investment Analysis and Portfolio Management, 7th edition, Frank K. Reilly and Keith C. Brown, Thomson/South-Western, 2003.

The Wall Street Journal Guide to Money and Investing, 3rd edition, Kenneth M. Morris and Virginia B. Morris, Fireside Publishing, 2004.

CHAPTER TEN

Portfolio Management Theory and Behavioral Finance

• • •

Portfolio management theory is much in vogue these days, although likely by its more widely-known name of *modern portfolio theory (MPT)*. It builds on a foundation of investor behavior assumptions first introduced by Harry Markowitz in 1952. These assumptions are separately expanded upon in this chapter when discussing so-called *Markowitz portfolio theory*, but were further refined and developed by others, most notably William Sharpe, a Nobel Laureate finance professor and the author of the *Sharpe formula* introduced in the previous chapter.

Upon completing this chapter, you should be able to:

- Explain Markowitz's portfolio theory, including the concepts of *efficient frontier* and the *optimal portfolio* for an investor
- Explain capital market theory
- Derive the *security market line* (SML) and discuss in what investment context it should be used
- Describe the underlying assumptions and forms of the *efficient market hypothesis* (EMH)
- Identify anomalies to the EMH
- Describe the basic principles of *behavioral finance* theory

BACKGROUND

A basic assumption of portfolio management theory is that an investor wants to maximize return from an investment for a given (or assumed) level of risk. Therefore, to truly optimize an investor's portfolio so as to achieve the highest possible return at the lowest possible risk, he or she must be open to the entire universe of investment choices. For example, less marketable investments such as coins, stamps, art, and antiques also need to be considered. In addition, the *relationship* between the returns on all these investments is also very important, since how they move in relation to one another (their *covariance*) is key to the proper diversification of a portfolio.

Portfolio management theory also assumes that investors are basically *risk-averse*, meaning that, given a choice between two assets with equal rates of return, they will select the asset with the *least amount of risk*. The purchase of an insurance policy to protect against potentially larger monetary losses in the future is evidence of the validity of this assumption. Further evidence of risk aversion is the difference in coupon rates demanded by investors as they accept greater risk in the form of a lower rated bond. For example, the coupon rate on bonds increases as an investor purchases speculative (or non-investment grade bonds) as compared to those bonds rated AAA or exhibiting little risk of issuer default. Accordingly, portfolio management theory assumes as a given that there is a *positive correlation* between expected return and total risk.

MARKOWITZ PORTFOLIO THEORY

Markowitz's approach to portfolio management was that an investor should evaluate investment options based on the investment's expected returns and risk (as measured by standard deviation). He showed that the variance of the portfolio's rate of return (standard deviation of expected returns) was a meaningful measure of investment risk and, subsequently, derived the formula for computing the variance of a portfolio. This formula not only reflected the importance of diversifying investments to reduce the total risk of a portfolio, but also showed the investor *how* to go about achieving this result. Markowitz also was the first to derive the concept of an *optimal portfolio,* defined as one that exhibits the *smallest portfolio risk* for a given level of expected return or the *largest expected return* for a given level of portfolio risk.

The Markowitz portfolio management theory is based on several fundamental assumptions. They are as follows:

1) Investors consider each investment opportunity as being represented by a probability distribution of expected returns over a specified holding period.

2) Investors estimate the risk of the portfolio on the basis of the variability of expected returns.

3) Investors base decisions solely on expected return and risk, therefore their *indifference curves* are a function of expected return and the expected variance (or standard deviation) of returns only.

4) Investors base their indifference to alternative investments on the maximization of wealth

over a specified period, and this indifference diminishes as they get beyond this period.

5) For a given level of risk, investors prefer higher returns to lower returns.

Accordingly, the Markowitz theory established the principle that *a single asset or portfolio of securities is considered to be efficient if no other asset or portfolio offers a higher expected return with the same or lower risk.*

The last chapter presents the formula for the standard deviation of a two-asset portfolio. It also notes that the general formula for a portfolio with more than two (many) assets merely substitutes the Greek letter for Sigma (Σ) for the number two to extends the analysis and derives the standard deviation of a portfolio. Markowitz was responsible for developing the standard deviation (total risk) of a portfolio formula and for proving that the resulting risk encompasses not only the variance of the individual assets but *also* includes the covariance between the pairs of individual assets in the portfolio. So, under the theory, what happens to the portfolio's standard deviation when an investor *adds* a new security to the portfolio? Specifically, one of the major effects is that the covariance changes between the returns of this asset and the returns of every other asset that is already in the portfolio. As a result, the relative weight of these numerous covariances is substantially *greater than* the additional asset's own variance of returns and that the critically important factor to consider is *not* the new asset's own variance but *its average covariance with all the other investments in the portfolio.*

Efficient Frontier

If we examined a number of asset combinations (as in the typical portfolio) and plotted their expected returns for every given level of risk assuming all the possible combined weights, we would develop a series of curves. The envelope curve that includes the best of these combinations is referred to as the *efficient frontier.* Specifically, this curve *represents that set of portfolios that has the maximum rate of return for every given level of risk.* In pictorial terms, the efficient frontier looks like this:

Figure 10-1

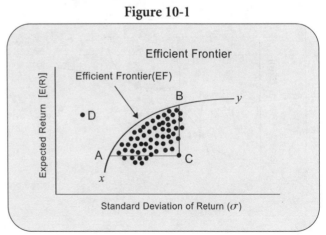

Every portfolio that resides on the efficient frontier has either a higher rate of return for equal risk or lower risk for an equal rate of return than another portfolio below or underneath the frontier. For example, in Figure 10-1, we would say that Portfolios A and B are both equally efficient and *dominate* Portfolio C. In other words, Portfolios A and B dominate Portfolio C because:

1) Portfolio A has an equal expected rate of return as Portfolio C but with a significantly lower level of risk assumed by the investor

2) Portfolio B has an equal level of assumed risk by the investor as Portfolio C but with a significantly higher expected rate of return

Accordingly, Portfolio C may be said to be *inefficient*; it is *attainable*, but *inefficient*.

With respect to Portfolio D in Figure 10-1, it is said to be *unattainable*. That is, since it resides above the efficient frontier, it is arguably *efficient*, but the expected return is not *attainable* as it is located outside the universe of portfolios available to the investor. Point D also cannot exist for any extended period of time under the Markowitz assumptions.

Finally, because of the benefits of diversification to minimize total risk among imperfectly correlated assets, we would expect the efficient frontier to consist of portfolios or combination of assets rather than individual securities. However, there are two notable exceptions to this statement: each end point of the frontier represents an individual security with the lowest total risk and highest expected rate of return, respectively. These are shown in Figure 10-1 as Assets X and Y, respectively.

Optimal Portfolio

Per the Markowitz theory, the efficient frontier provides the investor with all possible sets of efficient portfolios (or possible choices); however, the frontier does *not* tell the portfolio manager the particular portfolio (or one choice) that the investor should construct. Rather, the specific portfolio chosen (or optimal combination of assets taking into account the investor's expected return and level of assumed risk) depends on the investor's *utility function* or how much risk he or she is willing to assume for a desired level of reward. This utility function is represented graphically by one or more *indifference curves*. Figure 10-2 below shows two sets of indifference curves plotted in combination with the efficient frontier.

Figure 10-2

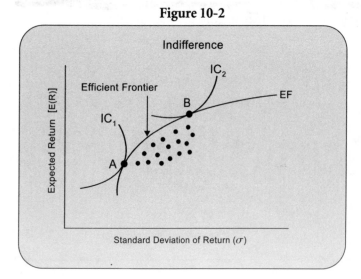

Two investors will choose the same portfolio only if their indifference curves are identical.

Different investors typically have different indifference curves. If the investor is exceedingly risk-averse, his or her indifference curve tends to be *very steep*, indicating that a large amount of additional expected return is necessary to bear additional risk. This is shown in Figure 10-2 as IC_1. In contrast, if his or her indifference curve is relatively *flat*, the investor is less risk averse, meaning that only a small or modest amount of additional expected return is necessary to assume more risk. This type of curve is shown in Figure 10-2 as IC_2. In practical terms, an investor with an indifference curve of IC_1 would likely be characterized as having a conservative risk tolerance level and an investor with an indifference curve of IC_2 would be termed as having a moderate, perhaps aggressive, tolerance for risk.

Nevertheless, we are still left without an answer to our question: which particular portfolio will the investor choose? To know this, we analyze where the investor indifference curve *intersects* with that of the efficient portfolio. Although, in reality, each investor has a number of indifference curves, for purposes of illustration, we have shown only one. The point at which the indifference curve is tangent (or intersects) with the efficient frontier is referred to as the investor's *optimal portfolio*. In Figure 10-2, this is shown as Point A for the investor with the indifference curve IC_1 (the *more* risk-averse investor) and Point B for the investor with the indifference curve IC_2 (the *less* risk-averse investor). The conservative investor's highest utility point is at Point A, which represents a portfolio with less risk and a lower amount of expected return; the more aggressive investor's highest utility point is at Point B, which represents a portfolio with more risk and commensurate higher amount of expected return.

One should also note that sometimes the optimal portfolio for an investor is known as his or her *mean-variance optimization*. This is because, as may easily be seen from the vertical and horizontal axis of Figures 10-1 and 10-2, the labels expected return (mean) and standard deviation (variance) are used.

CAPITAL MARKET THEORY

Capital market theory extends Markowitz's portfolio theory and develops a model for pricing all risky assets. The final product, referred to as the *capital asset pricing model* (CAPM) provides the portfolio manager (and investment advisor) with a basis for making an investment decision. That is, since CAPM generates the investor's *required rate of return*, this may be compared to the investment's *expected rate of return* to determine whether a purchase (or sale) of the risky asset should be made.

Since capital market theory builds on Markowitz portfolio theory (really, both theories constitute what we now know as *modern portfolio theory*), it requires the same assumptions concerning investor behavior, along with a few others. Accordingly, the assumptions underlying capital market theory are:

1) All investors are considered to be efficient investors whose objective is to target his or her *optimal portfolio*.

2) All investors have the same expectations; that is, they estimate identical (normal) probability distributions for future rates of investment return.

3) Investors can always borrow or lend money at the risk-free rate of return as represented by the yield on U.S. short-term securities and, specifically, that of the 90-day Treasury bill; in the CAPM formula (to be subsequently presented), the risk-free rate is shown as r_f.

4) All investors have the same one-period investment time horizon; a difference in this time period requires investors to derive minimization of risk strategies and invest in risk free assets that are consistent with their new horizon.

5) All investments are infinitely divisible, meaning that it is possible to buy or sell fractional shares of any asset or portfolio.

6) There are no taxes or transaction costs involved in buying or selling assets, meaning that these expenses are not relevant in investment decision-making.

7) There is no inflation or any change in market interest rates, or all changes in either investor-behavior factor are fully anticipated.

8) *Capital markets are in equilibrium,* meaning that all investments are properly priced taking into account the commensurate level of investor risk; thus, CAPM establishes a theoretical baseline by which to evaluate an investment's suitability for any investor.

Having noted all of these underlying assumptions, it now should be stated that the single major factor that permitted Markowitz portfolio theory to evolve into capital market theory was the concept of a risk-free asset. Indeed, the inclusion of a risk-free asset return in the CAPM formula was a major breakthrough allowing the portfolio manager a baseline figure from which to measure the amount of stock and market risk premium required by the investor to make a particular investment.

Capital Market Line (CML)

Using Markowitz portfolio theory, as we have seen, an investor develops a portfolio along the *efficient frontier* of all possible choices of investments. He or she is, thus, in the *macro world* as the quality of individual securities (the *micro world*) are, theoretically, now *not* the focus of immediate attention. The macro aspect of capital market theory is represented by the development of a so-called *capital market line (CML)*. This line specifies the relationship between the risk and return on a portfolio when a perfectly risk-free asset is added. Therefore, r_f, as represented in most textbooks as the 90-day Treasury bill rate, is situated at the far left position of the CML and on the vertical axis labeled *expected return percentage*. As an investor proceeds along the CML, which is a straight line, since both expected return and total risk *increase in a linear fashion* per capital market theory, he or she adds additional risky assets to make up a portfolio. Then, at the far right position along this line, the investor's portfolio is seen to consist of *all* or 100% risky assets (for example, the use of margin or borrowing from the investor's broker/dealer to purchase all assets). In pictorial terms, the CML with requisite formula looks like this:

Figure 10-3

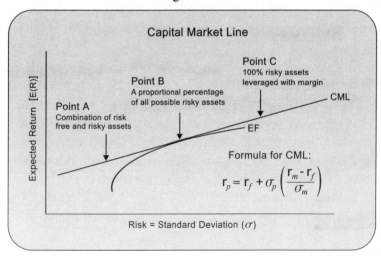

You should notice several important relationships and facts as you analyze Figure 10-3:

1) First, in effect, the CML becomes a new efficient frontier which now includes the risk-free asset.

2) Second, the old Markowitz efficient frontier remains for theoretical purposes and intersects or becomes tangent to the CML at Point B. This point reflects a proportional percentage of all possible risky assets chosen by the investor based on his or her

indifference curve. Also, at that point, the investor who invested all of his or her portfolio in that proportional percentage would have the same expected return and total risk as the overall market. Indeed, Point B is said to represent the *optimal risky portfolio* for a given investor.

3) Finally, as the investor moves from Point B (point of tangency) toward the risk free rate, the percentage of 90-day Treasury bills (the risk free asset) in his or her portfolio would *increase*. As a result, many investors (those who are relatively risk-averse) would be at some Point A since it reflects their desired risk tolerance. Conversely, those investors who move from Point B to Point C would *reduce* their ownership of 90-day Treasury bills and invest in more risky assets, such as longer term bonds.

You should also note that the slope of the CML is the market price of risk for efficient portfolios or the price of risk in a capital market that is presumed to be in equilibrium. In other words, the linear shape of the CML indicates the additional return that the market demands for each percentage increase in a portfolio's total risk as measured by its standard deviation.

Security Market Line (SML)

The second component of capital market theory is specification of the relationship between the expected return and the risk of *an individual asset or security*. At the *micro* level of the theory, this relationship is referred to as the *security market line* (*SML*). The capital market line (CML) depicts the risk-return trade-off at the level of an overall market that is assumed to be in equilibrium. As such, however, the CML applies only to efficient (or diversified) *portfolios* and *cannot* be used to assess the equilibrium expected return on a *single* security. Rather, this is the purpose of the SML. The SML, when using the capital asset pricing model (CAPM) as its applicable equation, indicates what should be the expected return on a risky asset and/or an inefficient (non-diversified) portfolio. Also, since the expected rate of return is determined under capital market theory to be in the context of a properly-priced market (one that is in equilibrium) the expected return for any investment asset is implicitly equivalent to the required rate of return for the investor.

In the security market line (SML), the vertical axis (as in that of the capital market line representation) is expected return. However, unlike the CML where the horizontal axis is represented by standard deviation, in the SML that axis uses the *beta coefficient* (*beta*) of the individual asset. In pictorial terms, the SML with requisite formula looks like this:

Figure 10-4

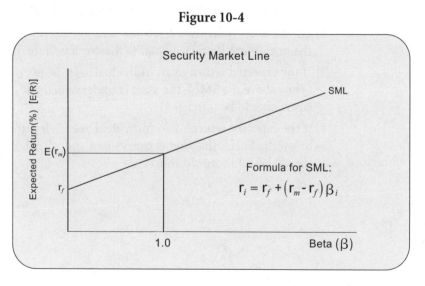

Security Market Line

Formula for SML:
$$r_i = r_f + (r_m - r_f)\beta_i$$

As previously noted, if security markets are in equilibrium, all individual assets (whether risky or not) should plot along the SML. However, what happens if investors determine that an asset does *not* fall on the SML (in other words, the asset is not perfectly priced)? In that case, let us now add two assets, X and Y, and plot each as either above the SML or below the SML as follows:

You should notice several very important implications as you analyze Figure 10-5:

Figure 10-5

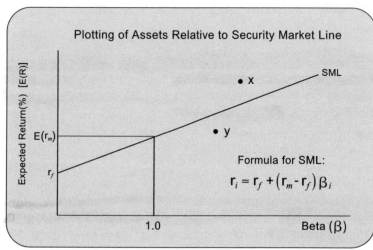

1) Since Security X is plotted *above* the SML, it is *undervalued* because it offers *more expected return* than investors require, given its level of systematic risk as measured by beta. Accordingly, Security X will likely be purchased by investors, subsequently driving *up* its price. As more and more of Security X is purchased, its expected return will be driven *down*, until, ultimately, it is at the level reflected by the SML.

2) Since Security Y is plotted *below* the SML, it is *overvalued* because it offers *less expected return* than investors require, given its level of systematic risk as measured by beta. Accordingly, Security Y will likely be sold (or sold short) by investors, subsequently driving *down* its price. As more and more of Security Y is sold, its expected return will be driven *up*, until, ultimately, it is at the level reflected by the SML.

We will discuss how to value individual assets using the capital asset pricing model (CAPM) in much greater detail in chapter 14 of this text (Asset Pricing Models), however, here it is important to realize that:

1) The SML is the pictorial representation of CAPM.

2) On the SML, individual assets are said to be properly priced; that is, the expected return of the investment is exactly *equal to* the required rate of return demanded by the investor.

3) If the expected return of an individual asset is more than the investor's required return (plots above the SML), the asset is undervalued and, all other investment factors remaining equal, should be purchased.

4) If the expected return of an individual asset is less than the investor's required return (plots below the SML), the asset is overvalued and, all other investment factors remaining equal, should be sold (or sold short).

Market and Stock Risk Premium

We can now analyze even further the particular types of risk that are necessary to entice an investor to invest in a particular asset or security. Specifically, if we know what the current risk free rate of return is (as represented by the 90-day Treasury bill rate), what is the incremental percentage necessary to motivate the individual to purchase the asset? In the capital asset pricing model, this is known as the *stock risk premium* and may be found by determining the amount equal to:

$$\text{Stock Risk Premium} = (R_m - R_f)\,\beta$$

Where R_m is equal to the return on the market, R_f is the risk free rate of return and β is the beta coefficient of the individual security.

> **Example 10-1:** Assume that the return on the market is 10% and that the 90-day Treasury bill rate of return is 4.5%. Further, you have previously computed the beta coefficient of Stock X to be 1.20. Therefore, the stock risk premium associated with Stock X is 6.60% [(0.10 - 0.045) x 1.20].

In turn, this means that an investor interested in purchasing Stock X would require an annual return of 6.60% in excess of what he or she could achieve simply by purchasing a risk free asset as represented by the 90-day Treasury bill rate.

If we wish to know only the broad risk of investing in the market, we can determine this by calculating the *market risk*. This is found by breaking down the *stock risk* even further and separating out the ($R_m - R_f$) component or, in Example 10-1, (0.10 - 0.045) as equivalent to 5.5%. In turn, this means that our investor needs at least an annual rate of return of 5.50% to invest in the market, generally, and another premium of at least 1.10% (6.60% - 5.50%) to purchase Stock X, specifically.

EFFICIENT MARKET HYPOTHESIS (EMH)

An *efficient capital market* is one in which security prices adjust rapidly (some would argue immediately) to the arrival of new information and, therefore, the current prices of securities reflect all information known about the security. As a result of this premise, a well-known academic theory referred to as the *efficient market hypothesis* (EMH) has developed. This hypothesis suggests that investors cannot expect to outperform the overall market *consistently* on a risk-adjusted basis. Finally, day-to-day changes in the market prices of securities follow a *random walk* and cannot be predicted with any reliable degree of accuracy. Therefore, since prices move in this independent manner, any trading rules or security analysis (such as technical analysis) trying to find a pattern to this walk is considered to be of *no value*.

There are three basic assumptions underlying the premise of an efficient capital market. They are as follows:

1) A large number of profit-maximizing participants analyze and value securities on a daily (or close-to-daily) basis; therefore, it is fruitless to try and outperform such a large representation of time and intellect.

2) New information related to one security occurs independently from that of another.

3) Profit-maximizing investors adjust security prices rapidly to reflect the effect of new information; further, this price adjustment is unbiased, meaning that a potential investor cannot predict with any certainty where the market will over- or under-adjust the security's eventual trading value.

Finally, at the heart of an efficient capital market is a belief that the *expected returns inherent in the current trading value of a security reflects its systematic risk*, meaning that investors who buy securities at today's market price receive a rate of return consistent with their perceived risk of investing. Stated another way, all securities should lie on the security market line (SML) so that their expected returns are consistent with the assumption of systematic risk as reflected by their beta coefficient.

Most of the early academic research related to efficient capital markets was based on the *random walk hypothesis*, which argues that changes in stock prices occur without any predictable pattern. Extensive empirical analysis was performed, but little basic theoretical assumptions were ever stated. This changed in 1966 when Eugene Fama announced his *efficient market hypothesis* (EMH) and divided his empirical results into three sub-hypotheses or forms depending on the information that was received by the investor. Respectively, in order of their rigidity, the forms were named: 1) the *strong- form EMH*; 2) the *semi-strong form EMH*; and 3) the *weak-form EMH*.

Strong-Form EMH

Essentially, the strong form of the efficient market hypothesis (EMH) assumes a *perfect market*, in which all information is cost-free and available to all investors at the same time. Specifically, the form holds that stock prices fully reflect *all information from public and private sources*. Therefore, even those investors with access to insider information are unlikely to consistently outperform the overall market. In addition, neither the fundamental nor technical analysis approach to security selection (see chapter 15 of this textbook) will achieve superior performance.

The strong form encompasses both the weak-form and the semi-strong form of the hypothesis and asserts that security prices adjust very rapidly to the release of new public information. Whether an investor fully understands the assertions of the strong form of the EMH, he or she who practices passive investment management by purchasing only index funds is tacitly agreeing with the validity of the strong-form EMH.

Semi-Strong Form EMH

This is a variation of the strong form of the hypothesis, but instead of holding that security prices reflect both public and private information, the semi-strong form asserts that *only public information is considered.* Therefore, an investor with access to insider information *may* outperform the market. Such public information includes all non-market information, such as earnings and dividends announcements, price-to-earnings (P/E) ratios, stock splits, news about the economy, and political views. The form suggests that investors who base their decisions on any important new information after it is public should not achieve above-average risk-adjusted profits from their transactions since the security price already reflects such information. Like the strong form of the hypothesis, neither fundamental nor technical analysis is accorded much credibility in the semi-strong variation.

The semi-strong form of EMH encompasses the weak form of the theory because all the market information considered by the weak form, such as security prices, rates of return, and market trading volume, has already been made public.

Weak-Form EMH

The weak form of the hypothesis assumes that current security prices fully reflect all *historical price data, but not data from outside the market* (such as that generated from analyzing company financial statements, the relevant industry, or the economy as a whole). Because it assumes that current market prices already reflect all security market information, the weak form implies that historical market data should have no relationship with future rates of return. As a result, technical analysis is of no use; however, credible fundamental analysis in security selection *may* achieve above-average risk-adjusted returns. In addition, those investors with access to insider information (though illegal) may also generate superior long-term performance.

The weak form does not incorporate the other forms of the hypothesis (strong or semi-strong), but remains *independent* both as to its underlying assumptions and with respect to the market factors that are considered.

In summary, the three forms of the EMH, with the relevant information each considers in establishing security market prices, are as follows:

Form of EMH	Information Reflected in Price
Strong	Technical and fundamental analysis as well as insider information
Semi-Strong	Technical and fundamental analysis
Weak	Technical analysis

Remember that, given the assumptions of the EMH, if the information is already reflected in the security market price, it is of no value with respect to its potential to out-perform the broader market indexes.

Academic Studies Testing the Forms

As with most theories and/or hypotheses in investments, the academic evidence supporting the EMH is mixed. However, several studies have supported the assumptions of the EMH and, specifically, the weak form of the theory. As a result, it is likely fair to assert that credible fundamental analysis may generate superior risk-adjusted rates of return over time. In addition, experience also suggests that access to insider information will yield investor profits; otherwise, security laws restricting such access would not be in effect.

Nevertheless, still other studies have produced findings that do *not* support either the hypothesis or any of its forms. These are known as *anomalies* and, by definition, are in contrast to what would be expected if the market were indeed totally efficient. Some of these anomalies (with commentary on their implications for investors) are now discussed.

Anomalies to the EMH

1) *Price-earnings (P/E) effect:* This anomaly suggests that higher returns are attainable with portfolios consisting of securities with low price-earning (P/E) ratios. Indeed, considering the evidence, it does appear that firms trading at low price-to-earning multiples may generate higher rates of return over time than that of firms whose stock does not exhibit this characteristic. This is likely because growth companies enjoy high P/E ratios; the market tends to overestimate the growth potential of those companies and thus overvalues them, while simultaneously under-valuing low growth firms with low P/E ratios.

2) *Small-firm effect (a.k.a. the neglected firm effect):* This anomaly relates to the number of security analysts that follow smaller-sized companies. Specifically, with fewer analysts following a stock or security, the value of that stock may not be efficiently priced and may result in an undervalued offering. An example of this is typically foreign or international stocks where the opportunity for a significant price gain may be possible.

3) *The January effect:* This anomaly has been observed for decades and has, at its genesis, a unique trading rule for those investors interested in taking advantage of tax selling. Investors, particularly institutions, tend to engage in tax selling at the end of the calendar year, thereby harvesting capital losses on stocks that have declined in price. After the new year, the tendency is then to reacquire these stocks (after waiting for at least 30 days to avoid the wash sale tax rule) or to buy other stocks that look promising. Accordingly, this scenario generates negative (downward) pressure on stock prices in November and December of the previous calendar year and positive (upward) pressure in January of the subsequent calendar year.

4) *The Value Line Enigma: Value Line* is a large well-known publication and advisory service that publishes financial information on over 1,700 stocks. A rank of "1" is the most favorable recommendation given by *Value Line* and "5" is the least favorable. Studies have shown that stocks rated "1" tend to outperform the market and that stocks rated "5" significantly under perform the market. Hence, the enigma: this phenomenon should not occur if the EMH was totally valid.

5) *Analysts recommendations:* Finally, there is evidence in favor of the existence of superior security analysts who may possess private information. This evidence is provided by two studies finding that the price of stocks mentioned in the *Wall Street Journal* column entitled "Heard on the Street" experience a significant change on the day that the column appears.

Efficient Markets and Security Analysis

As should be appreciated by now, advocates of EMH do *not* attribute any validity to the technical analysis theory of attempting to determine future security prices. Indeed, the assumptions of technical analysis are directly *contradictory* to the belief that markets are inherently efficient. A basic premise of technical analysis is that stock prices move in predictable patterns over time. Furthermore, *technicians* believe that when new public information comes to the market, it is *not* immediately available to everyone; rather, such information is disseminated downward from professional investors and institutions to the greater mass of *uninformed* investors. Finally, the process of analyzing information and then acting on it takes time; therefore, stock prices move to a new *support level* in a gradual manner, thereby causing trends in the direction of stock prices that persist over many years.

The belief in the pattern of price adjustments, as articulated by technical analysts, is anathema to EMH proponents who believe that security prices adjust to new information (public, private, or both, depending on which form of the hypothesis is being advocated) *very rapidly.* EMH advocates do not assert that market prices adjust perfectly, which implies a chance of over- or under-adjustment (and an opportunity for inefficiency). Nevertheless, since by the time information has been made public, this price adjustment has already taken place, a purchase or sale of a security using technical trading rules should not generate any abnormal rate of return beyond that of the overall market.

In contrast to technicians, *fundamental analysts* believe that, at any given point in time, there is a basic *intrinsic value* for the aggregate stock market, as a whole, and for an individual security. This value depends on underlying economic, industry, and company-specific factors that may be discerned from study and research. Therefore, if an investor can do a superior job of determining a security's intrinsic value, profit-making opportunities exist. As has been suggested, the weak form of EMH incorporates this result, with academic studies indicating some demonstrable support for its validity.

BEHAVIORAL FINANCE

We conclude our discussion of portfolio management theory by analyzing a recent branch of financial economics known as *behavioral finance.* This field of study argues that investors are not nearly as rational as traditional finance theory asserts. Rather, they may be motivated by psychological factors, such as the *herd effect* of not wanting to be left behind in the event of a market upturn. Accordingly, for investors that are curious about how emotions and biases influence security market prices, behavioral finance offers some interesting descriptions and explanations.

For example, studies have shown that if an individual is offered the choice of a sure $50 or, after the flip of a coin, the possibility of winning $100 (doubling his or her money) or winning nothing, the individual will most often choose the sure $50. Conversely, offer this same individual the choice between a sure loss of $50 or, after the flip of a coin, the possibility of losing $100 or nothing, and he or she will then likely choose the coin toss. Why is this so? Behavioral finance advocates explain this result by emphasizing the importance of *prospect theory*, which contends that investors *fear losses much more than they value gains*. Another psychological bias mentioned by *behaviorists* influencing investor behavior is that of *confirmation bias*. This means that investors tend to look for information that supports their previously established opinion and decision. As a result, they tend to overvalue the stocks of currently popular companies, such as a firm that has introduced a yet unproven technology. (Of course, this means that they also tend to undervalue the stocks of overlooked companies, as supported by the *neglected firm effect* anomaly to efficient market hypothesis as previously discussed.)

Other examples of behavioral finance in practice are the propensity of investors to hold on to stocks that have lost value for far too long, and sell *winning* stocks (that is, those that portend significant capital appreciation) much too soon. Again, this is likely explained by the typical investor's inherent fear of losses and, specifically here, converting a *paper loss* into a *real loss* for income tax purposes.

Finally, behavioral finance has also made analysts aware of an *escalation bias*. This bias causes investors to contribute more money into a failing stock or mutual fund than into investments that are outperforming the market average. This results in the relatively popular investment strategy of *averaging down* on a stock that has declined in value since its initial purchase, rather than selling it and admitting one's mistake. For example, if a particular stock was a good *buy* at $50, this same stock must now be a *real steal* once it has fallen in price to $30. Obviously, at this point, the investor should now reassess his or her motivations for buying the stock in the first instance. However, because of *escalation bias*, the investor tends to ignore any real, negative market forces weighing down the stock's value and focus only on any imaginary, false positives that cause him or her to buy even more of the same losing position.

In summary, advocates of behavioral finance have yet to come up with a coherent model that actually predicts the future rather than one that merely explains, with the benefit of hindsight, what the market did in the past. Nevertheless, it does provide a new, additional factor to consider in portfolio management theory: that being the implication of psychological and economic principles for the improvement of financial decision making.

IMPORTANT CONCEPTS

Markowitz Portfolio Theory

Capital Market Theory

Modern Portfolio Theory (MPT)

Efficient frontier

Optimal portfolio

Indifference curve

Capital Market Line (CML)

Security Market Line (SML)

Capital Asset Pricing Model (CAPM)

Required rate of return

Market risk premium

Stock risk premium

Efficient Market Hypothesis (EMH)

Strong-form EMH

Semi-strong form EMH

Weak-form EMH

Anomalies to EMH

Price-earnings (P/E) effect

Small-firm (neglected firm) effect

January effect

Value line enigma

Technical analysis

Fundamental analysis

Behavioral finance

QUESTIONS FOR REVIEW

1. According to portfolio management theory, if an investor is given a choice between two assets with equal rates of return, but with different levels or risk, which asset will he or she choose? Why?

2. Define an *efficient portfolio* as first derived by Harry Markowitz.

3. What are the five fundamental assumptions of Markowitz portfolio management theory?

4. What portfolio management principle was first established by Markowitz?

5. What is the *efficient frontier*? Why should it be important for the average investor?

6. How does a portfolio manager theoretically go about selecting the *optimal portfolio* for his or her client?

7. Capital market theory extends Markowitz portfolio theory and develops a model for pricing all risky assets. What is the model and what is its importance for the portfolio manager?

8. What are three additional assumptions of capital market theory that build on Markowitz portfolio theory? (Note: Eight assumptions are listed in the text; choose the three that you consider to be the most important.)

9. What are the macro and micro components, respectively, of capital market theory? What is each attempting to measure?

10. If a security is plotted above the SML, what does this mean? What does it mean if a security is plotted below the SML?

11. How does one determine what the stock risk premium that is associated with the making of an investment?

12. What are the three basic assumptions underlying the premise of an efficient capital market?

13. What does the efficient market hypothesis suggest about capital markets and why might this be important to any investor?

14. Explain what market or non-market information is considered in each of the following forms of EMH:

    • Strong form
    • Semi-strong form
    • Weak form

15. According to academic studies, which form of EMH, if any, may have some validity?

16. Explain each of the following anomalies to the EMH:

    • Price-earnings (P/E) effect
    • Small-firm effect
    • January effect
    • Value line enigma

17. If an individual believes in the EMH, is technical analysis useful? Explain.

18. What is behavioral finance and what does it possibly add to portfolio management theory?

19. Define each of the following theories or concepts put forth by behaviorists (those who advocate behavioral finance in explaining investor behavior):

    • Prospect theory
    • Confirmation bias
    • Escalation bias

SUGGESTIONS FOR ADDITIONAL READING

Tools and Techniques of Investment Planning, Stephen R. Leimberg, Robert T. LeClair, Robert J. Doyle, Jr., and Thomas R. Robinson, The National Underwriter Company, 2004.

Investments: An Introduction, 7th edition, Herbert B. Mayo, Thomson/ South-Western, 2002.

Investment Analysis and Portfolio Management, 7th edition, Frank K. Reilly and Keith C. Brown, Thomson/South-Western, 2003.

The Wall Street Journal Guide to Money and Investing, 3rd edition, Kenneth M. Morris and Virginia B. Morris, Fireside Publishing, 2004.

CHAPTER ELEVEN

Measures of
Investment Return

• • •

The second part of the risk/return tradeoff that is fundamental to investments is, of course, return. Indeed, the rate of return on an investment is often focused on the extent that it overshadows the first very important part of the tradeoff. In other words, how much risk does the investor need to assume in order to achieve the desired rate of return? Furthermore, return may be measured in many different ways and it is often difficult to know which method to select. That is the purpose of this chapter: to analyze the many different methods in measuring return and to use each method consistently in determining an appropriate investment vehicle, such as stocks, bonds, or mutual funds, in which to invest.

Upon completing this chapter, you should be able to:

- Calculate a specified measure of investment return
- Differentiate between those measures of return dealing primarily with stocks and mutual funds versus those dealing primarily with bonds
- Describe and compute certain portfolio measures of return, notably the Jensen (Alpha), Treynor, and Sharpe ratios

SIMPLE VS. COMPOUND RATES OF RETURN

The *simple annual rate of return* for an investment is computed by dividing its total return (its total gain or loss relative to the initial dollar investment) by the number of years that the investor has held the asset. Essentially, the simple annual rate of return is the rate of return equal to an investor's holding period of exactly one year, regardless of the length of time the investor has actually held the investment. For example, assume that the total return on an investment is 60% and that the investor has held the asset for 5 years. Therefore his or her simple annual rate of return is 12% (or 60 ÷ 5). If the investor has held the asset for less than a year, a corollary type of return known as the *annualized rate of return* is used. The example below describes this type of simple return.

> **Example 11-1:** Jerry purchases a $1,000, 3-month Treasury bill (90-day maturity date) for $900. He therefore has a total return of 10% ($100 ÷ $1,000) for the 90 day period. This converts to an annualized rate of return of 40.56% [.10 ÷ 90 = .0011 x 365= .4056 x 100= 40.56%]

In contrast to the simple annual rate of return, the *compound annual rate of return* assumes that the interest and principal on an investment is reinvested rather than always equated to a one-year holding period. Specifically, the compound annual rate of return for a given holding period (represented by *n* in the formula) is computed by adding one to the holding period (1 + n), raising this sum to the *n*th power (known as the *n*th *root*) and subtracting one. An example of how to compute the compound return follows:

> **Example 11-2:** Continuing with the facts of Example 11-1, now assume that Jerry continues to reinvest the interest and principal at the 90-day holding period/annualized rate of .0011% for the entire year (use 360 days instead of 365 for simplicity purposes). Therefore, each initial dollar of investment would grow to $1.0044 or ($1.0011)^4 by the end of one year. Accordingly, the compound annual rate of return is 44% or (1.0044 - 1 = 44%), which is *greater than* the simple annual (annualized) rate of return of 40.56%.

Which of these returns is better to use, the simple annual or compound annual rate of return? The answer to that question depends on how the investor intends to use the measurement.

If the objective of the investor is to estimate the future annual returns of an investment based on historical performance, the *simple* annual rate of return option is the preferable measurement. This is because the simple return is an unbiased estimate of future returns for a single year. However, if the investor is wishing to estimate the average annual rate at which his or her money would grow over a *period of years*, the *compound* annual rate of return is a better measure. In addition, since mutual funds quote the compound annual measurement in their advertisements and sales literature, the compound rate is also preferable when comparing the longer-term performance of one mutual fund against that of another mutual fund.

ARITHMETIC VS. GEOMETRIC AVERAGE ANNUAL RETURNS

The *arithmetic average annual return* is similar in concept to the simple annual rate of return, except that the arithmetic average takes into account multiple years or holding periods. It is computed by dividing the sum of a series of annual returns by the number of years of actual returns. For example, assume that an investment returned 12%, 16%, and a negative 6% over three years. This means that its arithmetic average annual return is 7.33% [(12% + 16% + - 6%) ÷ 3= 7.33%].

The *geometric average annual return* takes into account the time value of money in the same manner as does the compound annual rate of return. That is, to compute the geometric average annual return, add one to each period's return, calculate the product of those sums over the applicable time period, use the *n*th root of each product (using *n* as the number of years), and subtract one. We then take this product multiplied by 100 to convert into percentage terms. An example follows:

> **Example 11-3:** Using the same returns as the example in the previous paragraph relating to the arithmetic return, we begin with the three annual returns of 12%, 16%, and a negative 6%. Accordingly, adding 1 to each return gives us 1.12, 1.16, and .94 (or 1-.06), which in turn yields a product of 1.2212. We then take the third root of 1.2212 (since there are three returns) and subtract one. This gives us 6.89% [$(1.2212)^{1/3}$ -1 = 1.0689 - 1 = .0689 x 100 = 6.89%. This result is *less than* the arithmetic average since we have already *discounted* all the returns into present-year dollars. (Note: To compute the number of 1.0689 on your HP 10 B II financial function calculator, enter: 1.2212; Shift; y^x; .3333; =; 1.0689).

If an investor wishes to ascertain the impact of time on a same-dollar type of investment (that is, with no additional contributions or periodic withdrawals), the *geometric average annual rate of return* calculation should be used.

TIME-WEIGHTED VS. DOLLAR-WEIGHTED RATES OF RETURN

The *time- weighted rate of return* is the geometric annual rate of return measured on the basis of the current year value of the investment asset. As noted, because the time-weighted method incorporates the geometric (not arithmetic) average, thereby taking into account a same-dollar type of analysis, it is the preferred method for analyzing the true annual performance of portfolio managers. Such managers have no control over either contributions to or withdrawals from the fund, which may distort the rate of return measurement accordingly. If there are no interim cash flows (investor deposits or withdrawals) to a mutual fund, the time-weighted return, compounded annually, determines the true ending value of the investment asset.

Let us look at an example using the time-weighted rate of return to determine the investor's actual return taking into account the time value of money.

Example 11-4: An investor buys a share of XYZ mutual fund for $25. This share pays a dividend of $1.50 during the first year that the investor owns the fund. At the end of the first year, he purchases a second share for $30. At the end of the second year, these shares are still worth $30 and have not paid a dividend for that year. Now, assume that the investor sells the shares at the end of the second year. Accordingly, his time-weighted rate of return on the shares is 12.25%. This result is calculated as follows: [($30- $25) + $1.50] ÷ $25= 0.26; 0.26 +1= 1.26; [(1.26)$^{1/2}$ -1=1.1225-1= 0.1225 x 100= 12.25%. (Note: To compute the number of 1.1225 on your HP 10 B II financial function calculator, enter 1.26; Shift; y^x; .5000; =; 1.1225. Using 2 as the *n*th root also means that you can derive the same result by solving for the square root of 1.26 instead.)

In contrast, the *dollar- weighted rate of return* is the compounded annual rate of return that discounts a portfolio's terminal value and interim cash flows back to an initial value. It is equivalent to the portfolio's *internal rate of return (IRR)*. However, the dollar-weighted rate of return has several weaknesses as elaborated below:

1) It assumes that the cash flows are *not reinvested at any rate*. Instead, the computation inherently asserts that the interim cash flows are consumed when paid and never enter into the analysis again.

2) It may be misleading for purposes of portfolio performance return measurement since the method is influenced by the timing and presence of additional contributions (and/or investor withdrawals) that are beyond the control of the portfolio manager. Conversely, however, if investors wish to know the compounded annual rate of return on an investment where additional contributions and/or withdrawals have taken place, the dollar-weighted rate of return method should be used.

The dollar-weighted rate of return/internal rate of return method is typically used where there are a series of *unequal* cash flows, as is usual with most mutual funds that pay dividends. An example follows:

Example 11-5: Joe invested $10,000 in ABC mutual fund two years ago. The fund paid quarterly dividends of $200, $225, $175, $180, $160, $235, $245, and $220 at the end of each quarter, all of which were withdrawn on receipt. At the time of the last dividend payment, ABC mutual fund had grown to a value of $10,350. Accordingly, the dollar-weighted rate of return/internal rate of return for Joe's investment in the fund is 9.78% computed as follows using the HP 10 B II calculator: $10,000 +/- CFj; $200 CFj; $225 CFj; $175 CFj; $180 CFj; $160 CFj; $235 CFj; $245 CFj; $10,570 (which is the $10,350 ending value PLUS the final dividend of $220) CFj; Shift; IRR/YR times 4 =9.7822. (Note: Rather than multiplying the IRR by 4, you could have alternatively changed the P/YR setting on your HP 10 B II calculator to 4; the IRR then would be computed in annual terms and there would be no need to multiply the result.)

Finally, because the negative returns in the dollar-weighted computation receive a greater weight than in the time-weighted formula (where such returns are weighted *equally*), the resulting dollar-weighted return will normally be *lower* than that of the time-weighted return. This is another reason why time-weighting of investor contributions is usually preferred in evaluating the long-term performance of portfolio and mutual fund managers.

NOMINAL VS. REAL (INFLATION-ADJUSTED) RETURNS

The *nominal rate of return* on an investment is simply its actual or stated rate of return (like the coupon rate on a bond) earned over a given period of time *without* accounting for inflation. Conversely, the *real rate of return* does take inflation into account in its computation. Accordingly, the financial planner should use the real rate of return whenever possible so as to use constant or current year dollars. Examples of when the real rate of return computation should be used are in performing retirement and insurance needs analysis as well as in doing education funding for a client and his or her children.

The real rate of return is computed by dividing (1 + Nominal Rate of Return) by (1 + Inflation Rate) and subtracting one. Then, to convert this back to percentage terms, the product is multiplied by 100. It may be shown in a practical formula as follows:

$$r_{real} = \frac{(1 + r_{nominal})}{(1 + I)} - 1 \times 100$$

Where $r_{nominal}$ is the nominal (before-tax) rate of return and I is the inflation rate.

> **Example 11-6:** Mark has purchased a 10-year corporate bond with a coupon rate of 6.75%. Inflation has averaged 3.5 over this same time period. Therefore, Mark's real (inflation-adjusted) rate of return on the bond is 3.14% computed as follows: $[(1+.0675) \div (1+.035)] -1 \times 100 = 3.1401\%$.

Note that there is a more expedient method to compute the real rate of return used in actual practice wherein one simply subtracts the inflation rate from the given nominal rate. For example, using the facts of Example 11-6, Mark's real return using the shortcut method would be calculated as (6.75% less 3.5%) or 3.25%. As may be seen, this is quite close to the mathematically correct answer of 3.14%.

After-Tax and After-Tax Inflation-Adjusted Rate of Return

A variation of both the nominal and real rate of return computation is that of the after-tax and after-tax inflation-adjusted rate of return.

To compute the after-tax rate of return on an investment:

$$r_{after-tax} = r_{nominal} \times (1 - \text{investor's marginal tax rate})$$

If the investor also pays state income taxes, a separate factor equal to (1 - state marginal income tax rate) is included in the computation. Finally, to return to percentage terms, multiply the result by 100.

Example 11-7: Susan is earning a before-tax (nominal) return of 15% on a recently purchased investment. She is in a 33% federal and a 4% state marginal income tax bracket. Accordingly, Susan's after-tax rate of return on the investment is 9.65% computed as follows: 0.15 x [(1 - .33) x (1 - .04)] = 0.15 x [0.67 x 0.96] = 0.15 x 0.6432 = 0.0965 x 100= 9.65%. (Note: This computation assumes that Susan deducts state income taxes as an itemized deduction on her federal income tax return. If she does not itemize, the after-tax rate of return is slightly less.)

The computation for the after-tax inflation-adjusted rate of return incorporates both the real (inflation-adjusted) rate of return formula and that of the after-tax rate.

Example 11-8: Continuing with the facts of Example 11-7 except (for simplicity purposes) Susan now resides in a state that does *not* impose income tax. In addition, assume that inflation is running at a 3% annual rate currently. Therefore, Susan's after-tax inflation-adjusted rate of return on her investment is 6.85% computed as follows: 0.67 x 0.15 = 0.1005+1 = 1.1005 ÷ 1.03 = 1.0684 - 1 = 0.0684 x 100 = 6.85%.

It should be noted that the after-tax rate of return formula is only relevant where the earnings on the investment are currently subject to either federal or state income taxes or both. Since many investments are held in a tax-deferred account (like a qualified retirement plan or traditional IRA), the after-tax formula generally cannot be used until the date of the account's distribution. However, this is not the case with the real or inflation-adjusted rate of return formula. It may be used whenever inflation is present and where the planner is attempting to communicate the present value of future year dollars eroded by the loss of real purchasing power.

RETURNS DEALING PRIMARILY WITH STOCKS AND MUTUAL FUNDS

Total Return

The term *total return* is used by financial services professionals to mean the total gain or loss on an investment over a given time period as compared to the initial dollar investment expended by the investor (at the beginning of the time period). As such, this type of return consists of several components as follows:

1) The cash inflows to (or outflows from) the investment; a common example of a cash inflow is the payment of a dividend by the stock or mutual fund

2) Any price or capital appreciation (or capital depreciation) on the investment; a common example is the increase in share value of a growth stock or growth mutual fund

3) Any debt reduction (or increase); an example is debt repayment on residential or commercial real property owned by the investor

4) Any net tax savings (or additions) incurred by the investor; an example is the tax savings on interest and depreciation on rental real estate property

The first two are the most common components of total return (and the ones most thought of by investors who understand the term). In turn, whether an investor values interest or dividends (income) or changes in the market value of the investment (capital appreciation) depends primarily on his or her tax status and cash flow needs. For example, a retiree in a low tax bracket and with a relatively fixed income will likely value interest and dividends more highly than that of potential capital appreciation; alternatively, a young wage-earner in a higher tax bracket will likely value growth-type investments (potential capital appreciation) more highly than those that generate taxable interest and dividends. Regardless, either is included in the *total return* generated by the investment.

Risk-Adjusted Return

The concept of a *risk-adjusted return* uses the inputs first introduced in the previous chapter on measurement of risk (chapter 9). Among these inputs are standard deviation (total risk) and beta coefficient (systematic risk). Accordingly, several popular methods exist to measure an investment's risk-adjusted return, with the final result dependent on whether standard deviation or beta is used as the denominator. However, whichever method is used, it should compare stocks or mutual funds of the same characteristics and peer group. For example, since beta relates a mutual fund's volatility to an accepted benchmark—usually the Standard & Poor's index of 500 stocks—it should *not* be used in a risk-adjusted return computation where a benchmark is not a relevant point of comparison.

To compute the risk-adjusted rate of return of a stock or mutual fund using beta in the denominator, divide the stock or fund's nominal rate of return by its beta coefficient. An example follows:

> **Example 11-9:** JEM Mutual Fund has returned 6% annually over the course of the last year and features a beta of 0.50. Therefore, its risk-adjusted return is 0.12 (or 0.06 ÷ 0.50). This compares to KRF Mutual Fund that has returned 8% annually in the last calendar year but exhibits a beta of 0.80. Therefore, the risk-adjusted return of KRF fund is 0.10 (0.08 ÷ 0.80). Accordingly, on a risk-adjusted rate of return basis, JEM Mutual Fund has outperformed KRF Mutual Fund. This is the case, even though on an unadjusted basis, KRF Mutual Fund has a higher nominal annual rate of return.

Holding Period Rate of Return

The holding period rate of return of an investment is likely the most misunderstood measurement in investment practice today. By definition, the holding period return (HPR) is simply the total return for the given period over which the investment is held or owned. However, HPR has a major weakness since it fails to consider the *timing* of when the cash flows actually occurred. As a result, if the holding period of the investment is more than one year, the HPR *overstates* the true return of the investment *on an annual basis*. Conversely, if the investment's holding period is less than one year, the HPR *understates* the true annual return.

Example 11-10: Joe purchases 200 shares of XYZ stock for $10,000. During the years that Joe has owned these shares, he has received dividend payments of $4,000. Yesterday, Joe sold all 200 shares for a total price of $20,000. Accordingly, Joe's holding period return (HPR) is 140% [{($20,000 + $4,000) - $10,000} ÷ $10,000]. Nevertheless, without knowing the total period during which Joe owned the stock, we cannot compare his purchase of XYZ stock to other potential investments to determine if it was a good or bad decision.

The formula for holding period rate of return is not easily described, but in practical application, it may be written as:

$$\frac{(EV+I) - BV}{BV} \times 100$$

Where EV is equal to the ending value of the investment, I is equal to the periodic interest or dividends (income) from the investment and BV is equal to the beginning value of the investment.

In descriptive language, the HPR is calculated by subtracting the original cost of an investment (its beginning value) from its ending value, after adding any intervening income or dividends, then dividing that sum by the investment's beginning value and , finally, converting the product into percentage terms (or multiply it by 100).

Example 11-11: Assume that Sara purchased 100 shares of stock during the previous calendar year at $50 per share and that a 3% dividend was declared on the stock for that same year ($1.50 per share). At the beginning of the next year (after holding the stock for more than one year), Sara sells the stock for $55 per share. Therefore, her HPR (total return) is 13% computed as follows: [($55 + $1.50) - $50] ÷ $50 = $6.50 ÷ $50= 0.13 x 100 = 13%.

How is HPR computed if, for example, Sara had bought the shares of stock in a margin account established by the broker-dealer on her behalf? Intuitively, it would seem that, since she now has less money at risk, her holding period return should increase. However, let us expand on Example 11-11 by assuming a margin interest rate of 8% and that the stock now increases by 25% in the one-year period she owns the stock. Also assume that the initial margin requirement is 50% as specified by Regulation T of the Federal Reserve Board.

Example 11-12: Sara now has only $2,500 at risk (or half of the initial purchase price of $5,000, which is $50 per share x 100 shares from Example 11-11). So that is the *beginning value* (initial investment) component of the HPR formula. In addition, since she has borrowed the remaining $2,500 at an 8% annual interest rate, she incurs an interest expense of $200 (2,500 x 0.08). Therefore, she has to pay back her broker-dealer in the amount of $2,700 ($2,500 margin amount + $200 interest). Finally, the *ending value* of the stock is $6,250 ($5,000 x 1.25).Accordingly, the numerator of the HPR formula now looks like this: [($6,250 - ($2,500 + $200) - $2,500] = $1,050. When we divide that product by Sara's beginning value investment amount of $2,500, our final HPR is 42% ($1,050 ÷ $2,500= 0.42 x 100 = 42%).

As you can see from comparing the HPR derived in Example 11-12 to that HPR computed in Example 11-11, Sara has increased her HPR by 29% (42% - 13%), therefore proving the truth of our initial intuition. However, of course, Sara's potential downside risk is also magnified by using leverage (margin) in the stock purchase. That is, the potential negative HPR is also increased if margin is used and the price of the underlying stock *declines*, rather than increases as it did in Example 11-12.

Finally, it should also be noted that we can compute the after-tax HPR by adding Sara's marginal tax bracket (25%) into the analysis and then applying the after-tax formula of (1 - marginal tax rate). For example, using the information in Example 11-11, we can compute Sara's after-tax HPR to be 11.05% as follows:

$5,500 Ending Value (100 shares x $55 share)
+ $150 Dividend Income (100 shares x $1.50 per share dividend)
- $5,000 Beginning Value (100 shares x $50 share)
$ 650 Taxable Gain
x .85 (1 - .15; note that the stock is a long-term capital gain asset)
$552.50 After-Tax Gain

$552.50 After-Tax Gain ÷ $5,000 Beginning Value = .1105 x 100 = 11.05% After- Tax HPR

RETURNS DEALING PRIMARILY WITH BONDS

Current Yield

The *current yield* of a bond is the return represented by the amount of interest income paid in relation to the market value of the bond. It is calculated by dividing the annual interest payment on the bond (as reflected in its *coupon rate* multiplied by the par value of the bond, normally $1,000) by the bond's current market price. After this product is found, it is then multiplied by 100 to state the yield in percentage terms. In formula terms, the computation is as follows:

Current Yield (CY) = $\dfrac{\text{Annual Interest in Dollars}}{\text{Bond's Market Price}}$

Example 11-13: Jeff has a bond with a coupon rate of 8.25% that is currently trading at 96.5% of par (par of $1,000). Therefore, the current yield on Jeff's bond is 8.55% computed as follows: $82.50 ÷ $965 = 0.0855 x 100 = 8.55%.

Note that in Example 11-13, the bond is trading at a *discount* to its par value. As a result, the bond's current yield will always *exceed* its nominal yield (as reflected by the bond's coupon rate of 8.25%). Conversely, if the bond were trading at a *premium* to its par value (that is, the market price was more than $1,000), the bond's current yield will always be *less than* its nominal yield (as reflected by the bond's coupon rate).

Yield to Maturity

The *yield to maturity* (YTM) on a bond takes into account both the market price of the bond as well as any capital gains or losses on the bond if it is held to maturity. The current yield of a bond and its YTM are equal *only* if the bond is currently selling for its principal amount or par. YTM is the same as the dollar-weighted rate of return/internal rate of return concept that was discussed earlier, but in the context of a bond or fixed-income security. Finally, the YTM computation assumes that the investor reinvests all coupons received from the bond equal to the computed YTM. In effect, therefore, the computation assumes that the reinvestment rate is the yield to maturity.

The yield to maturity formula is inherently complex and serves little purpose when the computation may be done easily with the assistance of a financial function calculator, like the HP 10 B II, or computer software. An example follows:

> **Example 11-14:** Terry has purchased a market discount bond for $850 (par value of $1,000) with a coupon rate of 7%. The bond pays interest semi-annually and matures in 15 years. Therefore, the yield to maturity (YTM) on Terry's bond is 8.83 % computed as follows and with keystrokes shown for the HP 10 B II calculator: 2, Shift, P/YR ; $850 +/- PV; $1,000 FV; $35 PMT; 15 Shift x P/YR; solve for I/YR= 8.83%.

Note that the YTM should always be calculated as if the bond makes semi-annual interest payments (unless, of course, the facts of the problem specifically state that the bond returns interest payments annually). This same assumption is also to be made *even if* the bond is a zero-coupon bond and returns no (cash) interest payments on a periodic basis.

Yield to Call

Many corporate bonds, as well as some government bonds, are callable. This means that, in times of falling interest rates, companies will choose to replace, or *call*, their old, more expensive bonds and issue new bonds in their place at the lower interest rate. The cost to the issuer for doing this is referred to as the *call premium* on the bond.

The actual formula for computing the *yield to call* (YTC) on a bond is the same as that for the yield to maturity (YTM) *except* that the principal value of the bond at its maturity date is replaced by the *call price* and the maturity date is replaced by the first potential call date. In addition, using the so-called *yield ladder*, if a bond is selling at a discount, the YTC is typically *higher* than its YTM (and *lower* if the bond is selling at a premium). There is an exception to this rule for bonds selling at a premium where the call premium is so high that it causes the YTC to be greater than that of the bond's YTM. However, normally, if the premium bond's call premium is low or equals the par value of the bond (that is, there is no call premium), then the YTM will be greater than YTC and follows the general rule.

Like yield to maturity, the yield to call (sometimes referred to as *yield to worst* in the financial services marketplace) may be easily computed with the assistance of a financial function calculator. A sample computation using the HP 10 B II calculator follows:

Example 11-15: Josh has recently purchased a 10-year maturity $1,000 bond originally issued at par in the secondary marketplace for $1,150 (a premium bond). The bond carries a coupon rate of 8% and interest is paid semi-annually. It has a call price of $1,050 and may be called in five years. Therefore, the yield to call (YTC) on Josh's bond is 5.42% computed as follows: 2, Shift, P/YR; $1,150 +/- PV; $1,050 FV; $40 PMT; 5 Shift x P/YR; solve for I/YR = 5.42%.

You should also note that this same bond has a YTM of 5.98% (2, Shift, P/YR; $1,150 +/- PV; $1,000 FV; $40 PMT; 10 Shift x P/YR; solve for I/YR= 5.98%) and is therefore consistent with the general rule that the YTM will exceed the YTC on a premium bond.

Taxable Equivalent Yield (TEY)

Finally, some bonds (such as municipal bonds) return tax-free income. As a result, investors need to have a method of comparing the yield (return) on these bonds to those that are fully taxable (like a corporate issue). The formula that is used to make this comparison is the municipal bond's *taxable equivalent yield* (TEY) as follows:

$$\text{Taxable Equivalent Yield} = \frac{\text{Tax Free Nominal Yield}}{(1 - \text{marginal tax rate})}$$

Again, after finding this product, it is then multiplied by 100 to state the result in percentage terms.

Example 11-16: James is the owner of municipal bond with a stated coupon rate (nominal yield) of 5.5%. He is in a 33% federal income tax bracket and resides in a state that does not have state income taxes. (Of course, most states do have income tax, which would then need to be added to the resulting marginal tax rate.) Therefore, the taxable equivalent yield (TEY) on James' municipal bond is 8.21% [0.055 ÷ (1 - .33) = 0.055 ÷ 0.67= 0.0821 x 100 = 8.21%].

You should also note that the TEY formula is the *reverse* of the after-tax rate of return formula previously discussed. That is, in the after-tax rate of return formula, the before-tax (nominal) return on the fully taxable bond is *multiplied* by (1 - investor's marginal tax rate) instead of *dividing* the tax-free (nominal) yield by this same fraction. Therefore, we derive the same 5.5% as stated in Example 11-16 as the after tax return, but using the inverse method [0.0821 x (1-.33) = 0.0821 x 0.67 = 0.0550 x 100 = 5.50%].

PORTFOLIO MEASURES OF RETURN

The theoretical foundation for using the Jensen (alpha), Treynor, and Sharpe measures to evaluate the performance of a portfolio was first introduced in chapter 9 of this text. However, the formulas (and examples of computation) were not provided there; accordingly, to do so is the purpose of the last sections of this chapter.

Jensen Ratio (Alpha)

The Jensen ratio (also known as *alpha*) is a measure of the risk-adjusted value added by a portfolio manager. Specifically, alpha is measured as the portfolio's actual or realized return in excess of that predicted by the capital asset pricing model (CAPM). See chapter 10. An alpha of *zero* indicates that the portfolio earned its expected rate of return given its level of assumed risk (as measured by beta). A *positive* alpha indicates that the portfolio manager has added value on a relative basis; conversely, a *negative* alpha indicates that the portfolio manager has not performed as well as predicted by CAPM and in relation to his or her peers. Note that alpha (like the Treynor method that is upcoming) assumes a diversified investor portfolio since beta is included among its formula inputs. Standard deviation (used by the upcoming Sharpe method) does *not* assume a diversified portfolio.

The formula for the Jensen method of portfolio measurement (alpha) is:

Formula 11-1: Jensen Index of Portfolio Performance

$$\alpha_p = r_p - \left[r_f + (r_m - r_f)\beta_p \right]$$

Where r_p is the portfolio's realized return and the remainder of the formula is the capital asset pricing model (CAPM).

> **Example 11-17:** Assume that DEF portfolio has a realized rate of return of 17% over the last several years and a beta coefficient of 0.72. The realized rate of return for the overall market over this same time period is 18% and the risk-free rate is 6%. Accordingly, the alpha of the DEF portfolio is 2.36% computed as follows: [.17- {.06 + (.18 - .06).72} = .17 - {.06 + .0864} = 0.17 - 0.1464 = 0.0236 x 100 = 2.36%.

In turn, this means that the portfolio manager of DEF portfolio has added value and exceeded the portfolio return that would have been predicted by the capital asset pricing model (CAPM).

Treynor Ratio

Given our previous discussion of portfolio management theory (see chapter 10), we are aware that most investors are risk-averse. Therefore, portfolio performance can and should be evaluated on a risk-adjusted basis. In risk-adjusted measures, the portfolio return is compared to its risk. The Treynor ratio evaluates this return in the context of an assumed diversified portfolio and measures any excess return relative to *systematic* risk (thereby using beta as its risk measurement).If the ratio/index number is relatively high, it indicates that the portfolio manager has achieved a return considerably above the risk-free rate. In addition, when comparing the index number obtained from the ratio against that of a benchmark index (such as the S& P 500 index of stocks) we can determine whether the manager produced better or worse risk-adjusted returns than the benchmark.

The formula for the Treynor method of portfolio measurement is:

Formula 11-2: Treynor Index of Portfolio Performance

$$T_p = \frac{r_p - r_f}{\beta_p}$$

Where r_p equals the portfolio's realized return, r_f is the risk-free rate of return and β_p is the beta of the portfolio.

> **Example 11-18:** LMN portfolio has a realized return of 16% over the last several years and a beta of 1.10. Three month Treasury bills (the proxy for the risk-free rate) are currently yielding 5%. The S& P 500 index has a realized return of 14% and a beta of 1.00. Therefore, the Treynor ratio for LMN portfolio is 10 [(16-5) ÷ 1.1]. During this same time period, the benchmark's index was 9 [(14 - 5) ÷ 1.0]. Accordingly, this means that the portfolio manager for LMN generated a *better* risk-adjusted return than that of the benchmark.

Sharpe Ratio

Like the Treynor ratio, the Sharpe ratio evaluates risk-adjusted return, but (unlike Treynor) it does this in the context of an assumed *non-diversified* portfolio. Therefore, it measures any excess return produced by the portfolio manager relative to *unsystematic risk* (thereby using standard deviation as its risk measurement). If the ratio/index number is relatively high, it indicates that the portfolio manager is considerably above the risk-free rate. In addition, when comparing the index number obtained from the ratio against that of a benchmark index (but here one that is relatively non-diversified, like a sector fund), we can determine whether the manager produced better or worse risk-adjusted returns than the benchmark.

The formula for the Sharpe method of portfolio measurement is:

Formula 11-3: Sharpe Index of Portfolio Performance

$$S_p = \frac{r_p - r_f}{\sigma_p}$$

Where r_p equals the portfolio's realized return, r_f is the risk-free rate of return and σ_p is the standard deviation of the portfolio.

Example 11-19: Continuing with the facts of Example 11-18, except now the risk-adjusted return of LMN portfolio is compared against PLF sector fund with a realized return of 12% and a standard deviation of 4.5. In addition, assume that the standard deviation of LMN portfolio is 6.25. Therefore, the Sharpe ratio for LMN portfolio is 1.76 [(16 - 5) ÷ 6.25]. During this same time period, the benchmark's index was 1.56 [(12-5) ÷ 4.5]. Accordingly, this means that the portfolio manager for LMN also generated a *better* risk-adjusted return than that of the benchmark (now the relatively non-diversified sector fund).

Information Ratio

There is still another method to compute the amount of risk-adjusted return value that is added (or lost) by the portfolio manager. This is known as *the information ratio* and uses a different hurdle rate for determining the amount of excess return generated by the portfolio manager. Specifically, the ratio uses the excess return of the portfolio less that of the benchmark compared to the standard deviation of this excess return. Therefore, the ratio analyzes whether the portfolio manager has as least added percentage units of return beyond that of the total risk assumed when developing the portfolio.

The formula for the information ratio is:

$$IR = \frac{r_p - r_B}{\sigma_{excess}}$$

Where r_p equals the portfolio's realized return, r_B is the benchmark's realized return, and σ_{excess} is the standard deviation of the excess return.

> **Example 11-20:** Continuing with the facts of both Examples 11-18 and 11-19, we see that LMN portfolio has achieved a realized return of 16%. Further, we see that the benchmark sector fund reports a realized return of 12%. Finally, the standard deviations of LMN portfolio and the benchmark sector fund are 6.25 and 4.5, respectively. Therefore, the information ratio for the LMN portfolio is 2.29 [(16 - 12) ÷ (6.25 - 4.5) = 4 ÷ 1.75 = 2.29]. The positive information ratio is, thus, further evidence that the portfolio manager has been adding value beyond that possible simply by investing in the benchmark sector fund.

IMPORTANT CONCEPTS

Simple annual rate of return

Annualized rate of return

Compound annual rate of return

Arithmetic average annual return

Geometric average annual return

Time-weighted rate of return

Dollar-weighted rate of return

Internal rate of return (IRR)

Nominal rate of return

Real (inflation-adjusted) rate of return

After-tax rate of return

After-tax inflation-adjusted rate of return

Total return

Risk-adjusted return

Holding period rate of return

Current yield

Yield to maturity (YTM)

Yield to call (YTC)

Taxable equivalent yield (TEY)

Jensen ratio (alpha)

Treynor ratio

Sharpe ratio

Information ratio

QUESTIONS FOR REVIEW

1. Contrast the simple annual rate of return to the compound annual rate of return. Which one of these two types of return will generate the greater percentage return and why?

2. If an investor has held an investment asset for less than a year, what measure is used to compute his or her return?

3. If an investor wishes to determine his or her percentage return on an investment asset without considering any additional contributions or periodic withdrawals, what type of return should he or she use? Explain why this is so.

4. What are the weaknesses inherent in the dollar-weighted rate of return computation? What is the preferred alternative to evaluate the performance of a portfolio manager?

5. When would you typically use the internal rate of return method to compute the return on an investment asset?

6. A corporate bond exhibits a coupon rate of 5.5% with semi-annual interest payments. What is this type of return called?

7. What is the formula for real (inflation-adjusted) rate of return and where might you use this type of return in the personal financial planning process?

8. Rick lives in New York City. His federal marginal tax rate is 25%, his New York State marginal tax rate is 7% and his New York City marginal tax rate is 2.5%. If he buys U.S. Treasury bonds with a 5% coupon rate, what is his after-tax rate of return?

9. What components make up an investor's total return on an investment asset? What are the two most common of these components?

10. What is the formula for risk-adjusted return? When should it be used in investment practice?

11. What is a major weakness of the holding period rate of return measurement?

12. If margin is used to purchase a stock and its price increases from the date of purchase, will the investor's holding period of return be more or less than if margin had not been used? Explain.

13. If a bond is trading at a premium to its par value, will the bond's current yield be more or less than its nominal yield? Explain.

14. Define what is meant by the term yield to maturity of a bond. To what general rate of return concept is it the same or similar?

15. When would a corporation be likely to call any previously issued bonds?

16. If a bond is selling at a discount to par, is its yield to call likely higher or lower than its yield to maturity? Explain.

17. Julie is the owner of a municipal bond with a nominal yield of 5%. She is in the 35% federal marginal income tax bracket only. What is the taxable equivalent yield (TEY) on Julie's bond?

18. Explain the input factors that are used in each of the following measures of portfolio return:

    * Jensen ratio (alpha)
    * Treynor ratio
    * Sharpe ratio

19. Assume that a mutual fund exhibits an alpha of negative two. Is this a positive or negative reflection on the performance of the portfolio manager? Explain why this is the case.

20. What is the hurdle rate used in the information ratio to determine whether value has been added (or lost) by the portfolio manager?

SUGGESTIONS FOR ADDITIONAL READING

Tools and Techniques of Investment Planning, Stephen R. Leimberg, Robert T. LeClair, Robert J. Doyle, Jr., and Thomas R. Robinson, The National Underwriter Company, 2004.

Investments: An Introduction, 7th edition, Herbert B. Mayo, Thomson/ South-Western, 2002.

Investment Analysis and Portfolio Management, 7th edition, Frank K. Reilly and Keith C. Brown, Thomson/South-Western, 2003.

The Wall Street Journal Guide to Money and Investing, 3rd edition, Kenneth M. Morris and Virginia B. Morris, Fireside Publishing, 2004.

CHAPTER TWELVE

Valuing Equity Securities

• • •

There are two general methods for valuing the theoretically proper price or trading value of an equity security (a stock): 1) those analytic formulas that attempt to determine the *intrinsic value* of the stock and 2) those market-based methods that attempt to estimate the *relative value* of the stock with reference to the value of other similar securities. There are several individual approaches under either general method, all of which are discussed in this chapter. However, in the intrinsic value approaches, a significant determinant of the value of the stock is the investor's *required rate of return* (sometimes referred to as the investor's *hurdle rate*). While this determinant has already been mentioned with respect to portfolio management theory (see chapter 10), it is the subject of much further discussion in the upcoming chapter 14 concerning asset pricing models and their use in investment planning.

Upon completing this chapter, you should be able to:

- Compute the intrinsic value of a stock using a specified discounted cash flow model
- Describe the variations of the dividend discount model of stock valuation
- Determine the value of a stock or other asset using the discounted earnings (capitalized earnings) method of valuation
- Compute the relative value of a stock using a specified market based model
- Define the book value of a company and determine how it is computed using an asset based model of valuation

DISCOUNTED CASH FLOW MODELS/INTRINSIC VALUE

The *intrinsic value* of a stock is, by definition, the present value of its future cash flows discounted at a risk-adjusted interest rate. However, unlike a bond where the future cash flows are known (typically in the form of semi-annual interest payments promised the bondholder) the future cash flows from a stock are essentially unknown. Since cash flows from a stock consist primarily of discretionary dividend payments on the part of the issuing corporation, they can, at best, only be estimated. However, dividends are not the only type of cash flow that may be used in a discounted cash flow (intrinsic value) approach. *Free cash flow to equity* may also be estimated. Free cash flow to equity is the excess of cash flow that the underlying corporation generates from operations in excess of the necessary capital investment in the corporation's assets. As a result, this free cash flow may or may not be distributed to shareholders in the form of dividends.

There are four approaches to determining the intrinsic value of a stock. The first three of these approaches discount future cash flow in the form of *dividends*. They are: 1) the constant growth dividend discount model; 2) the multi-stage (variable) growth dividend discount model; and 3) the no-growth (perpetuity) dividend discount model. The fourth approach, the discounted free cash flow model, discounts *free cash flow to equity* and may be used to determine the intrinsic value of a stock where a dividend has not been paid, and is not expected to be paid.

Constant Growth Dividend Discount Model

The constant growth dividend discount model is used to determine the intrinsic value of a stock where its dividends are growing at a constant rate. The formula for the model is as follows:

Formula 12-1: Constant Growth Dividend Discount Model

$$V = \frac{D_1}{r - g}$$

Where V is the intrinsic value of the stock, D_1 is the dividend paid for the next year (the first dividend to be paid in the future), r is the investor's required rate of return and g is the constant growth rate of the dividend payments. The numerator of the formula may also be rewritten as $[D_0 \times (1+g)]$ where D_0 is equal to the *current year's dividend* (the dividend that is paid now or was most recently paid) and g is the assumed constant growth rate of the dividends. In other words, you should note that $[D_0 \times (1+g)]$ is *equivalent to* D_1 in applying the constant growth dividend formula.

Example 12-1: Assume that ABC stock is currently paying a dividend of $2.00 and that the dividend is expected to grow at a constant rate of 6%. Further, assume that the investor's required rate of return is 10%. Therefore, under the constant dividend growth model, the intrinsic value of ABC stock to this investor is $53.00 per share computed as follows: [{2 x (1+.06)} ÷ (.10 - .06) = 2.12 ÷ .04 = $53.00].

You should note that the first iteration of the constant growth formula was used in deriving this answer. This is because the problem states that a *current year dividend* (period 0) of $2.00 was paid. However, if the example had instead stated that a dividend of $2.12 ($2.00 x 1.06) in the *next year* (period 1) was to be paid, the numerator result in the formula (and, ultimately, the final answer) would have been the same.

As noted, the constant growth dividend discount model assumes that the growth rate of dividends declared by the issuing firm is constant. In practice, this is generally *not* the case. Nevertheless, the model is often used at least as a starting point in the proper valuation of a company's stock. As assumed by the model, the growth rate of the dividends (g) cannot be greater than the investor's required rate of return (r). If the investor's required rate is greater than the dividend's growth rate, the model becomes meaningless since the denominator (and hence the intrinsic value of the stock) turns negative. The model also assumes that the investor's required rate of return is known and never changes. This is likely *not* a realistic assumption since this rate is highly dependent on the general level of current (and expected) market interest rates.

The model does permit a means of comparison regarding whether the stock should be purchased at its current trading value. For example, in Example 12-1, we determined the intrinsic value of ABC stock to be $53.00 per share. Therefore, if ABC stock was selling in the secondary market for $55.00 per share, and given the assumptions of the model, an investor should likely *not* purchase the stock since it would be considered to be overvalued. We can also determine what the expected return of the stock should be if we know the constant growth rate of its dividends. This is done by using a form of expected return formula relevant to the constant growth model as follows:

$$E_r = \frac{D_0(1+g)}{P} + g$$

Where E_r is the expected return, D_0 is the current year dividend, g is the constant growth rate of the dividend, and P is the current price or trading value of the stock.

Finally, note what this form of the expected return form is demonstrating: It is taking the dividend yield of the stock (or {$D_0(1+g)/P$}) and adding it to the growth rate of the company's dividends.

Example 12-2: Continuing with the facts of Example 12-1, but assuming that the current price of ABC stock is $55.00, we determine the expected return of the stock to be 9.85%. The relevant computation is as follows: E= [{$2.00 x (1+0.06)} ÷ (55) + 0.06 = 0.0385 + 0.06 = 0.0985 x 100 = 9.85%]

You should also note that we would have anticipated that the expected return for ABC stock (9.85%) would be *less than* the investor's required return (10%) since the stock is currently *overvalued* in the secondary market (that is, a current price of $55.00 versus an intrinsic value of $53.00). We, therefore, may use the model as a basis for a tentative investment decision.

In summary, with respect to the constant growth dividend discount model:

1) If the market *lowers* the required rate of return for a stock (for example, market interest rates decline), the value of the common stock will *increase*

2) If the market *raises* the required rate of return for a stock (for example, market interest rates increase), the value of the common stock will *decrease*

3) If investors decide that the expected growth rate in dividends will be *higher* (for example, the earnings prospects of the issuing company have become more favorable), the value of the common stock will *increase*

4) If investors decide that the expected growth rate in dividends will be *lower* (for example, the earnings prospects of the issuing company have become less favorable), the value of the common stock will *decrease*

Multi-Stage (Variable) Growth Dividend Discount Model

The multi-stage (variable) growth form of the dividend discount model assumes that the growth rate of the stock's dividend is *not constant, but rather changes* (either up or down). This is also known as trying to determine the intrinsic value of a stock with temporary supernormal or subnormal growth. To determine the value of such stock, you must combine time value of money techniques with the constant growth model. Therefore, in analyzing the initial years of growth, you first compute the present value of the dividends of each year of the super or subnormal growth period. Next, you compute the remaining value of the stock using the constant growth model and discount this lump sum amount back to the present. (Remember, however, this is still only the case if the constant growth dividend rate is *less than* that of the investor's required rate of return). Third, all of the present values of the initial years of growth (Step 1) are added together with the present value lump sum amount using the constant growth model (Step 2) to determine one final (combined) intrinsic value of the stock (Step 3).

Let us work through an example expanding on the ABC stock valuation first described in Example 12-1:

Example 12-3: As noted in Examples 12-1 and 12-2, ABC stock is currently paying (in year 0) a dividend of $2.00 per share. Now assume, however, that the dividend is expected to grow for three years at 6% and then at 7% thereafter. Further assume that the investor's required rate of return is 9%. Using the multi-stage growth dividend discount model, the intrinsic value of ABC stock to this new investor is $104.14 computed as follows:

Step 1: Compute present value of stock for each of the first three years individually:

D_1 : $2.12 FV ($2.00 x 1.06); 1 N; 9 I/YR ; Solve for PV= $1.95

D_2 : $2.25 FV ($2.12 x 1.06); 2 N; 9 I/YR ; Solve for PV= $1.89

D_3 : $2.38 FV ($2.25 x 1.06); 3 N; 9 I/YR ; Solve for PV= $1.84

Total PV= $5.68

Total PV using the dividend growth rate for first three years: $5.68 (sum of each of PV's)

Step 2: Use constant growth model to compute remaining expected intrinsic value of stock at beginning of year 4 (end of year 3) and discount back to present value:

$$V = \frac{\$2.38\ (1+.07)}{.09-.07} = \frac{\$2.55}{.02} = \$127.50$$

$127.50 FV; 3 N; 9 I/YR; Solve for PV= $98.46

Step 3: Add Step 1 and Step 2 present value amounts to determine final intrinsic value:

$5.68 + $98.46 = $104.14

As noted earlier, in practice, it is generally atypical for companies to sustain constantly growing dividends. Indeed, it is much more probable that the future growth rate of dividends will *decline* over the years. In practice, companies tend to grow early in their life cycle, but as they mature their earnings growth rates tend to slow down, stop, or even decline. Company dividend payout rates then tend to follow suit. Accordingly, the multi-stage model may be more relevant for use than that of the constant growth model. Nevertheless, the constant growth model is usually the focus of examination questions and does effectively communicate how the intrinsic value of a dividend-paying stock or mutual fund is actually derived.

No Growth Dividend Discount Model

There is yet a third form of the dividend discount model that assumes that the growth of the dividend is constant forever or has *zero growth*. As a result, this form of the model is known as the *no growth dividend discount model* or *perpetuity model*. It is based on the formula for a perpetual annuity where the dividend is not increasing over time. To determine the value of this type of dividend stream, simply substitute zero for g in the constant growth form of the model as follows:

$$V = \frac{D_1}{r - 0}$$

This form, in turn, may be written as:

$$V = \frac{D_1}{r}$$

The new form of the model is the dividend for the first period divided by the investor's required rate of return. However, since the dividend is assumed to be forever constant, it could be the dividend for *any* period.

An example in applying the use of this form of the dividend discount model follows:

> **Example 12-4:** Assume that ABC stock *always* pays a $2.00 dividend and the investor's required rate of return is 10%. Therefore, the intrinsic value of ABC stock to this investor where there is zero growth of the dividends is $20.00 per share computed as follows: ($2.00 ÷ 0.10 = $20.00). This should be compared to the $53.00 per share computed in Example 12-1 where there was a constant 6% dividend growth. Accordingly, this means that the growth potential of ABC stock was worth $33.00 per share ($53.00-$20.00) to our investor.

Finally, you should note that the zero growth form of the dividend discount model is also used when computing the intrinsic value of preferred stock. This is because, as noted in chapter 3 of this text, preferred stock is in perpetuity and has *no* specified maturity date. Thus, once computing the intrinsic value of the preferred stock, an investor should inquire about its current market price and determine whether the stock is overvalued or undervalued. He or she can then use this information in making a possible investment decision.

Discounted Free Cash Flow Model

What happens if a company's stock does not pay a dividend? In this case, *none* of the previous three forms of the dividend discount model will work. As a frequent alternative, a company's free cash flow to equity is then discounted to find the intrinsic value of its stock. Free cash flow to equity (FCFE) is the company's operating cash flow less its current year's capital investments and debt repayments (including any outstanding or cumulative preferred dividends payable) Accordingly, this is the cash flow that is potentially available for distribution by the company in the form of a dividend. Many growth-type companies, however, choose to retain and reinvest this cash flow rather than pay it out annually as dividends to shareholders.

The FCFE model is mathematically equivalent to the constant growth form of the dividend discount model except that the current year's dividend (or D_0) or next year's dividend (D_1) is replaced by the FCFE on a per share basis. Therefore, the formula for the model may be written as follows:

$$V = \frac{FCFE_1}{r-g} = \frac{FCFE_0\,(1+g)}{r-g}$$

Example 12-5: Frank Corporation has an estimated free cash flow to equity (FCFE) for next year of $4.00 per share. In addition, its FCFE is expected to grow at the rate of 3% per year for the next several years. Your client has a required rate of return of 12%. Therefore, the intrinsic value of Frank Corporation's stock to your client is $44.45 computed as follows: [$4.00 ÷ (.12-.03) = $4.00 ÷ .09 = $44.45].

As with the constant form of the dividend discount model, the FCFE model may be expanded for multiple or variable growth rates in the future simply by replacing dividends with FCFE per share. As a result, the FCFE model is also used to value closely held businesses where earnings are frequently manipulated by the owner for income tax or compensation reasons.

DISCOUNTED EARNINGS MODEL/CAPITALIZED EARNINGS

Each of the previous models has discounted cash flows, whether in the form of dividends or free cash flow to equity. However, there is still another way to determine the value of an investment asset, although it is most frequently used to compute the value of an *entire company* (or property) rather than the individual shares of the company's stock. This method, known as the *capitalized earnings method*, discounts the value of the company's earnings instead of its cash flows and is computed as follows:

$$V = \frac{E}{R_d}$$

Where V is the estimated value of the company (or property), E is equal to the annual earnings of that company (or property), and R_d is the capitalization or discount rate, encompassing both a required rate of return for the investor plus an anticipated growth factor for the subject asset.

Example 12-6: Reed is attempting to value a commercial real estate rental property that generated net operating (before-tax) earnings of $250,000 last year. Further, he has determined a capitalization rate of 8% to use in valuing this property. Accordingly, Reed will likely pay no more than $3,125,000 to purchase the property ($250,000 ÷ 0.08) since this is consistent with his required rate of return, as well as allowing for the anticipated capital growth of the subject property.

Of course, the *higher* the capitalization rate, the *lower* the amount that the investor is willing to pay for the company or property. This makes sense since the investor is essentially discounting the price (present value) of the company for a greater assumed risk or required rate of return. As a result, we can also analyze this risk factor by using a multiple of earnings approach or the *reciprocal* of the capitalization rate.

Example 12-7: In Example 12-6, we observed that Reed determined that a capitalization rate of 8% was appropriate in valuing the subject property. In turn, this equates to a multiple of earnings of 12.5 years (100 divided by 8) before Reed will recover his initial investment. Alternatively, if Reed had used a capitalization rate of 10%, the multiple of earnings would have been 10 years

(100 divided by 10), thereby reflecting the additional risk that Reed believed that he was assuming and, accordingly, *reducing* the price that he would pay for the subject property to $2.5 million ($250,000 divided by .10).

Finally, in using this method to value the intrinsic value of a company, care must be taken to analyze its true or justifiable annual earnings. For example, a small closely held corporation may reduce earnings by paying out excessive salaries to the owner/employees and/or other forms of hidden compensation (such as paying rent to the owner/employees for the corporate use of personally owned property). They may do this, in part, to achieve a greater compensation or rental expense deduction for corporate income tax purposes. As a result, a potential investor will need to account for these differences in adjusting the earnings to a more realistic level, in turn impacting what he or she may be willing to pay for the targeted company.

MARKET BASED MODELS/RELATIVE VALUE

In contrast to the various discounted cash flow models that attempt to estimate the *intrinsic value* of a stock, it is also possible to estimate the stock's *relative value* by comparing its price to that of other similar securities. This is done by referencing the stock's current trading value (price) to relevant variables that affect a stock's value, such as earnings per share, earnings growth, free cash flow, and sales. Accordingly, the following relative valuation models are now discussed: 1) price to earnings per share (P/E); 2) price to earnings divided by growth (PEG); 3) price to free cash flow (P/FCF); and 4) price to sales (P/S). We begin with the P/E model, also known as the *earnings multiplier model*, since it is the most popular relative valuation measure.

Price to Earnings (P/E) Model

An alternative to the dividend discount model (intrinsic value) approach is the price to earnings (P/E) relative valuation method. As noted previously, none of the dividend discount model forms will work if the company does not pay (or does not expect to pay) a dividend. Therefore, one way investors may estimate value is by determining how many dollars they are willing to pay for a dollar of expected earnings (as typically represented by the estimated earnings of the company during the following 12-month period). This estimation of value relies on the premise that the stock's value (market price) has some relationship to the earnings per share generated by the issuing company.

The formula for the P/E ratio to value stocks is:

$$V = EPS \times P/E \text{ ratio}$$

Where V is the estimated market price of the stock, EPS is the earnings per share of the stock and P/E ratio is the price to earnings relative valuation ratio established by the market or industry to which the stock belongs.

Example 12-8: RDF stock is trading in the secondary marketplace for $50.00 per share. Its earnings per share over the next 12-month period are estimated to be $3.00 per share and a fundamental securities analyst has determined the relevant P/E ratio for the stock's peers to be 20. Therefore, using the P/E ratio approach, RDF stock should be trading for $60.00 per share ($3.00 times 20) and is *undervalued* in relation to its market peers.

In theory, the P/E valuation model is determined by three factors as follows:

1) The expected dividend payout ratio of the stock (that is, its dividends divided by its earnings)

2) The estimated required rate of return that all marketplace investors have determined for the stock (or the "r" that is included in the forms of the dividend discount model)

3) The expected growth rate of dividends for the stock (or "g" as included in the dividend discount models)

However, similar to the constant growth dividend discount model summary, a small difference in either the required rate of return demanded by marketplace investors (r) or the expected growth rate of the stock's dividends (g) will have a relatively large impact on the applicable P/E ratio. In addition, the spread between r and g is the main determinant of the *size* of the ratio. For example, assume that the expected dividend payout ratio for a stock is 50% of earnings, r is 13%, and g is 8%. The resulting P/E ratio is, therefore, 10 or the dividend payout ratio of 50% (0.50) divided by (r-g) or, here, (0.13-0.08) or 0.05. If, instead, the market adjusts the r for the stock to 12% (0.12) and g increases to 9% (0.09), the resulting P/E ratio increases to 16.7 or [0 .50 ÷ (0.12 - 0.09) = 0.50 ÷ 0.03 = 16.7]. We have, therefore, *increased* the ratio by an index number of 6.7 (16.7 - 10) simply by *decreasing* the spread between r and g from 5 (0.13 - 0.08) to 3 (0.12 - 0.09).

Finally, as we have shown, the P/E ratio associated with a stock is primarily influenced by the investor's perception of risk (as measured by his or her required rate of return) and the expected dividends growth rate of the stock. There is an *inverse* relationship between investor risk and the anticipated P/E ratio. Therefore, *higher (lower) risk* relative to other companies should result in a *lower (higher) P/E ratio.* Conversely, there is a *direct* relationship between the expected dividends growth rate of the stock and the anticipated P/E ratio. Therefore, *higher (lower) expected growth* relative to other companies should result in a *higher (lower) P/E ratio.*

Price to Earnings Divided by Growth (PEG) Model

We can also expand the price to earnings (P/E) model to compare a subject company's earnings growth rate to that of its peer companies. For example, if a subject company has a higher growth rate than that of its peers, perhaps it deserves a different relative measure of valuation where this superior rate of growth is recognized. Therefore, another commonly used model is that of assessing a company's P/E ratio relative to its growth, also known as its *PEG* (price to earnings divided by growth) ratio. Specifically, this model's equation is written as follows:

$$PEG = \frac{P}{E} \div g$$

Example 12-9: Continuing with the facts of Example 12-8 and RDF stock, we note that its value is estimated by referencing a P/E ratio of 20 for its marketplace peers. However, now assume that RDF Company estimates a growth rate of 10% in earnings for the next year. Accordingly, RDF's PEG ratio is 2.00 [20 ÷ 10].

We may now compare RDF Company to its peers in terms of growth of earnings and determine: 1) whether the P/E ratio applied to value RDF is justifiable in relation to its peers and 2) whether its stock is a good value (again, relative to its peers). For example, if JAB Company (a marketplace peer of RDF) has an expected growth rate in earnings of 9% and was valued using a P/E ratio of 18, then it would appear that the higher P/E ratio applied to value RDF stock was justifiable given its corresponding higher growth rate. However, if WLA Company (another peer of RDF) had an expected growth rate of 8% and was valued with a P/E ratio of only 14, then its stock would appear to be a better value in terms of price relative to earnings and growth (that is, WLA features a PEG ratio of 1.75—or 14 ÷ 8— in comparison to RDF's PEG ratio of 2.0).

As with most valuation measures, there are also several caveats to be aware of when using the PEG model. First, any company's expected growth figures are normally available only for a short period of time (for example, no more than five years). Therefore, companies with a lower growth rate but estimated over a longer period of time (say, 10 years) are penalized by use of the ratio. Second, the PEG ratio does not take into account the relative investor *risk* when investing in one company's stock versus another company's stock. Third and finally, the PEG equation assumes a linear or *lockstep* relationship between a company's growth and its applicable P/E ratio, which may or may not actually occur in reality.

Price to Free Cash Flow (P/FCF) Model

Another relative measure that may be used to value a company's stock is that of how effectively it uses its free cash flow to generate earnings growth. This is known as the price to free cash flow (P/FCF) model and is computed as follows:

$$\frac{P}{FCF} = \frac{1 + g}{r - g}$$

Where P is the price of the company stock, FCF is the free cash flow of the company, g is the expected growth rate of the company's earnings, and r is the required rate of return of the potential investor.

Example 12-10: Again, we continue with the performance numbers of RDF stock that we have noted so far in Examples 12-8 and 12-9. Specifically, RDF stock has an expected growth rate in earnings of 10%. Further, however, we now assume that the potential investor's required rate of return considering an investment in RDF stock is 14%. Therefore, the price to free cash flow (P/FCF) ratio of the stock is 27.50 [(1 + 0.10) ÷ (0.14 - 0.10) = 1.10 ÷ 0.04 = 27.50].

Then, as with the other relative valuation measures, we compare this P/FCF ratio to that of RDF's marketplace peers to determine if its stock appears to be overvalued or undervalued. For example, if RDF was selling for $50 and exhibited a P/FCF ratio of 27.5 compared to BMG stock (its marketplace peer) selling for the same price but with a P/FCF ratio of 25, the investor may well determine that RDF stock was a better buy (or undervalued). In addition, the P/FCF ratio measure does have the advantage that some consideration of investor risk in making the purchase (in this case, the systematic risk of the stock as measured by its beta coefficient) is taken into account.

Price to Sales (P/S) Model

The final market-based method of relative valuation that we will consider is that of a company's stock price to its sales. More popularly known as the price to sales model, it is computed as follows:

$$\frac{P}{S} = \frac{\text{Profit Margin times Dividend Payout Ratio times } (1 + g)}{r - g}$$

Where P is the price of the company stock, S is the company's annual sales, Profit Margin is the company's earnings divided by its sales, Dividend Payout Ratio is the percentage of its earnings paid out as dividends computed as [common dividends paid per share divided by earnings available for common shares], g is the expected growth rate of the company's earnings, and r is the required rate of return of the potential investor.

> **Example 12-11:** Continuing to build on our previous examples of 12-8, 12-9, and 12-10, now assume that RDF Company exhibits a profit margin of 30% (0.30) and a dividend payout ratio of 50% (0.50). The other inputs, that is, an expected growth rate of company earnings of 10% (0.10) and the potential investor's required rate of return of 14% (0.14), remain the same. Therefore, the price to sales (P/S) ratio for RDF stock is 4.1250 computed as follows: [{0.30 × 0.50 × (1 + 0.10)} ÷ (0.14 - 0.10) = 0.1650 ÷ 0.04 = 4.1250].

As with the other measures discussed to this point, the P/S ratio of RDF stock is then compared to its industry peers to determine whether the stock appears over or undervalued relative to those peers. Again, similar to the P/E ratio analysis, a potential investor may wish to invest in a stock whose price to sales ratio is *low* in comparison to its peers with the expectation that this ratio will improve, thereby driving up the price of the underlying stock. However, and this is still a major warning, with any ratio analysis type of valuation, these are *relative* measures. Therefore, the industry peers against whom any stock is being compared may themselves be overvalued. As a result, an *undervalued* stock may simply be *less overvalued* than its industry peers. But, such stock may *still be overvalued* with respect to the aggregate market and may *not* be a good *buy*.

In summary, before proceeding to one last measure using an *asset based approach* to valuation, that of computing a company's *book value*, we list the intrinsic and relative valuation methods commonly used in determining the estimated sales price of an equity security.

Figure 12-1

Intrinisic Value Methods	Relative Value Methods
1. Constant Growth Dividend Discount Model	1. Price to Earnings(P/E) Ratio
2. Multi-Stage(Varianble) Dividend Discount Model	2. Price to Earnings Divided by Growth (PEG) Ratio
3. No Growth/Perpetuity Dividend Discount Model	3. Price to Free Cash Flow (P/FCF) Ratio
4. Discounted Free Cash Flow Model	4. Price to Sales(P/S) Ratio

ASSET BASED MODELS/BOOK VALUE

The *book value* of a company refers to the amount of equity available to its shareholders, that is, the amount that shareholders have invested over time in the company. Specifically, book value is determined by subtracting company liabilities from company assets. However, many of these assets are reported on the company balance sheet at what the company paid for them (historical cost) less any accumulated depreciation, which often times does *not* reflect the current fair market value of those assets. As a result, most companies sell for *more than* their book or accounting value. Additionally, many companies who already are operating as a *going concern* are more valuable in that capacity rather than as the mere sum of their assets minus liabilities (or their book value). This is because of the company's intangible value to a potential buyer, otherwise known as company *goodwill.*

As mentioned, a company balance sheet (similar to the personal statement of financial position that is prepared by the financial planner) reflects the assets owned by the company and the liabilities (or claims against) those assets. After these assets and liabilities are shown (and after they are typically further broken down into current and long-term holdings), the stockholder's equity portion is reported. Then, once the total amount of shares outstanding with existing stockholders is known, the *book value per share* may be computed. Alternatively, the book value per share may be used to compute a relative valuation measure known as the *price to book value (P/BV) ratio*, which is then compared to the company's industry peers to assist in making an investment decision.

Let us look at a typical (abbreviated) company balance sheet and compute the resulting book value per share:

Xeta Omega, Inc.
Corporate Balance Sheet
For Fiscal Year Ending December 31, 2005

Assets		Liabilities	
Cash	$1,500,000	Accounts Payable	$ 100,000
Inventory	$5,000,000	Notes Payable	$ 900,000
Equipment	$2,000,000	Total Liabilities	$1,000,000
Total Assets	$8,500,000		
		Stockholders Equity (150,000 Shares Outstanding)	$7,500,000
		Total Liabilities and Equity	$8,500,000

Example 12-12: Using the information from the corporate balance sheet for Xeta Omega, Inc., we are now able to compute a $50.00 book value per share for the corporation as follows: Stockholders Equity of $7,500,000 ÷ 150,000 Shares Outstanding = $50.00 book value per share.

Finally, you should note the difference between a stock's market value, its intrinsic value, and its book value. All have been discussed in this chapter and are defined as follows:

- A stock's *market value* is also known as its price or trading value, but is specifically the price of the stock as determined by investors in the secondary marketplace.
- A stock's *intrinsic value* is its discounted present value based on future cash flows (or some other relevant factor) as determined by formula.
- A stock's *book value* is the amount of a company's stockholder equity divided by the total number of shares outstanding.

IMPORTANT CONCEPTS

Market value

Intrinsic value

Constant Growth Dividend Discount Model

Multi-Stage (Variable) Growth Dividend Discount Model

No Growth/ Perpetuity Dividend Discount Model

Discounted Free Cash Flow Model

Discounted Earnings Model/Capitalized Earnings

Capitalization rate

Relative value

Price to Earnings (P/E) Valuation Model

Price to Earnings Divided by Growth (PEG) Valuation Model

Price to Free Cash Flow (P/FCF) Valuation Model

Price to Sales (P/S) Valuation Model

Book value

Price to Book Value (P/BV) ratio

QUESTIONS FOR REVIEW

1. What are the two general methods used to determine the *proper* price of a stock?

2. Define what is meant by the term *intrinsic value* of a stock.

3. What are the three forms of the dividend discount model?

4. What model should be used to determine the intrinsic value of a stock that does not pay (or expect to pay) a dividend?

5. With respects to the inputs of the constant growth dividend discount model, there is a basic assumption. What is it?

6. Using the constant growth dividend discount model, assume that you determine the intrinsic value of a stock to be $50.00 per share. If the stock is currently trading for $55.00 per share, what is your likely investment decision? Explain.

7. What is the reciprocal form of the constant growth dividend discount model and what is it that you are trying to determine?

8. Given the assumptions of the constant growth dividend discount model, if market interest rates increase, what happens to the intrinsic value of a share of common stock?

9. What are the three computational steps in determining the intrinsic value of stock if the multi-stage form of the dividend discount model is used?

10. Assume that a stock is expected to pay a $1.00 dividend in perpetuity. If the investor's required rate of return is 12%, what is the intrinsic value of this stock?

11. Define a company's *free cash flow*. Why might this determination be relevant?

12. If Investor A uses a capitalization rate of 15% in determining how much he would pay for a company and Investor B uses a rate of 12%, which investor is willing to pay more for the company? Explain why this is so.

13. What are four *relative valuation* methods used to determine what should be the market value of a stock?

14. In theory, what are the three factors that determine what price/earnings (P/E) ratio to use in estimating the market value of a stock?

15. If a stock has a lower expected dividends growth rate as compared to another company's stock, what is the corresponding effect on the P/E ratio that should be used?

16. Why might it be advisable to use the PEG ratio rather than the P/E ratio to determine the relative valuation of a stock?

17. What is an advantage of the P/FCF relative method of stock valuation?

18. A company's profit margin and dividend payout ratio is used in what method of stock valuation?

19. Why does a company often sell for more than its *book value*?

SUGGESTIONS FOR ADDITIONAL READING

Tools and Techniques of Investment Planning, Stephen R. Leimberg, Robert T. LeClair, Robert J. Doyle, Jr., and Thomas R. Robinson, The National Underwriter Company, 2004.

Investments: An Introduction, 7th edition, Herbert B. Mayo, Thomson/ South-Western, 2002.

Investment Analysis and Portfolio Management, 7th edition, Frank K. Reilly and Keith C. Brown, Thomson/South-Western, 2003.

The Wall Street Journal Guide to Money and Investing, 3rd edition, Kenneth M. Morris and Virginia B. Morris, Fireside Publishing, 2004.

CHAPTER THIRTEEN

Valuing Debt Securities

. . .

W̲e now proceed to methods used to value the other major type of security, that of the corporate debt obligation (a bond). Unlike stock, the valuation of a bond is relatively easy since the future cash flows are contractually set. Indeed, in the basic valuation formula for a bond (reproduced below), the only unknown is the investor's required rate of return (r_B) necessary to make such a purchase. Subsequently, after introducing you to the bond rating agencies and some fundamental concepts used in bond valuation, the remainder of this chapter is devoted to measuring the change in the price of a bond given a respective change in market interest rates.

Upon completing this chapter, you should be able to:

- Explain bond ratings, including the definition of an *investment grade* bond
- Compute the intrinsic value of a bond using time value of money principles
- Discuss yield curves and the term structure of interest rates
- Apply the concepts of Macauley and modified duration in describing the interest rate sensitivity of a given bond
- Compute the estimated change in price of a bond using duration
- Define bond convexity and how it is used in the valuation of a bond
- Explain portfolio immunization
- State the basic principles of duration in bond portfolio management

BOND RISKS AND RATINGS

Bonds are subject to their own set of investment risks, just as all types of fixed-income securities are. As noted previously in chapter 9, when discussing sources of investment risk, most of these constitute types of systematic risk that can only be minimized (not eliminated) if a bond investment is made. Among these types of systematic risk are reinvestment rate risk, interest rate risk, and purchasing power risk, which impact all forms of corporate, government, and municipal bond issues. However, government bonds do *not* possess another type of investment risk referred to as *default risk*, that is, the risk that a creditor may seize the underlying collateral of the bond (if any) and sell it to recoup the principal. In addition, government bonds do not possess *credit risk* or the risk that the issuer cannot make interest and principal payments.

The credit risk associated with a corporate bond may be minimized by investing only in *investment grade* (or non-speculative grade) bonds. So how does one go about establishing the creditworthiness of a bond? This is the function of bond rating agencies, most notably the private firms of Standard & Poor's and/or Moody's Investors Service (Moody's). Each of these firms rates a corporate bond issue and determines whether it is high or medium investment grade or, alternatively, speculative (non-investment) grade. Additionally, each firm assigns a rating to those bonds where the issuer has gone into default and is currently not able to make principal payments. Table 13-1 below provides a summary of all ratings currently used by either Standard & Poor's or Moody's.

TABLE 13-1

	Standard & Poor's	Moody's
Investment Grade:		
High Grade	AAA-AA	Aaa-Aa
Medium Grade	A-BBB	A-Baa
Non-investment Grade:		
Speculative	BB-B	Ba-B
Default	CCC-D	Caa-C
Overall Range:	AAA-D	Aaa-C

Of course, it should be noted here that, like all entities whose job it is to make judgment calls, bond rating agencies are at times incorrect! For this reason, it is recommended that financial planners conduct their own due diligence regarding the creditworthiness of bonds and use the rating agencies primarily as a crosscheck to or confirmation of their own conclusions.

BOND VALUATION AND CONCEPTS

Basic Valuation Formula

The basic formula used to determine the value of a bond is as follows:

$$\text{Bond Value} = \frac{CF_1}{(1+r_B)} + \frac{CF_2}{(1+r_B)} + \dots + \frac{CF_t}{(1+r_B)^t}$$

Where CF is the future cash flows (semi-annual interest payments) from the bond and r_B is the investor's required rate of return on the bond.

In turn, to project r_B, we should note the rating of bonds of the particular risk class and add the applicable risk premium associated with a bond similar to that of the nominal risk-free rate of interest.

> **Example 13-1:** Assume that a 20 year $1,000 par value corporate bond features a 7 percent coupon and pays interest semi-annually to the bondholder. This bond carries a Standard & Poor's bond rating of BB (or speculative grade). The nominal risk-free rate of interest is 5%. The risk premium curve for 20-year corporate bonds over the nominal risk-free rate is: 1% for those bonds rated AA; 2% for bonds rated A; 3% for BB's: and 4% for B-rated bonds. Accordingly, the required rate of return for an investor is 8% (the nominal risk-free rate of interest of 5% plus the applicable risk premium for BB rated bonds of 3%).

Once we have determined this required rate of return, we can perform a time-value-of-money computation to determine the bond's value of $901.04 as follows: In 2 Payments per year (2 P/YR); $1,000 FV; $35 PMT; 8 I/YR; 20 Shift X P/YR; solve for PV= $901.04.

You should note that we should have anticipated that the bond would be trading at a *discount to par* since the investor's required rate of return of 8% exceeds that of the bond's coupon rate of 7%. This is indeed the case as the bond is valued at (and should be trading for) only $901.04.

This same type of computation may be done if, instead of the investor's required rate of return, we know the yield to maturity (YTM) for similar bonds in the secondary marketplace.

> **Example 13-2:** A 3-year $1,000 par value corporate bond has a coupon rate of 12% and pays interest semi-annually. If the yield to maturity (YTM) for similar quality bonds in the secondary marketplace is 10% annually, the bond should be selling for $1,050.76 computed as follows: In 2 P/YR; $1,000 FV; $60 PMT; 10 I/YR; 3 Shift X P/YR; solve for PV= $1,050.76.

Again, we could have anticipated that the bond would be trading at a *premium to par* since the yield to maturity for similar quality bonds of 10% was below that of the subject bond's coupon rate of 12%. This is indeed the case as the bond is valued at (and should be trading for) $1050.76.

Yield Ladder (Comparison of Yield to Maturity, Coupon Rate and Current Yield of a Bond)

Given that we now understand the basic formula used to compute the present value of a bond, we can compare the bond's yield to maturity to that of its coupon rate and current yield in each of three situations as follows:

1) Where the bond is currently trading at a premium to par value

2) Where the bond is currently trading at par

3) Where the bond is currently trading at a discount to par value

Let us look at an example using the same coupon rate (or nominal yield, NY) and maturity date for a bond in all three situations, changing only the bond's current trading value or selling price:

Example 13-3:

Situation #1: Assume that a 20-year $1,000 par value corporate bond with an 8% coupon rate (CR) and that pays interest *annually* is currently trading in the secondary market at a price of $1,100. Therefore, its current yield (CY) is 7.27% ($80 ÷ $1,100) and yield to maturity (YTM) is 7.05% [In 1 P/YR; $1,100 +/- PV; $1,000 FV; $80 PMT; 20 N; solve for I/YR= 7.05%].

Situation #2: Assume that a 20-year $1,000 par value corporate bond with an 8% coupon rate (CR) that pays interest *annually* is currently trading in the secondary market at a price of $1,000. Therefore, its current yield (CY) is 8% ($80 ÷ $1,000) and yield to maturity (YTM) is 8.00% [In 1 P/YR; $1,000 +/- PV; $1,000 FV; $80 PMT; 20 N; solve for I/YR= 8.00%].

Situation #3: Assume that a 20-year $1,000 par value corporate bond with an 8% coupon rate (CR) that pays interest *annually* is currently trading in the secondary market at a price of $900. Therefore, its current yield (CY) is 8.89% ($80 ÷ $900) and yield to maturity (YTM) is 9.10% [In 1 P/YR; $900 +/- PV; $1,000 FV; $80 PMT; 20 N; solve for I/YR= 9.10%].

Therefore, as we have computed, the following relationships apply:

1) Premium Bond: YTM < CY < CR/NY

2) Par Bond: YTM=CY=CR/NY

3) Discount Bond: YTM > CY > CR/NY

Or, if placing these relationships on a so-called yield ladder, the following results:

Yield Curves/Term Structure of Interest Rates

The *term structure of interest rates* (or the yield curve as it is more popularly known) is a theory that relates the term of maturity of a sample of same quality (rated) bonds to their yield to maturity *at a given point in time*. Therefore, the theory represents a cross section of yields for a category of bonds that are comparable in all respects but their date of maturity. Different yield curves may be constructed for Treasury bonds, government agency bonds, municipal bonds, AAA rated corporate bonds, and so on. However, the accuracy of the yield curve will depend on the overall comparability of the bonds in the sample.

Figure 13-1

The Yield Ladder

Discounted Bonds
(yields higher than coupon)

YTM
CY
More — NY — CR
Less
CY
YTM

Premium Bonds
(yields lower than coupon)

There are four basic types of yield curves that are pictured below:

In most instances, the positive or normal yield curve will predominate. This means that bond yields will increase as their maturity dates lengthen. This makes sense since, as maturities lengthen, investors will demand a premium for the extra risk (both interest rate and purchasing power risk) associated with *tying up* their money for longer periods of time. However, at times, any of the other types and shapes of curves may be present. For example, in the early 1980's when the Federal Reserve Board was tightening short-term credit (driving up interest rates) to slow the economy and combating inflation, the bond markets observed a negative yield curve. Indeed, as this book is being written, the yield curve is quite flat or turning even a bit negative, which raises concerns of a possible upcoming economic recession.

Figure 13-2

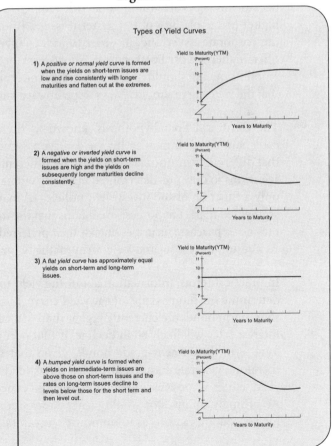

Types of Yield Curves

1) A *positive or normal yield curve* is formed when the yields on short-term issues are low and rise consistently with longer maturities and flatten out at the extremes.

2) A *negative or inverted yield curve* is formed when the yields on short-term issues are high and the yields on subsequently longer maturities decline consistently.

3) A *flat yield curve* has approximately equal yields on short-term and long-term issues.

4) A *humped yield curve* is formed when yields on intermediate-term issues are above those on short-term issues and the rates on long-term issues decline to levels below those for the short term and then level out.

Similar to the efficient market hypothesis (EMH) and its various forms discussed in chapter 10 of this textbook, the term structure of interest rates theory also has several iterations. Specifically, there are three different academic arguments about why yield curves mutate into one of the four basic shapes pictured in Figure 13-2.

The first of these arguments is the most plausible and is known as the *expectations hypothesis*. According to this hypothesis, the shape of the yield curve results from the interest rate expectations of secondary market participants. More specifically, it maintains that any long-term interest rate simply represents the geometric average or mean of the current and future one-year interest rates and should be expected to prevail over the maturity of the bond. In effect, the term structure consists of a series of intermediate and long-term interest rates, each of which is a reflection of the geometric average of current and expected one-year interest rates. Accordingly, the expectations hypothesis can explain the shape of *any* yield curve. As an example, investor expectations for increasing short-term future interest rates result in a positive or rising yield curve; conversely, investor expectations for declining short-term future interest rates will cause long-term rates to fall below current short-term rates, and the yield curve will turn negative. Similar explanations may be proffered for the flat and humped yield curves.

The second argument or explanation is referred to as the *liquidity preference hypothesis*. This hypothesis holds that long-term bonds should provide higher returns than shorter-term obligations because investors are willing to sacrifice some yield to invest in short-term bonds in order to avoid the higher price volatility of longer-term issues. In other words, bondholders prefer short-term loans to the corporate issuer and, in order to induce investors to lend money longer-term, it is necessary to offer higher yields. Furthermore, short-term bonds can more easily be converted into predictable amounts of cash should unforeseen market or economic events occur. As a result, the hypothesis argues that the yield curve should always slope upward and that any other shape is only a temporary aberration.

The third and final hypothesis, known as the *segmented market hypothesis*, is the least-plausible explanation regarding why any yield curve assumes its given shape. Specifically, this hypothesis asserts that different institutional investors have different maturity needs that lead them to restrict their bond selections to only pre-determined maturity segments. That is, the shape of the yield curve is ultimately only a function of the investment policies of major institutional investors. In its strongest form, the segmented market hypothesis maintains that the maturity preferences of these investors are so fixed that they never purchase securities outside their preferred maturity range to take advantage of yield differentials. As a result, the short- and long-term maturity portions of the bond market are effectively segmented.

In practical terms, information about the yield to maturities on existing bonds may help an investor determine the future shape of the yield curve. For example, if the yield curve is negative (the yields on short-term bonds are currently higher than that of long-term bonds), historical evidence suggests that interest rates will likely soon decline. If that occurs, an investor is most likely to profit by purchasing long-term, investment-grade bonds, given that their market prices will increase substantially and, therefore, generate significant capital gains for his or her overall bond portfolio. Conversely, if the yield curve is positive, there is a market expectation of an eventual increase in interest rates. Accordingly, an investor would want to reposition his or her portfolio to short-maturity bonds with higher coupon rates so as to minimize the capital losses caused by the eventual increase in rates.

BOND DURATION AND CONVEXITY

The *duration* of a bond is defined as the average time that it takes the bondholder to receive the interest and principal from a bond in present value dollars. It is an important number for all bond investors to know since it is a measure of the bond's price volatility compared with those issues of equal coupon rates and different maturity dates. In addition, the concept of *modified duration* may be used to estimate the change in the price of a bond given a commensurate change in market interest rates. Finally, an understanding of duration may be used to *immunize* or protect a bond portfolio from interest rate fluctuations and reinvestment rate risk.

The Computation of Bond Duration

The computation of duration uses the following formula:

Formula 13-1: Macauley Duration / Duration

$$D = \frac{1+y}{y} - \frac{(1+y) + t(c-y)}{c\left[(1+y)^t - 1\right] + y}$$

Where y is the yield to maturity (YTM) per period of the bond, c is equal to the coupon rate per period of the bond, and t is the number of periods until the bond's maturity. If the compounding period is semi-annual, then the number of periods (t) is twice the number of years, and the coupon rate (c) and YTM (y) are half the annual rates. The application of this formula may be seen more simply in the following example.

> **Example 13-4:** Assume that a three-year $1,000 par value ABC corporate bond, paying interest *annually*, is selling on the secondary market for $974.23. The bond has a coupon rate of 7% and a yield to maturity (YTM) of 8%. Accordingly, the bond's duration is 2.8 years computed as follows:

Year	Cash Flow (CF)	PV of CF (at 8%)	PV x # of Years
1	$70.00	$64.81	$64.81
2	$70.00	$60.015	$120.03
3	$1,070.00	$849.40	$2,548.20
Total		$974.23	$2,733.04

Then, divide the total present value of the bond's future cash flow ($2,733.04) by the market price of the bond ($974.23) to derive the specified duration of 2.8 years. (You should also note that the duration of the bond, 2.8 years, is less than its maturity date of 3.0 years. This result will *always* hold.)

You can also compute the duration of 2.8 years found in Example 13-4 by entering the following keystrokes on the HP 10 B II financial function calculator:

1.08 shift , y^x

3 , - , 1, x ,

.07 , + ,

.08 , =, shift, STO, 1

.07 , - ,

.08 , x ,

3, + ,

1.08 , ÷ , RCL, 1 , = , shift , STO , 2

1.08 , ÷ ,

.08 , - , RCL , 2, = ,

2.8053

Entering a rather complex equation such as this can be a challenge when using a financial function calculator, particularly if entering all the inputs at once. Therefore, an alternative method is to break up the equation into logical bits and pieces, and calculate those first. Then, combine these individual entries into the one cumulative process shown. This method may take longer, but it tends to minimize human error when entering the necessary inputs into your calculator.

Macauley Duration

If duration is computed by discounting cash flows using the yield to maturity of a bond (as in Example 13-4) and the result is expressed in years, it is called *Macaulay duration*. Macauley showed that the duration of a bond was a more appropriate measure of time characteristics than the term to maturity of the bond because duration considers both the repayment of the bond's principal at maturity as well as the size and timing of its coupon payments prior to final maturity. In addition, he proved several important relationships between duration and the various features of a bond as follows:

1) *There is an inverse relationship between the bond's coupon rate and its duration.* A bond with a larger coupon rate will have a shorter duration because more of its total cash flows come earlier in the form of interest payments.

2) *There is a positive or partially-direct relationship between the bond's term to maturity and its duration.* Therefore, a bond with a longer term to maturity will almost always have a higher duration. However, the relationship is *not totally* direct since, as the maturity date increases over time, the present value of the bond principal declines in value.

3) *A zero coupon bond will have a duration equal to its term to maturity.*

4) *There is an inverse relationship between the bond's yield to maturity (YTM) and its duration.* Therefore, a bond with a higher yield to maturity will have a lower duration. This is because the higher yield will *discount* the future cash flows more severely; in turn, the shorter-term cash flows will dominate the calculation, thereby leading to a shorter duration.

Finally, Macauley also showed that a call provision can have a dramatic effect on a bond's duration. This is because such provision can change the total cash flows for a bond and, thus, significantly change its duration. In addition, there is a great amount of uncertainty associated with a callable bond; specifically, it is very difficult to estimate when the call option will be exercised (and the cash flows of the bond impacted) since it is a function of changes in market interest rates.

Modified Duration

An adjusted measure of duration called *modified duration* may be used to approximate the interest rate sensitivity of a bond. Specifically, modified duration equals Macauley duration divided by 1 plus the current yield to maturity divided by the number of payments in a year (y). In formula terms, this may be written as:

$$D_{mod} = \frac{\text{Macauley duration}}{1+y}$$

where y is the current yield to maturity of the bond in question.

For example, if our bond in Example 13-4 had made semi-annual interest payments (that is, two payments per year instead of one), its modified duration would be 2.6923 (or 2.7) computed as follows:

$$D_{mod} = \frac{2.8}{1 + 0.08/2}$$

$$= \frac{2.8}{1 + 0.04}$$

$$= 2.6923 \text{ (or 2.7)}$$

Modified duration measures the approximate relative *change in the bond price for every 100 basis point (1%) change in annual interest rates*. Accordingly, since there is an inverse relationship in bond yields and their prices, the change in the price-of-bond formula may be written as follows:

Formula 13-2: Estimated Change in Price of Bond

$$\frac{\Delta P}{P} = -D\left[\frac{\Delta(1 + y)}{1 + y}\right]$$

Where ΔP is the change in the bond price, Dmod is modified duration, Δ (1+y) is the change in market interest rates, and y is the yield to maturity (YTM) of the bond in question.

You should also note that in Formula 13-2, a negative sign is included before D or modified duration. This expresses the inverse relationship between bond yields and bond prices previously mentioned.

Estimated Change in Bond Price

It should be apparent by now that the first step in determining the estimated change in a bond's price is to convert its Macauley duration into modified duration. Therefore, consider the following extension of Example 13-4 using ABC corporate bond:

Example 13-5: As before, ABC bond has a Macauley duration of 2.8 years and a yield to maturity (YTM) of 8%. Now assume that you expect market interest rates to decline by 75 basis points (.75% or 3/4 of 1%) over the next year. In addition, now assume that ABC bond returns *semi-annual* interest payments. Therefore, the estimated percentage change in the price of ABC bond if interest rates decline by 3/4 of 1% is + 2.02%. This is computed in two steps as follows:

1) Compute ABC Bond's modified duration:

$$D_{mod} = \frac{2.8}{1 + 0.08/2}$$

$$= \frac{2.8}{1 + 0.04}$$

$$= 2.6923 \text{ (or 2.69)}$$

2) Compute estimated percentage change in price of ABC bond:

$$\frac{\Delta P}{P} = -(2.69) \times \frac{-75}{100}$$

$$= (-2.69) \times (-0.75)$$

$$= +2.0175 \text{ (or + 2.02\%)}$$

This computation indicates that the price of ABC bond should increase by approximately 2.02% in response to the 75 basis point decline in market interest rates. If the trading value of the bond (price) was now $950 before the decline in interest rates, its value after the decline in interest rates should be $969.19 ($950 x 1.0202).

Conversely, if market interest rates had *increased* by these same 75 basis points, we would expect the price of ABC bond to decrease by 2.02% to a trading value of $930.81 [($950 x (1 - 0.0202) or $950 x 0.9798].

Finally, you should note that, for CFP ® examination purposes, it is likely that the duration number given to include in the estimated change in price bond formula will *not* be specified as modified duration. If not, you should assume that the duration given is that of modified duration unless the terminology Macauley duration is used. In that case, you will need to convert Macauley duration to modified duration as in the first step of Example 13-5 above.

Bond Convexity

Convexity is a measure of the curvature of the relationship between a bond's yield to maturity and its market price (value). Specifically, convexity helps explain the change in bond prices that is not accounted for simply by the bond's duration. Convexity is determined by taking the Macauley duration computation one step further and multiplying (PV x t) by (t+1). For example, let us go back to Example 13-4 where we determined the present value of all cash flows taken multiplied by the number of years (t) to be $2,733.04. Specifically, these were shown in the last column as:

	PV x Year (t)
Year 1	$64.81
Year 2	$120.03
Year 3	$2,548.20
Total	$2,733.04

We then multiply each of these amounts by (t+1) and derive the following:

	PV x Year (t) x (t+1)
Year 1	$129.62
Year 2	$360.09
Year 3	$10,192.80
Total	$10,682.51

This total ($10,682.51) is then divided by the price of the bond ($974.23 in the example) multiplied by the number of compounding periods (1) squared multiplied by (1 + y, or 1.08) squared. Therefore, in summary, we find the convexity of our bond in Example 13-4 to be 9.40 computed as follows:

$10,682.51 ÷ [($974.23 x 1) x (1.08)^2] = $10,682.51 ÷ [($974.23) x (1.1664)] = $10,682.51 ÷ $1,136.34 = 9.4008.

Consequently, we can use this number as an input in the following formula to compute the price change of a bond attributable to the effect of convexity:

Price Change Due to Convexity = 1/2 $\times$ Current Bond Price $\times$ Convexity $\times$ (Δ in Yield)^2

Therefore, in applying this formula to our ABC bond in Example 13-5 currently trading at $950 before a 3/4 of 1% decline in market interest rates, we compute the bond's price change due to convexity to be 0.4465 (0.45) as follows:

Convexity Change: 1/2 $\times$ 950 $\times$ 9.4008 $\times$ (.0075)^2

$$= 1/2 \times 950 \times 9.4008 \times .0001$$

$$= 475 \times 9.4008 \times .0001$$

$$= 4{,}465.38 \times .0001$$

$$= 0.4465 \text{ or } 0.45$$

In turn, when combining the effect of modified duration with convexity computed for the ABC bond, we find the more precise change in the bond's price to be +2.07% for a new trading price of $969.64 as follows:

Change in Yield: - 75 basis points

Modified Duration Change (from Example 13-5): +2.02% $\times$ 950 = +19.19

Convexity Change (from above computation): 0.45

Combined Effect: $950.00

$$\underline{+ \ 19.19} \text{ (Duration)}$$

$969.19

$$\underline{+ \ \ 0.45} \text{ (Convexity)}$$

$969.64 (Price Change of +2.07%)

Finally, you should note that convexity is *always* a good result for bond investors, regardless of whether market interest rates increase or decrease. If interest rates decrease, then convexity will accentuate the increase in the price change of the bond. However, if interest rates increase, convexity will lessen the decline in the price. (The proof of this latter statement is beyond the scope of this text.)

In graphical representation, we can illustrate the improvement that convexity adds to the estimated change in the price of a bond formula using duration like this:

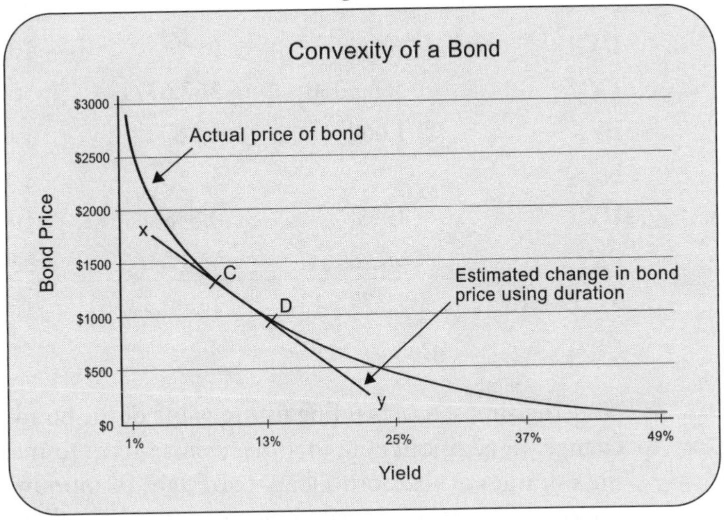

Finally, as could be anticipated given the similarity between duration and convexity, the relationships between convexity and bond attributes are the same as those proven by Macauley. That is:

Figure 13-3

Convexity of a Bond

1) *There is an inverse relationship between the bond's coupon rate and its convexity;* that is, a lower coupon means a higher convexity

2) *There is a direct relationship between the bond's term to maturity and its convexity;* that is, a longer maturity means a higher convexity

3) *There is an inverse relationship between the bond's yield to maturity (YTM) and its convexity;* that is, a higher yield means a lower convexity

PORTFOLIO IMMUNIZATION

Portfolio immunization is a passive investment strategy that has as its objective the safeguarding of bond portfolios against interest rate volatility and its corresponding effect on bond prices. Specifically, immunization involves structuring a bond portfolio such that bond price changes (because of interest rate movements) and cash flows for reinvestment (reinvestment rate risk) offset one another. A portfolio is said to be *immunized* if the duration of the bond portfolio is made equal to a pre-selected time horizon (investment period) of the investor. For example, an investor with a time horizon of 10 years that wants to immunize his or her portfolio does not choose bonds with a 10 year *maturity date*, but bonds with a *duration* of 10 years. Therefore, the further away that the portfolio's duration is from the investor's time horizon, the greater the interest rate risk incurred by the investor.

Let us look an example to prove the assertion that duration is the operative characteristic in portfolio immunization:

Example 13-6: Assume that a bond portfolio has an average yield to maturity of 10%, an average 6% coupon rate and an average term to maturity of 6 years. The portfolio is also structured so that it has an aggregate duration of 5.00 years. Now, assuming that market interest rates increase or decrease 50 basis points (1/2 of 1%), here are the resulting future values of the portfolio: (Note: All computations are performed on an HP 10 B II calculator. Also note that these computations are for purposes of illustration only; you will likely *not* have to perform these computations on the CFP ® Certification Examination.)

INITIAL CHANGE IN INTEREST RATES

	<u>10.0%</u>	<u>9.5%</u>	<u>10.5%</u>
PMT	$60	$60	$60
N	5	5	5
I/YR	10%	9.5%	10.5%
$FV_{5.0}$	366.3060	362.6771	369.9696
FV	1,060	1,060	1,060
N	1	1	1
I/YR	10%	9.5%	10.5%
$PV_{5.0}$	963.6364	968.0365	959.2760
TOTAL $FV_{5.0}$	1,329.9424	1,330.7136	1,329.2456

Note the almost exact ending future value of the bond portfolio ($1,329) *regardless* of the interest rate change. In addition, note that the average term to maturity of the portfolio (6 years) is greater than the duration of the portfolio. Accordingly, in immunizing the portfolio, a manager should integrate bonds of different maturity dates, but combine them so that the average maturity date *exceeds* the duration used to match the investor's time horizon.

Macauley duration also measures the precise point in time when the interest rate risk and the reinvestment rate risk of a bond portfolio offset one another. As a result, if an investor purchases a bond and sells it when the bond reaches its duration (for example, 5.00 years above), any loss in its value because of interest rate increases should be exactly offset by the increase in the reinvestment earnings of the interest payments from the bond. Similarly, if interest rates decrease, there will be loss of reinvestment earnings from the bond, but its value (market price) will increase to offset this loss.

Finally, as should be anticipated, portfolio immunization may be easily accomplished with the use of only zero coupon bonds (*zeros*). This is because zeros have a duration equal to their term to maturity. Further, zeros have no reinvestment rate associated with the bond's interest payments, since there are no interest payments ever actually received by the investor.

USING DURATION TO MANAGE BOND PORTFOLIOS

Building on the previous relationships discussed with respect to the impact of duration in bond portfolio management, we can now state the following:

> 1) *The smaller the bond's coupon rate, the greater its relative price fluctuation.*
>
> 2) *The longer the bond's term to maturity, the greater its relative price fluctuation.*
>
> 3) *The smaller the bond's yield to maturity, the greater its relative price fluctuation.*

In turn, these relationships lead us to some basic principles used to maximize a bond portfolio's rate of return when interest rates are expected to change. If the investor expects a *decline* in market interest rates, he or she should attempt to construct a portfolio of *long maturity bonds with low coupon rates.* This will provide the investor with a portfolio that has the *maximum interest rate sensitivity* to take advantage of the capital gains experienced by bonds from the decrease in market interest rates. Conversely, if the investor expects an *increase* in market interest rates, he or she should attempt to construct a portfolio of *short maturity bonds with high coupon rates.* This will provide the investor with a portfolio that has the *minimum interest* rate sensitivity to minimize the capital losses experienced by bonds from the increase in market interest rates.

IMPORTANT CONCEPTS

Default risk

Credit risk

Investment grade bond

Non-investment grade (speculative) bond

Present value of a bond

Par bond

Discount bond

Premium bond

Yield to maturity

Current yield

Coupon rate / nominal yield

Yield ladder

Yield curve/term structure of interest rates

Expectations hypothesis

Liquidity preference hypothesis

Segmented market hypothesis

Macauley duration / bond duration

Modified duration

Change in bond price using duration

Bond convexity

Portfolio immunization

Interest rate risk

Reinvestment rate risk

Zero coupon bond

QUESTIONS FOR REVIEW

1. What are the three types of investment risk that impact all forms of bond issues?

2. How can the credit risk associated with a corporate bond be minimized?

3. When is a bond considered to be of *investment grade* and what does this mean in so far as the likely coupon rate offered by such bond in comparison to other bonds?

4. Is it easier to determine the present value (intrinsic value) of a stock or to determine that of a bond? Explain your reasoning.

5. KZZ $1,000 corporate bond has a 5-year maturity and carries a coupon rate of 8%. It pays interest semi-annually. The yield to maturity for similar quality bonds is 6%.

   Answer the following questions:

   a) What is the present value of KZZ bond?

   b) Should the bond be selling at a discount or premium to its par value and why?

6. If a bond is selling in the secondary market at a discount to par, will its yield to maturity be more or less than its current yield? Explain.

7. Explain each of the four basic types of yield curves. Which one of these types is usually predominant and why?

8. What are the three academic arguments or hypotheses attempting to explain why the yield curve assumes its given shape? Which one of these arguments is likely the most plausible?

9. Define what is meant by the term *bond duration*. Why is this important?

10. What are the three inputs used in the computation of bond duration formula?

11. Is the duration of a bond more or less than the bond's maturity date? Explain.

12. What are the four important relationships proved by Macauley in explaining the importance of duration to a bond investor?

13. How does modified duration differ from Macauley duration? In what formula is modified duration used?

14. Assume that the modified duration of JDD bond is 3.62 and that market interest rates increase by 50 basis points (1/2 of 1%). What is the estimated change in the value (market price) of JDD bond?

15. What concept is used to more closely approximate the change in the value of a bond given a respective change in market interest rates?

16. What are three relationships between the convexity of a bond and the attributes of that bond?

17. What is the objective of *portfolio immunization* and what is the operative characteristic in such an investment technique?

18. Is it more or less difficult to immunize a portfolio if the portfolio consists only of zero coupon bonds? Why?

19. What are the three basic relationships between the attributes of a bond and the bond's relative price fluctuation?

20. If market interest rates are expected to increase, what type of bond portfolio should be constructed by an investor? Why?

SUGGESTIONS FOR ADDITIONAL READING

Tools and Techniques of Investment Planning, Stephen R. Leimberg, Robert T. LeClair, Robert J. Doyle, Jr., and Thomas R. Robinson, The National Underwriter Company, 2004.

Investments: An Introduction, 7th edition, Herbert B. Mayo, Thomson/ South-Western, 2002.

Investment Analysis and Portfolio Management, 7th edition, Frank K. Reilly and Keith C. Brown, Thomson/South-Western, 2003.

The Wall Street Journal Guide to Money and Investing, 3rd edition, Kenneth M. Morris and Virginia B. Morris, Fireside Publishing, 2004.

CHAPTER FOURTEEN

Asset Pricing Models

• • •

This chapter covers several models that have been developed to arrive at an estimated price for assets or the derivatives of those assets. Specifically, four models are addressed, the first two of which may generally be used to value *any* investment asset or security. These are the capital asset pricing model (CAPM) and the arbitrage pricing theory (APT). In contrast, the other two models that are considered may only be used in the valuation of *options* (or the derivative of an asset). These are the binomial options pricing model and the relatively well-known Black-Scholes valuation model.

We have been introduced to the capital asset pricing model (CAPM) before, specifically in chapter 10 of this textbook. As such, we have learned that CAPM is the graphical representation of the security market line (SML) and may be applied in order to value individual securities by using the security's beta coefficient as the relevant measure of investor risk instead of standard deviation. CAPM also reflects what should be the expected return on any risky asset and is equal to the investor's required rate of return, given the model's assumption that capital markets are in equilibrium (or properly priced) at all times. Therefore, the purpose of the model is to quantitatively determine *the required rate of return for any investor.*

Upon completing this chapter, you should be able to:

- Compute the investor's required rate of return using the capital asset pricing model (CAPM)
- Explain the factors involved in valuing a security using arbitrage pricing theory (APT)
- Describe how to value an option using the binomial option pricing model
- Describe the factors influencing the market price of an option under the Black-Scholes option valuation method

CAPITAL ASSET PRICING MODEL (CAPM)

The capital asset pricing model (a basic tenet of modern portfolio theory) asserts that the expected return of any individual security should be the risk-free rate of return that is currently available to an investor *plus* an applicable premium for the risk associated with that particular security. In formula terms, this may be written as follows:

Formula 14-1: Capital Asset Pricing Model

$$r_i = r_f + \left(r_m \cdot r_f\right) B_i$$

where r_i is the expected return of the security (also equal to the investor's required rate of return since the market is assumed to be equilibrium), r_f is the expected risk-free rate of return in the secondary marketplace (normally as represented by the yield on the 90 day U.S. Treasury bill), r_m is the expected rate of return of the overall market and β_i is the beta coefficient of the individual security. In turn, the risk premium that is assumed to be sought by the investor consists of the *stock risk premium* associated with that security (equal to $\{r_m - r_f\}\beta$) and the overall risk of investing in the broader market or the *market risk premium*, (as measured by $\{r_m - r_f\}$.

> **Example 14-1:** Assume that the stock of Tour Tempo, Inc. has a beta coefficient of 1.2. Also assume that the expected return on the market is 8% and that the expected 90-day Treasury bill (T-bill) rate is 3.5%. Accordingly, under the capital asset pricing model (CAPM), the expected return of the security is 8.90% computed as follows: 3.50% + (8% -3.50%)1.2 = 3.50% +5.40% = 8.90%. In addition, given the assumptions of the model, we also know that 8.90% is the required rate of return that investors demand before investing in this particular security.

As expected, the required rate of return for individuals to invest in Tour Tempo, Inc. (8.90%) is higher than the expected return on the overall market (8%). However, this makes sense given that the risk premium (specifically, the stock risk premium) is more than the market risk premium with a beta of the stock in excess of 1.0. Specifically, the stock risk premium to invest in Tour Tempo, Inc. is 5.40% [(8% - 3.50%) x 1.2] whereas the market risk premium is only 4.50% (8% - 3.50%). Alternatively, this would *not* be the case if the beta of Tour Tempo, Inc. was only 0.5. In that instance, its stock risk premium would be only 2.25% [(8% - 3.50%) x 0.5] as compared to its market risk premium of 4.50% (8% - 3.50%).

We can also use the required rate of return found in Example 14-1 (or 8.90%) as an input in the constant growth dividend discount model (see chapter 12) to determine the intrinsic value of Tour Tempo, Inc. stock. Thus, assuming that the expected growth rate of Tour Tempo's dividend payout is 5% and that the stock is currently paying a dividend of $1.50 per share, we determine the stock's intrinsic value to be $40.38 as follows:

$$V = \frac{D_0(1+g)}{r-g} = \frac{\$1.50(1+0.05)}{(0.0890-0.05)} = \frac{\$1.50(1.05)}{(0.0390)} = \frac{\$1.5750}{(0.0390)} = \$40.38$$

As noted in chapter 10, when discussing portfolio management theory, since beta is one of the inputs in the capital asset pricing model (CAPM), the model in operation assumes that the investor owns a *diversified* portfolio. Accordingly, the CAPM accounts only for the impact of *systematic risk* and does *not* consider *unsystematic risk* or investor risk that has been *diversified away*. Again, this is reasonable since, in a diversified portfolio using negatively or low positively correlated securities, one stock's losses should be offset by another stock's gains.

As a part of modern portfolio theory (MPT) whose major contribution to investment practice was a consideration and measurement of investor risk in making an investment decision, the capital asset pricing model is quite valuable. Specifically, it allows us to compute the required rate of return for an investor and compare it to an investment's expected rate of return. For example, if the investor's required rate of return is *more than* the investment's expected return, the investment should likely *not* be made. Conversely, if his or her required rate of return is *less than* the investment's expected return, perhaps a buy decision is warranted.

However, as with most models and theories, the CAPM should only be used as a starting point in valuing a security. This is because the model relies on a number of assumptions, any one of which may be invalidated by academic researchers over time. Still, the model has, in large part, existed to date simply because of the robustness of its theoretical underpinnings and intuitive logic. As a result, an investor should likely consider carefully the product of the model and, perhaps, use its required rate of return as a so-called *hurdle rate* before making any security investment.

ARBITRAGE PRICING THEORY (APT)

As we have discussed, the capital asset pricing model (CAPM) is built around a consideration of a single risk factor: the *beta coefficient* of a stock or mutual fund. Specifically, that factor measures the volatility of an investment asset's return relative to the market (otherwise known as the asset's *systematic risk*).

In contrast, arbitrage pricing theory (APT), as developed by Stephen A. Ross, includes *multiple* risk factors in its determination of the expected rate of return of an investment asset. Further, unlike CAPM, the individual factors that contribute to the return derived under the APT are *unexpected* and *not pre-specified*. While there may be many of these unexpected factors, academic research has identified that four are pre-eminent. These are:

1) Unexpected inflation (sometimes known as inflation risk)

2) Unexpected shifts in the risk premium that is sought by investors (confidence risk)

3) Unexpected changes in the investor's preference for short versus long-term investments (time horizon risk)

4) Unexpected changes in the overall level of the economy's industrial production (business cycle risk

In the APT formula, each of these unexpected factors is represented by the capital letter F (*factor*) and then a subscript number to identify that each factor is unique. Each factor is then preceded by a representation of how much the asset or security (in decimal terms) is sensitive to the risk factor. This is also known as the *sensitivity coefficient* of the asset or security or *b*. Finally, the risk-free rate of return (again, like in CAPM, usually represented by the 90-day Treasury bill rate) is used as the constant *a* in the formula. This makes intuitive sense since, like CAPM, APT is trying to quantify how much additional risk premium must be offered to the investor to entice him or her to actually purchase the asset or security.

The generic form of the APT model or formula can, thus, be written as follows:

$$r_i = a + b_1 F_1 + b_2 F_2 + b_3 F_3 + b_4 F_4 + \ldots\ldots b_n F_n$$

where r_i is the expected return of the asset or security, *a* is the constant or risk-free rate of return, *b* is the sensitivity coefficient of the unexpected risk factor, F is one of the four previously mentioned unexpected risk factors (expressed in percentage terms or *price of risk*) and F_n are still more unexpected risk factors (with b_n the associated coefficient of the security's sensitivity to that additional unexpected risk factor or factors).

You should note that the factors and coefficients used in the APT model are typically determined by academic statistical analysis that is beyond the scope of this textbook. Furthermore, as with other theoretical models, they are based on *past* investment performance and events, which may or may not be valid with respect to the future.

Example 14-2: Continuing with the scenario first presented in Example 14-1, assume that you are attempting to determine the expected return for Tour Tempo, Inc. stock. However, you now wish to use arbitrage pricing theory (APT) and its associated inputs to determine the stock's expected return. As before, the current risk-free rate of return in the marketplace is 3.5% (as represented by the 90-day Treasury bill rate). In addition, the unexpected risk factors and the sensitivity correlation of Tour Tempo, Inc. stock to those factors are as follows:

Risk Factor	Stock Coefficient (b)	Price of Risk (F)
Inflation Risk	-0.10	-3.00%
Confidence Risk	0.80	2.50%
Time Horizon Risk	1.20	-0.75%
Business Cycle Risk	1.50	4.00%

Therefore, the expected return for Tour Tempo, Inc. stock is 9.10% computed as follows: 3.5% + (-0.10 x -3.0%) + (0.08 x 2.5%) + (1.20 x -0.75%) + (1.50 x 4.0%) = 3.5% + (0.0030) + (0.0020) + (-0.0090) + (0.06) = 0.035 + 0.0560 = 0.0910 x 100 = 9.10%.

In turn, the expected return derived under the APT model may be compared to that determined using CAPM, allowing the financial planner the opportunity to separately analyze the impact of the risk factors unique to APT. Again, it needs to be emphasized that the factors used in the APT are *unexpected*, which therefore permits an even greater *cushion* of risk that may be taken into account by the planner.

Finally, in the APT formula, if the particular risk is expected (rather than unexpected as is the normal assumption) the risk factor in the formula is represented by a *zero*. The deviation from each of the risk factors considered in the model is then measured against that base. Thus, by identifying additional risk factors that may impact the expected return of a security, the arbitrage pricing theory suggests an alternative valuation model that may be used to arrive at the risk-adjusted price of that security,

BINOMIAL OPTION PRICING MODEL

Before we can ascertain a value for an option under this exceedingly complex method of pricing, we need to review the several characteristics of options that are important to determining their value. Among these are the option's exercise price, its expiration date, and the price of the underlying security (*derivative*) on which the option is written.

1. The option's exercise price: This is also known as the *strike price* of the option. It is the price at which the holder of the option can buy or sell the underlying security. Typically, the option contract is *standardized* so that there are several exercise prices available in excess of (or below) the current market price of the security. An *increase* in the exercise price *decreases* the value of a *call* option (right to *buy* the underlying security). Conversely, an *increase* in the exercise price *increases* the value of a *put* option (right to *sell* the underlying security). To explain why this is so for a call option, consider this example: If Mike wants to buy a call option on Dell stock (currently trading at $30 per share), and he has a choice between exercise prices for the option of $35, $40, or $45, the $35 option will likely be the most expensive to purchase and the $45 option will be the least expensive. This is because Dell's stock price has further to go before the call option will be *in the money* (that is, before it has accrued some amount of *intrinsic value*).

2. The option's expiration date: Standardized options are generally written for a time period of *nine months* from date of issue. Most options traded in the United States are *American style options*, meaning that they may be exercised at any time up to the expiration date of the option (or any time before the nine-month period expires). On the other hand, *European style options* may only be exercised on the expiration date of the option contract. An *increase* in the time to expiration of the option *increases* the value of a *call* option. Similarly, an *increase* in the time to expiration of the option *increases* the value of a *put* option. This is, of course, because the underlying stock price has more time to equal the option's exercise price and, thus, for the option to finish *in the money* (see chapter 7 of this textbook). (Note: This same direct relationship holds for the resulting value of both calls and puts if there is a *decrease* in the time to expiration of the option.)

3. The security underlying the option: As noted, this is the underlying security (or derivative) on which the value of the option is based, or that from which the option's value is derived. A standardized option contract typically represents 100 shares of common stock, also known as a *round lot* of the issue. An increase in the underlying security price will result in an increase in the value of a call option. In contrast, an increase in the underlying security price will result in a decrease in the value of a put option. (Note: The same direct/inverse relationship holds for call/put options if there is a decrease in the underlying security price.

A critical element of the binomial option pricing model, then, uses the underlying security price to estimate the value of the option written against such security. Specifically, this model asserts that future changes in the underlying security's price can always be simplified to one of two possibilities: an up movement or a down movement. For this reason, the binomial model is also sometimes referred to as the *two-state option pricing model.* Let us look at an example of the model in application.

Example 14-3: Assume that a call option with an expiration date of nine months has been written on XYZ stock. The exercise price of the option is $20.00. Over the nine-month time period, the underlying stock price is either expected to increase by 10% or decrease by 5% and its current price is also $20.00. Finally, the risk-free rate of interest is 4%. Using the binomial option, we derive the current value for the call option on XYZ stock to be $1.16 as follows:

1) The value of the option at the time of its expiration will be its intrinsic value. Therefore, if the price of the underlying security increases to $22.00 ($20.00 x 1.10), then the option will be worth $2.00 ($22.00 - $20.00) at the option's expiration date. Conversely, if the price of the underlying security falls to $19.00 ($20.00 x .95), the option will expire worthless and will have *no* or *zero* intrinsic value.

2) In the model, the current value of an option is the present value of the weighted average of the future call values. The risk-free rate is the rate for the single period over which the option values are being discounted, and Π is the weighting factor. The weighting factor is determined from the potential increase in the price of the underlying security using the following formula:

$$\Pi = \frac{(1+r) - d}{u - d}$$

where r is the risk free rate, d is the potential downside in the underlying price of the stock computed as one minus the downside percentage in decimal form, and u is the potential upside in the underlying price of the stock computed as one plus the upside percentage in decimal form.

3) Computing Π, therefore, results in:

$$\Pi = \frac{(1.04 - 0.9500)}{(1.10 - 0.9500)}$$

$$\Pi = \frac{0.09}{0.15}$$

$$\Pi = .60$$

4) We then use the weighting factor in the final formula for determining the current value of the option as follows:

Formula 14-2

$$C_0 = \frac{\pi(C_1^+) + (1 - \pi)(C_1^-)}{(1 + r)}$$

where Π is the weighting factor, C_1 is the expected future value of the call option and r is the risk free rate of interest.

Accordingly, we solve for the current value of the call option of XYZ stock as follows:

$$C_0 = \frac{0.60\,(2.00) + 0.40\,(0.00)}{1.04}$$

$$C_0 = \frac{1.20 + 0.00}{1.04}$$

$$C_0 = 1.1538 \text{ or, when rounded up, } 1.16$$

As will be recognized, the above example illustrates only a very simplified practical result, assuming only two possible underlying movements of XYZ stock. Of course, in reality, XYZ's stock price could attain virtually any price before the time of the option's expiration, not simply two prices. Therefore, the computation for the current value of the call option using the binomial model would be of little value unless it took into account several periods worth of two-step price movements. As a result, computer software and simulation is often used to assist in determining the option's value. In addition, the above example assumes a European style option that may only be exercised at the option's date of expiration. In contrast, an American style option may be exercised at any time *before* expiration; as a result, there can be *many* sub-periods where the current value of the option must be computed. This, of course, only adds to the complexity in deriving an appropriate value for the option.

BLACK-SCHOLES OPTION VALUATION MODEL

The binomial option pricing model is a *discrete* method for valuing options because it allows security price changes to occur in distinct upward or downward movements. However, it can also be assumed that security prices change *continuously* throughout time. This was the approach taken by Fisher Black and Myron Scholes in developing their relatively well-known model for valuing European-style options. Specifically, the model assumes that stock prices can be described by a statistical process known as *geometric Brownian motion*. Ultimately, this process is summarized by a volatility factor ascribed to the underlying security represented by the Greek symbol σ, like the standard deviation factor referenced in chapter 9 of this textbook.

While mathematically complex (indeed, the recitation of the actual formula is beyond the scope of this book), the Black-Scholes model does help us to understand the value of a call option as it relates to the five following factors:

1) The current underlying security price

2) The option's exercise price

3) The time to expiration of the option

4) The risk-free rate of return

5) The volatility of the underlying security

Functionally, the model holds that the value of the option is dependent on all five factors. However, the first and fourth factors are observable market prices while the second and third factors may be found by referencing the terms of the option contract. Therefore, as noted, the only variable that must actually be derived by the model itself is the volatility factor associated with the future price of the underlying security. Note that the model may only be used to value *call options and not puts*.

Figure 14-1 below summarizes the relationship between the five factors in the Black-Scholes model and the value of the call option:

Figure 14-1: Factors Influencing Value of a Call Option using Black-Scholes Model

An Increase In The:	Results In The Call Value:
Underlying Security Price	Increasing
Option's Exercise Price	Decreasing
Option's Time to Expiration	Increasing
Risk-Free Rate	Increasing
Underlying Security Volatility	Increasing

The logic behind the first three of these relationships is straightforward. Ergo, an increase in the underlying security price will *increase* the call's current value; a larger exercise price will *reduce* the call's value. Also, the *longer* that the option has until it expires, the *greater* the time premium component associated with the option's market value. Nevertheless, the last two relationships are not as apparent. Specifically, an increase in the marketplace risk-free rate of return will increase the value of the call option since it *reduces* the present value of the option's exercise price (in other words, the basic concept of a smaller present value, the greater the discount rate that is used). Similarly, when the volatility of the underlying security increases, the call becomes more valuable since this *increases* the probability that the option will have a greater *in the money* value when the option actually expires.

The Black-Scholes option valuation model is popular with investors for at least two reasons: 1) it is computationally convenient (and may easily be programmed into one's computer) and 2) it produces reasonable values under a variety of circumstances. Nevertheless, academic studies have shown that the volatilities of the underlying securities on which the options were written tend to be overly large when the associated call options are *in the money* and are inordinately small when the call options are currently *out of the money*. This means that in-the-money call options are priced *higher* in the marketplace by investors than the Black-Scholes model suggests and that out-of-the-money options are *not valued enough* per the terms of the model. In addition, the model assumes that the underlying stocks trade frequently; this attribute is inherent in the volatility factor used in the model's computation. Therefore, stocks that are less frequently traded or infrequently traded are *not* good candidates for the model. Finally, Fisher Black has commented that the model's assumptions of a constant risk-free rate and volatility level until the expiration date of the call option are almost certain to be violated in real life. As a result, the current option value derived by the model is best viewed only as an approximation.

IMPORTANT CONCEPTS

Capital Asset Pricing Model (CAPM)	Price of risk
Stock risk premium	Binomial Option Pricing Model
Market risk premium	American-style option
Systematic risk	European-style option
Arbitrage pricing theory (APT)	Two-State Option Pricing Model
Stock coefficient	Black-Scholes Option Valuation Model

QUESTIONS FOR REVIEW

1. What is the purpose of the Capital Asset Pricing Model (CAPM)? What is the graphical representation of such model?

2. What is the *stock risk premium* associated with the purchase of a security? What is the *market risk premium* associated with that same security? Why is each of these important in investment theory?

3. Complete the following sentence: CAPM accounts only for the impact of _____ risk and does not consider _____ risk.

4. Assume that after using CAPM you have determined that an investment's expected return is less than the investor's required rate of return. What is the likely course of action that you advise for this investor? Explain your conclusion.

5. What does the arbitrage pricing theory (APT) attempt to take into account that the CAPM does not consider?

6. What are the four unexpected factors that have been found to be pre-eminent in the calculation of an investment's expected return using arbitrage pricing theory?

7. If the risk factor in the APT formula is reflected as a zero, what does that mean?

8. What is the difference between an American-style and a European-style option?

9. If there is an increase in the exercise price of the option, what is the corresponding effect on the value of a call and put, respectively?

10. What is the assumption regarding the movement in the price of the underlying security in each of the following option valuation models:

    • The Binomial Option Pricing Model
    • The Black-Scholes Option Valuation Model

11. Why is the Binomial Option Pricing Model sometimes referred to as the *two state option pricing model*?

12. What is used as the discount rate in determining the value of an option under the Binomial Option Pricing Model?

13 What are the five factors or variables considered in the Black-Scholes Option Valuation Model? Which one of these factors has an *inverse* relationship to the value of a call option?

14. If the volatility of the underlying security increases, why does the call option become more valuable?

15. What are three problems with using the Black-Scholes Option Valuation Model to value a European-style call option?

SUGGESTIONS FOR ADDITIONAL READING

Tools and Techniques of Investment Planning, Stephen R. Leimberg, Robert T. LeClair, Robert J. Doyle, Jr., and Thomas R. Robinson, The National Underwriter Company, 2004.

Investments: An Introduction, 7th edition, Herbert B. Mayo, Thomson/ South-Western, 2002.

Investment Analysis and Portfolio Management, 7th edition, Frank K. Reilly and Keith C. Brown, Thomson/South-Western, 2003.

The Wall Street Journal Guide to Money and Investing, 3rd edition, Kenneth M. Morris and Virginia B. Morris, Fireside Publishing, 2004.

CHAPTER FIFTEEN

Investment Strategies

• • •

This is likely among the most practical (and least theoretical) chapters in the entire textbook. It considers the interesting subject of investment strategies, whether unique to the investor or investment advisor or part of generally-accepted practices. The chapter begins with a discussion of the importance of implementing a written investment statement to guide future investing and ends with a brief analysis of the popular theories of value and growth investing.

Upon completing this chapter, you should be able to:

- Explain the importance of an investment policy statement
- Identify common and appropriate benchmarks in evaluating investment performance
- Describe common strategies used in formula investing, including *dollar cost averaging*
- Explain types of bond swaps
- Identify strategies involving the timing of investment purchases and sales
- Describe short selling and how it may be effectively used by an investor
- Differentiate forms of security selection and security analysis
- Compute a margin call and the required equity amounts necessary in the use of leverage
- Contrast the basic principles underlying value investing to those of growth investing

INVESTMENT POLICY STATEMENTS

Possible investment strategies that should be pursued by an investment advisor on behalf of his or her client begin with the formulation of a complete and thorough investment policy statement. Such a statement should be developed in accordance with the client's investment goals and objectives, but it should also list the constraints or limitations that bear on those goals. Specifically, the *objectives* portion of the statement should include the desired return requirements of the investor's portfolio as well as a recitation of the level of risk that a client is willing and able to take. Of course, many clients do not know the level of risk that they are willing to assume, so it is up to the investment advisor to assist them in accurately expressing this risk. Because of this, many advisors have developed a risk tolerance questionnaire that they ask the client to complete before proceeding with the formal development of the investment policy statement.

The investor's desired rate of investment return and risk tolerance should be complementary. In other words, if the investor expresses little to no tolerance for risk, an investment in aggressive growth-type mutual funds is likely not appropriate. Furthermore, the desired rate of return should be achievable by the client and investment advisor. In this regard, many advisors will consult the historical rate of return of asset classes as guidance for what is possible. However, if they do so, they must quickly caution the client that the historical rate of return is no guarantee of the same or similar performance in the future. As a result, many advisors will also include in the investment policy statement an appropriate *benchmark* by which to measure the performance of their investment recommendations in the future. The choice of which benchmark(s) to use is the focus of the next section in this chapter.

Finally, the constraints or limitations that will possibly impede the achievement of the client's desired rate of return should be listed in the second major part of the investment policy statement. Specifically, many advisors use the following five constraints as a part of any statement:

1) The time horizon of the investor

2) The liquidity needs of the investor during this time horizon

3) The tax status of the investor's portfolio or accounts within the portfolio

4) Any laws and regulations that may bear on the investor's portfolio

5) Any unique circumstances of the investor, such as a possible upcoming inheritance (cash inflow) or substantial financial withdrawal (cash outflow)

Of these, the liquidity needs of the investor during the stipulated time horizon of the statement is likely most important. For example, if the investor would like to purchase a vacation home during this time horizon, the need for cash to do so must be factored into the statement. Similarly, if the client must allow for withdrawals so as to send his or her children to college (while, perhaps, also in the process of saving for his or her own retirement), this fact should also be considered.

APPROPRIATE BENCHMARKS

Although many investors use comparisons to other portfolio managers as a measure of performance, benchmarks should really include certain independent characteristics.

Among these are the following:

1) The benchmark selected should be unambiguous, with the composition and weighting of assets within the benchmark clearly stated.

2) The benchmark should be measurable, that is, it should be possible to monitor and calculate the benchmark's rate of return on a relatively frequent basis.

3) The benchmark should be consistent with the manager's investment style; for example, if the portfolio manager invests primarily in growth stocks, the selected benchmark index should also reflect this.

4) The benchmark should be reflective of current investment practice.

5) The benchmark should be selected *before* the beginning of the investment period or investor's time horizon.

Finally, if desired, the benchmark should be *investible*. This means that the investor should be able to invest in the benchmark as an alternative to employing the particular investment advisor or portfolio manager. However, there should be a level of comfort that runs both ways. Not only should the investor be given the option to invest in the benchmark as an alternative, but the investment advisor should also be comfortable that the benchmark used is indeed appropriate as a measuring device.

So what are some examples of what should be used as an appropriate benchmark? Appropriate *value weighted indexes* include the Standard & Poor's 500 index of the largest U.S. capitalization stocks, the Russell 2000 index of small capitalization stocks, and the Wilshire 5000 index of stocks used to measure overall U.S. market conditions. In addition, the European and Far East (EAFE) Index may be used to compare international stock performance. (Note that a value weighted index is the sum of the current market capitalization values of the securities within the index divided by the sum of those securities' market capitalization values in a designated base year.)

An appropriate *price weighted index* may be any of the Dow Jones indexes, including the widely watched Dow Jones Index of 30 industrial stocks. (Note that a price-weighted index is the sum of the current prices of the securities within the index divided by a previously announced adjusted divisor.)

FORMULA INVESTING

The term *formula investing* essentially means that an investor does not actively trade or manage his or her portfolio, but instead follows certain automatic rules regardless of market conditions. The most commonly-known of this type of investing is so-called *dollar cost averaging*, but there are other forms as well. We will now consider each.

Dollar Cost Averaging

Using dollar cost averaging, an investor decides to purchase additional shares of stock or shares in a mutual fund at regular intervals and, usually, in equal amounts. Often, this is accomplished through the use of an automatic withdrawal plan at the investor's bank or other financial institution. The purchase is made at the appropriate interval, no matter what the price of the investment may be at that time. In turn, since the dollar amount is typically the same regardless of market conditions or market prices at the time, this technique is referred to as *dollar cost averaging*.

The effect of this technique is to increase the number of shares gradually over a long period of time. In the event that the current price of the stock or mutual fund is less than or below that of the previous price, the investor has succeeded in purchasing more shares of the investment. Because more shares are acquired when the price of the stock or mutual fund declines, this has the result of *reducing* the average cost of a share. Subsequently, if the stock or mutual fund share price increases, the investor will earn more profits on lower-priced shares, thereby increasing his or her dollar-weighted rate of return.

Let us look at an example whereby an investor, Kent, uses the dollar cost averaging strategy to purchase additional shares rather than a lump sum purchase of all shares at one time.

Example 15-1: Kent purchases $10,000 of the ABC mutual fund shares in January, 2006 when its share price is $25.00. He therefore purchases a total of 400 shares ($10,000 divided by $25.00) with a cost basis of $25 per share. Now, instead, assume that Ken uses this same amount of $10,000 to make 10 separate purchases of $1,000 each over the next ten months when the price of ABC mutual fund shares is fluctuating as follows:

Month	Share Price	# of Shares Purchased
1/2006	$25.00	40.00
2/2006	$27.00	37.04
3/2006	$22.00	45.45
4/2006	$20.00	50.00
5/2006	$18.00	55.55
6/2006	$21.00	47.62
7/2006	$23.00	43.48
8/2006	$26.00	38.46
9/2006	$25.00	40.00
10/2006	$27.00	37.04
Total		**434.64**

Accordingly, as may be seen and computed, when using dollar cost averaging over the 10-month period, Kent has now purchased 434.64 shares of ABC mutual fund with a cost basis of only $23.00 per share ($10,000 divided by 434.64 shares). Because Kent was able to take advantage of market fluctuations, he therefore ends up with an additional 8.6% shares and associated market value.

It should be noted that dollar cost averaging works best when markets are declining or fluctuating, as Example 15-1 illustrates. It does *not* work well when the market is steadily increasing, since in that event, the investor would be better off buying as many shares as possible up front when the price per share is lower. In addition, even in a declining market, the investor should not automatically assume that the market price of the stock or mutual fund will eventually increase. Rather, a stock or mutual fund that is declining in price may result from an underlying corporate earnings problem or a weakness in that particular market sector (for example, technology). If this is the case, the investor needs to consider the ongoing expenditure of funds as a fixed cost that should not influence the purchase of any additional shares.

Share Averaging/Averaging Down

Some investors do not like to make periodic purchases of stock or mutual fund shares. Instead, they prefer to purchase additional shares only when the price of the shares *declines*. Accordingly, these investors are following a strategy of *averaging down*. This is a method by which the investor reduces the cost basis of an investment in one security by buying more shares as the price of that security decreases. As with dollar cost averaging, the investor will be rewarded if the price of the security subsequently increases. Of course, by only buying "on the dips" in the market, the investor may also miss out on a bull market, wherein share prices tend to move upward for a significant period of time. Finally, a variation of the averaging down strategy occurs when the investor purchases the same number of shares every time. If the investor does so, he or she is said to be following a policy of *share averaging*.

With dollar cost averaging, there is a greater total reduction in the average cost of shares than there is with share averaging. When the investor *dollar cost averages* the amount spent is held constant, but the number of shares purchased varies. Conversely, when the investor *share averages* the number of shares purchased is held constant, but the dollar amount varies. Since the investor purchases a fixed number of shares with share averaging regardless of how low the price falls, the average cost of the overall shares is *not* reduced to the extent that it is with dollar cost averaging. Share averaging is also, by definition, not as easy to *automate* (for example, by way of automatic monthly investing) as is dollar cost averaging since the amounts invested using share averaging are seldom the same.

Dividend Reinvestment Plans (DRIPs)

Dividend reinvestment plans (*DRIPs*) are offered by many large companies/stock issuers as a service to their shareholders. With such plans, dividends are automatically reinvested into the company's stock or consumed by the investor as cash. If the dividends are reinvested, the investor purchases additional shares of company stock without contacting a broker/dealer, who may charge a commission if these shares are purchased directly.

There are two general types of dividend reinvestment programs. The first (less popular) type exists when a bank acts on behalf of the company and all shareholders. The bank collects the cash dividends for the shareholders, pools all of the shareholder monies or contributions, and then purchases the additional shares in the open market. In the second (more popular) type of plan, the company issues new shares of stock in lieu of a cash dividend, with the money then reinvested by the company to satisfy future capital needs. While this latter type of plan was initially offered only by utility companies, which typically are in constant need of new operating funds, it is now the standard DRIP for most other types of companies and/or mutual funds.

Bond Ladders, Barbells, and Bullets

Bond ladders are a popular strategy for staggering the maturity of a client's bond investments and, subsequently, for establishing a schedule for reinvesting the proceeds as the bonds mature. For example, a $50,000 portfolio of bonds could acquire $5,000 worth of bonds that mature for each of the next 10 years. Therefore, if interest rates change, the prices of the bonds with the shorter terms to maturity will fluctuate less then the prices of the bonds with the longer terms to maturity (recall the discussion of duration in chapter 13). This has the effect of minimizing the impact of the price changes in the bonds due to interest rate fluctuations. As shorter-term bonds mature, their principal may subsequently be reinvested at higher market interest rates.

Ladders are popular among investors who want bonds as part of a long-term investment objective, such as seeking predictable income for retirement needs or saving for a young child's college tuition. However, investors should be aware that laddering may require the commitment of investment assets over time, and return of principal is not guaranteed with corporate (versus government) debt issues.

Bond barbells are a strategy for buying short-term and long-term bond issues. The long-term end of the barbell allows the investor to lock attractive long-term interest rates, while the short-term end ensures that the investor will have the opportunity to invest in other assets if the bond market experiences a downturn in value. For example, if the investor has $100,000 to invest, he or she might expend $50,000 to purchase bonds with maturities of one year and the other $50,000 to purchase bonds with a 10-year maturity date. As a result, if interest rate changes, the investor needs to replace only half of his or her bond portfolio. Expectations of lower interest rates would mean selling the short-term bonds (since their price will have increased the most) and investing the proceeds in longer-term bonds. If higher rates are anticipated, the investor would do the opposite: sell the longer-term bonds and reinvest the proceeds into shorter-term maturities.

Bond bullets are a strategy for having several bonds mature at the same time and minimizing the interest rate risk when the investor buys the bonds. For example, assume that an investor wants all her bonds to mature in 10 years, but is very concerned about the interest rate risk associated with such a purchase. Therefore, using the bond bullet strategy, she buys two bonds immediately, two bonds two years from now, and two more bonds four years from now. Accordingly, the bonds purchased immediately have a maturity date of 10 years, the bonds purchased two years later have maturity dates of eight years, and the bonds purchased four years later carry a maturity date of six years each. The bond bullet strategy is useful when the investor knows that she will need the proceeds from the bonds at a specific date, such as when a child begins college, but wants to protect bond principal at the same time.

BOND SWAPS

Bond swapping is the process of selling one debt instrument (a bond) and replacing it with another. Such swapping is done to save on income taxes, increase the yield to maturity (YTM) or current yield of the bond, or reduce the overall interest rate risk of the bond portfolio. As an example, a tax swap is an exchange that is motivated solely by current tax law considerations. To illustrate such a swap, assume that an investor purchases a $1,000 par value bond now trading in the secondary market for $800. If he swaps that bond for a similar quality bond selling for $800, he now has that same amount of money to invest, plus he is entitled to claim a capital loss of $200. If he is currently in a 25% marginal income tax bracket, he also generates an additional $50 ($200 x 0.25) in cash by virtue of the allowable capital loss. In addition, he can also use the sale proceeds to repurchase the swapped bond for $800 and hold that bond until its scheduled maturity date.

Other additional forms of bond swaps are as follows:

1) *Substitution swap*: This form of swap involves exchanging bonds with similar characteristics selling for different prices. It is done to increase the current yield of the bond.

2) *Inter-market spread swap*: This form of swap involves the exchanging of similar bonds with different coupon rates. It is done to increase the overall rate of return from the bond.

3) *Rate anticipation swap*: This swap attempts to take advantage of expected changes in interest rates. If rates are expected to increase, long-term bonds are swapped for short-term bonds. If rates are expected to decline, short-term bonds are swapped for long-term bonds to take advantage of the expected price increases for the longer-term issues and to lock in higher coupon rates.

4) *Pure yield pickup swap*: Here, a lower yield-to-maturity (YTM) bond is exchanged for a higher yield-to-maturity (YTM) bond. The new bond that replaces the old bond is either a longer-term bond or a lower-quality bond sufficient to generate a higher overall yield to maturity.

TIMING OF INVESTMENT PURCHASES AND SALES

Investment strategies also include the timing of the purchase of securities and their subsequent sale. A so-called *passive investor* actually does not try and time investment purchases and sales at all; rather, he or she practices what is known as a *buy-and-hold* strategy, remaining optimistic that over the long term a considerable profit will be generated, if historical performance is any guide. We now consider the buy-and-hold strategy as well as other timing methods.

Market Timing

Market timing is an attempt to predict the overall direction of the secondary securities market and take advantage of changes in the prices of those securities, either up or down. In the purest form of the strategy, the investor evaluates possible alternatives to the securities market, including real estate, and allocates his or her money accordingly. However, most commonly, the market timing strategy refers to when an investor times his or her purchases of securities while staying fully (or predominately) invested in the secondary market.

There are various trends in the economy or valuation measures of securities to use in assessing when the investor should be in or out of the market. Many of these are integrated into computer software that may be used to assist in the market timing process. The technical analysis method of security selection is also sometimes used in the process. However, historical studies have shown that an investor's rate of return is dramatically reduced if he or she is out of the market for the best 20 to 30 days of market performance. Further, to actually pinpoint exactly when these days will occur is exceedingly difficult to determine. Therefore, an investor or portfolio manager who practices market timing should proceed carefully and realize that such a strategy has not, to date, been proven successful over the long term.

Finally, the market timing strategy should not be confused with the portfolio rebalancing strategies that are currently practiced by many portfolio managers. Portfolio rebalancing is done by portfolio managers to keep the investor's asset allocation consistent with those originally agreed upon between the investment advisor and the client. Over time, given market fluctuations in value, the investor may "drift" from his or her original asset allocation and need to be repositioned. However, portfolio rebalancing is done to comply with investor goals and risk tolerance and does not depend on attempting to time the market to generate possible profits. Indeed, it primarily reflects a mechanical "buy low, sell high" strategy, wherein the assets that have appreciated the most are exchanged for assets that have appreciated the least. As such, portfolio rebalancing is predicated on the premise of *regression/ progression to the mean*, in which those assets that have outperformed will tend to under-perform in the future, whereas those assets that have underperformed will tend to over-perform in the future.

Buy-and-Hold

Passive portfolio management is essentially a long-term *buy-and-hold* strategy. The attractiveness of this strategy is supported by the efficient market hypothesis (EMH). As we have previously learned, in its strongest form, this hypothesis maintains that the current market prices of securities reflect all information (public or private) presently available to investors and that it is pointless to try and achieve superior portfolio performance.

A pure buy-and-hold strategy has several advantages. First, the investor minimizes his or her transaction costs in the acquisition and trading of securities. Over a longer period of time, this can add up to sizeable savings. Second, such a strategy will assist in managing an investor's income tax obligations. Specifically, if securities are held for more than one year from their date of purchase, they are entitled to long-term capital gain treatment. Currently (in the year 2006), the maximum long-term capital gain rate is 15%, as compared to an *ordinary income* maximum rate of 35%. Therefore, a tax savings of 20% can occur (30% if the individual is subject to the 5% long-term capital gain rate) by investing in this manner. Finally, a buy-and-hold strategy ensures that an investor will not be out of the securities market during an upturn in prices. As we have learned, this also means that the investor does not have to pursue the historically fruitless attempt to *time the market*.

Passive Investing/Indexing

In addition to the buy-and-hold strategy, *passive* portfolio management is characterized by a belief that a portfolio's return will be unable to beat a relevant market index, such as the S&P 500, over time. Therefore, *indexing* or investing in index mutual funds is characteristic of an investor who believes in passive management. The purpose of an indexed portfolio is not to beat the targeted index, but merely to match its long-term performance, less any management fees and/or transaction costs. One way to construct a passive or indexed portfolio is to simply buy-and-hold the securities in the index, at their appropriate weightings. This method is known as *replication*, and is characterized by a low tracking error with the actual index that is targeted. A second method of constructing such a portfolio is *sampling*, whereby several securities are chosen to be representative of the targeted overall index.

In contrast, *active* portfolio management is an attempt by the portfolio manager to outperform the benchmark portfolio or index on a risk-adjusted basis. Active portfolio management strategies include such approaches as *sector rotation*, which emphasizes investment in certain economic sectors or industries in response to the next market upturn, and *earnings momentum*, whereby a search for companies with above-average growth of earnings is practiced. When deciding whether to pursue an active management strategy, the investor must weigh its higher costs (in terms of fees and expenses) against the possibility of a higher risk-adjusted rate of return than that of passive indexing. Not surprisingly, academic studies have also shown that the benefits of indexing (passive management) *decline* as the investment expertise of the portfolio manager *increases*. There is also evidence that certain market segments (for example, small capitalization stocks and international stocks, to name two) may, in fact, benefit from active management. This would indicate that some market segments are less efficient than others.

SHORT SELLING

An investor who owns a security is said to be *long* as it relates to that security. Conversely, an individual who does not own the security and borrows it from a third party (normally, a broker-dealer) is said to be *short*. Therefore, a short-selling strategy involves the sale of securities *borrowed from* the investor's broker-dealer. Accordingly, there are several requirements that must be met before an investor may engage in short selling. These are as follows:

1) Short sellers must have a margin account with the broker/dealer.

2) While maintaining their short position, short sellers must reimburse the broker-dealer for any dividends or interest paid on the borrowed securities.

3) Short sales are permitted only on rising prices, referred to as an *uptick*; in other words, the short seller can only sell the borrowed security if the last trade price was less than the current trade price.

4) The net proceeds from the short sale, plus the required margin, are first held by the broker-dealer before being disbursed to the short seller.

So why does an investor sell short and what are the mechanics involved in doing so? An investor sells short because he or she believes that the market (and particular security *shorted*) will *decline* in price, and a profit can then be made on the subsequent repurchase of the security. Mechanically, when the price declines, the short seller instructs his or her broker-dealer to sell the borrowed security, then repurchase the security at the lower price and, finally, cancel (*cover*) the short position by replacing the borrowed security with the real security. The short seller profits by the difference between the price at which the borrowed stock was sold and the price at which it was repurchased. This difference constitutes either short-term or long-term capital gain, depending on the length of time (*holding period*) that the short seller owned the repurchased security. If the short seller closes out the short position by purchasing the securities after they have appreciated in value, he or she incurs either a short-term or long-term capital loss.

An alternative to engaging in short selling is simply to purchase a put option on the targeted security, thereby permitting the investor to sell the security if its price declines. In the event that the price of the security instead increases, the investor only sacrifices the amount expended to purchase the put option (that is, the option's premium). Therefore, an individual who sells short is *more at risk* than the investor who simply buys a put. Specifically, selling short is highly risky because if the price of the borrowed security increases, rather than declines, the seller will have to buy back the security at its higher price. However, if the short seller is correct in his or her anticipation that the price of the borrowed security will decrease in the relatively near future (note that there is no time limit on when a short sale must be closed out), the leverage potential involved in using borrowed money to repurchase the security will increase the percentage gain of the investor.

Example 15-2: Assume that your client, Jeb, sells short MEJ stock currently trading at $25 per share. He does this via a margin account established for him by his broker-dealer. The margin requirement (that is, the amount of the cash that must be deposited by Jeb) is 50%. If the price of MEJ stock declines to $20 and Jeb covers his short position by purchasing (or repurchasing) the stock at that price, he makes a $5 profit ($25 - $20). However, his actual percentage gain is 100% or the difference between the $12.50 that he had to deposit to sell short MEJ stock and the repurchased $25 sale price of the stock. Therefore, he has leveraged a 20% gain if he bought and sold the stock directly ($5 ÷ $25) into a 100% gain. (However, you should also note that if Jeb had been incorrect in his perception that the price of MEJ stock would decline, and if its price had instead increased to $60 per share before he covered his short position, he would have incurred a 140% loss [($60 - $25) ÷ $25]. Accordingly, an investor who engages in short selling should be aware of the amplified risk for loss as well as the potential for a significant gain.)

Short Selling Against the Box

Investors use short sales for *hedging purposes* (to limit the risk of investment loss) when they sell short *against the box*. (Note that additional hedging strategies are the subject of the next chapter, chapter 16, in this textbook). Selling short against the box means that an investor sells short securities that they also own (or are *long*) in their portfolio. This technique offers perfect negative correlation of securities because gains or losses that the investor holds in the long position are matched by gains or losses in the short position. As a result, the economic value of the investor's position does not change.

Originally, short selling against the box was used primarily for income tax reasons. That is, an investor who had an appreciated position in a security that he or she wanted to sell, but did not want to incur a taxable gain for income tax purposes, would enter into such a strategy. As a result, the strategy permitted the investor to defer the tax bill until the position was closed (perhaps to a later year when he or she was in a lower marginal tax bracket), while eliminating all economic risk in the meantime as if the position had been sold. However, under current tax law, short sales against the box are now treated as *constructive sales*, meaning that a tax gain on the appreciated long position must be recognized in the tax year in which the investor enters into the short sale. Accordingly, investors must now increase the basis of their long position by the amount of their realized gain, just as if they had actually sold and repurchased the securities, and begin a new holding period for income tax purposes.

SECURITY SELECTION AND ANALYSIS

An individual who practices active portfolio management is involved in active security selection. As such, this selection is made using the *fundamental analysis* of securities, the *technical analysis* of securities or, sometimes, both.

Fundamental Analysis

All fundamental analysts consider both particular company fundamentals and broader economic trends, although the order in which they do so (and the emphasis they place on each) depends on their orientation as either a *top down* or *bottom up* analyst (see subsequent discussion).

With respect to particular company fundamentals, a fundamental analyst concentrates on three critical financial statements: 1) the company balance sheet; 2) the company income statement; and 3) the company statement of cash flows. The *balance sheet* reflects the resources of the company (assets) and the claims against those resources (liabilities). The difference between the two is the retained earnings of the company, equivalent to the net worth of an individual on his or her statement of financial position. Of course, the amount of retained earnings is critical since it represents either capital for the future growth of the company (capital appreciation of its stock) or a possible source for future dividend payments to the company's stockholders. In addition, certain other ratios of interest to the fundamental analyst may be determined from analysis of the company balance sheet. The company *income statement* shows how profitable company operations were during a given period of time (usually quarterly). Typically, three years of statements are provided for the analysis of the fundamental analyst. Finally, the third important statement, *the statement of cash flows*, presents the actual cash received and paid out during the reporting period. Cash flow is important because it ultimately reflects the amount necessary to pay employees/workers, vendors, creditors, and company stockholders. The statement is normally divided into operating cash flows, investing cash flows, and financing cash flows.

With respect to economic trends, a fundamental analyst researches such factors as the gross domestic product (GDP), the unemployment rate, the consumer price index (CPI), and the producers price index (PPI). His or her goal in researching these factors is to predict the future direction of the economy and, therefore, the possible future direction of price movements in the stock of the particular company or industry sector that is being reviewed. In addition to the above *macro* economic factors, the fundamental analyst pays close attention to the actions of the Federal Reserve Board (the Fed) as it is in charge of the monetary supply and targets the overall interest rate reflected in the economy. Indeed, the Federal Reserve Open Market Committee (FOMC) that conducts *open market operations* on behalf of the Fed is a closely-watched barometer of Fed sentiment and the likely direction of future interest rates. If the FOMC is pursuing an expansionary monetary policy, it will *buy* U.S Treasury securities, ultimately driving market interest rates *down*; whereas, if pursuing a contractionary monetary policy, it will *sell* U.S. Treasury securities, ultimately forcing market interest rates *up*.

1. Top-Down Analysis

Top-down fundamental analysts begin with researching the overall economy and current state of the secondary market. Specifically, the analyst examines the overall economy and selects an industry that he or she believes will perform best over an upcoming time frame (for example, five years). The analyst then screens a database of securities to find acceptable companies in this industry. Finally, depending on his or her investment orientation (for example, a value or growth investor), the analyst narrows down (*targets*) the list of companies in the industry by focusing on companies that have the preferred characteristics. For example, a fundamental analyst that is following a *value* approach will target companies that have a low stock price relative to its earnings. An analyst that is pursing a *growth* approach will be more interested in companies that exhibit a potential for superior earnings growth with the current stock price being of less consequence.

2. Bottom-Up Analysis

Bottom-up fundamental analysts often call themselves *stock pickers*. This is because they attempt to identify the best securities to buy (and the right price at which to buy them) *regardless* of the market sector or industry. A bottom-up analyst typically begins, first, with an examination of the company fundamentals, often by screening large databases of securities. Once identifying securities of interest, he or she then considers the *prospect* for the company, the sector or the industry and, ultimately, the overall economy. Like the top-down analyst, the bottom-up analyst will select securities (*stock pick*) based on his or her investment orientation and then report the chosen securities to the field or company representatives via a periodically scheduled research letter.

3. Ratio Analysis

As noted, all fundamental analysts employ ratio analysis in analyzing the financial strengths or weaknesses of a company. These ratios are used to compare the financial performance and position of one company to another and, then, to make an investment decision regarding the purchase or non-purchase of its stock. The general categories that the ratios fall into are those that show the company's liquidity and solvency; efficiency in business operations; profitability; and price multiples (of its stock).

Likely the most important of the *liquidity and solvency ratios* is the company's *current ratio* as determined from the company's balance sheet. The current ratio is found by dividing the company's current assets by its current liabilities and shows the ability of the company to pay its short term liabilities or obligations to employees, suppliers, and creditors. While there is no rule of thumb for what is an appropriate ratio, certainly the higher the current ratio the better, as it reflects the overall solvency of the company. In addition, this ratio should be higher than one, but not so great as to indicate that company resources are being used inefficiently. Other liquidity and solvency ratios include a company's *debt ratio* (total liabilities divided by total assets) and the *times interest earned ratio*, computed by dividing the company's earnings before interest and taxes by its interest expense.

Efficiency ratios illustrate how effectively the company is managing its business operations. Accordingly, various turnover ratios are investigated, including the company's *accounts receivable turnover* (sales divided by average accounts receivable), its *inventory turnover* (cost of goods sold divided by average inventory), and the *total asset turnover* (sales divided by average total assets). Certainly for a manufacturing corporation (such as an automobile company), its inventory turnover is critical as it measures how often it depletes its current inventory and must generate more. A longer-than-normal time period of days of inventory on hand may indicate that a company is not being very efficient in its operations..

Profitability ratios are very important to the fundamental analyst since they measure how much money a company is making and the earnings that it may potentially distribute to shareholders. Generally, any company (whether manufacturing or service-related) will strive to have as high a *net profit margin* (net income divided by sales) as possible. Another frequently analyzed profitability ratio is a company's *return on equity (ROE)*, found by dividing its earnings available for common shareholders (after any preferred dividends are paid) by the company's common equity or book value. See chapter 12 for more on book value. Related to the company's ROE is its *dividends payout ratio*, determined by dividing its common dividends paid per share by its earnings available for common shareholders. You should note that the denominator for the company's dividend payout ratio is *the same* as the numerator for its ROE, thus the common relationship.

Example 15-3: Assume that the company balance sheet for Amalgamated Utilities, Inc. reflects the following:

Common equity: $40.00 per share
Common dividends paid: $2.00 per share
Earnings available for common shareholders: $5.00 per share.

Therefore, the return on common equity (ROE) for Amalgamated Utilities, Inc. is 12.5% or $5.00 per share divided by $40.00 per share and its dividend payout ratio is 40% or $2.00 per share divided by $5.00 per share. These ratios would then be compared to utility stocks generally to determine if Amalgamated was a relative *buy* (undervalued) or *sell* (overvalued) investment asset.

Finally, the *price multiples* used by fundamental analysts have been discussed before, most notably in the chapter on valuation of stock, chapter 12, in this textbook. A stock's *price earnings ratio* (its market price per share divided by its earnings per share) is a frequently-used method of relative valuation in determining whether a stock should be bought or sold. Other commonly used price multiples are the stock's *price to book value* and its *price to free or operating cash flow* (both computed on a per share basis).

Technical Analysis

As we learned in chapter 10, an individual who believes in all forms of the efficient market hypothesis (EMH) considers the approaches used in the technical analysis of securities to be of *no value*. Nevertheless, technical analysis assumes that important information is reflected in past market data such as price and trading volume that can be charted to uncover trends in future market activity. Because of their heavy reliance on charts or graphical representation of data, technical analysts are sometimes called *chartists*, but such analysts inherently believe that markets are *not efficient* and that value to an investor may be generated by their efforts.

In its simplest form, technical analysis involves the preparation of charting past price and volume data for a particular security or industry sector. As a result, these charts produce certain trends and concepts that may be used to determine the future activity in (and price of) the security. Such terms as the *moving average* of the security, its upwards and downwards *trendline*, and *head and shoulders formation* are used by technical analysts to explain when it may be preferable to buy or sell the security. Figure 15-1 below illustrates a head and shoulders bottom indicating a bullish reversal (up) of a previous downtrend in the market. A technical analyst would observe the second shoulder line indicated by past price movements of the security to determine when to buy. For example, if the price of the security increases *above* the second shoulder formation, the analyst would consider that to be a *buy signal*.

Figure 15-1

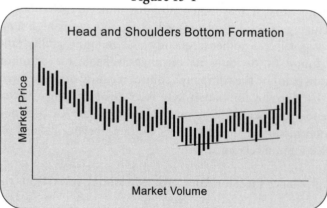

230 ⓅKaplan University

Support and *resistance* levels are also important to technical analysts. Stock prices may move within a narrow trading range for months or even years. The bottom of this trading range is known as the *support level* of the stock and the top of this trading range is known as its *resistance level*. See Figure 15-2 below. When a stock declines to its support level, the low price attracts buyers, whose buying then supports the price and keeps it from declining further. When a stock increases to its resistance level, the high price attracts sellers, whose selling then prevents the stock price from rising further. A decline through the support level is referred to as a *bearish breakout* and a rise through the resistance level is called a *bullish breakout*.

There are also certain theories used by technical analysts to describe overall market trends. Among these are:

Figure 15-2

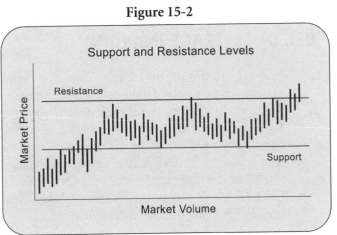

1) *The Dow Theory*: According to this theory, the primary trend in a bull market is a series of higher highs and higher lows. In a bear market, the primary trend is a series of lower highs and lower lows. Daily fluctuations in the market are considered irrelevant in predicting future behavior.

2) *The Odd-Lot Theory*: Typically, small investors engage in odd-lot (less than 100 shares at once) trading. Adherents of the odd-lot theory believe that investors invariably buy and sell at the wrong time. Therefore, when odd-lot traders buy (sell), odd-lot analysts are bearish (bullish).

3) *The Short Interest Theory*: Short interest refers to the number of market shares that have been sold short (see previous discussion on short selling). Therefore, because short positions must eventually be *covered*, some technical analysts believe that short interest reflects market demand. A high amount of short interest is considered bullish and a low amount of short interest is considered bearish.

4) *The Mutual Fund Cash Position Theory*: If a mutual fund portfolio manager is holding a great amount of cash (that is, if he or she remains relatively un-invested in the securities market), it is considered a bullish signal to the technical analysts. This is because, ultimately, this cash will find its way to the market and be used to buy outstanding shares of stock. Conversely, a low amount of cash is considered bearish to the analyst since the portfolio manager is already relatively fully invested in the market.

5) *Investment Advisory Opinions*: Many technical analysts believe that if a large proportion of investment advisory services are pessimistic (bearish) this signals the approach of a market trough and the onset of a bull market. Specifically, the technician's market trading rule resulting from this theory is that a 60 percent bearish sentiment among investment advisory services indicates a major market *bottom*, while a 60 percent bullish sentiment suggests a major market *top*.

6) *Barron's Confidence Index*: Published by *Barron's* financial newspaper, the Confidence Index is the ratio of *Barron's* average yield on 10 investment-grade bonds divided by the yield on the Dow Jones average of 40 lower-grade bonds. Technical analysts believe that the ratio is a bullish indicator when investors are investing in lower-quality bonds for the added yield, therefore causing the yield spread to decline and the Confidence Index to increase. Conversely, when investors are bearish, they avoid investing in lower-quality bonds, therefore causing the yield spread to increase and the Confidence Index to decline.

USE OF LEVERAGE (MARGIN)

Leverage involves the use of techniques that permit investors to benefit from an investment of a given amount by using less of their own money. In such manner, the investor can thereby increase both their dollar amount of profit and their percentage return (although at increased risk since the debt used to *lever* the investment must eventually be repaid). With respect to securities investing, leverage commonly translates to the use of *margin* and the establishment of a margin account by the investor with his or her broker-dealer. Therefore, a margin account permits an investor to borrow from the broker-dealer using stocks and other securities as security (collateral) for the loan. However, certain financial requirements must be met by the investor before he or she is allowed to engage in market trading involving the use of margin.

As with all security transactions, there are both advantages and disadvantages associated with the creation of a margin account by the investor. Likely, the major advantage of such an account is the ability of the investor to increase the size of his or her profit beyond that possible if only personal funds are used (see Example 15-4 below). In addition, the investor may increase his or her potential gain by the receipt of dividends received from the additional shares purchased with the use of leverage.

Example 15-4: Assume that Brad purchases 1,000 shares of CDO stock at $30 per share using $30,000 of his own money. Further assume that CDO stock appreciates to $40 per share when Brad sells all of his shares. Therefore, he has realized a gain of $10,000 ($40,000 less $30,000) on the stock. Alternatively, if Brad had bought CDO stock through a margin account with a 50% initial margin requirement, his gain would have increased considerably. For instance, he could have purchased an additional 1,000 shares of the stock while still only using $30,000 of his own money. If his 2,000 share total then appreciates the same $10 per share, his gain is now $20,000 ($80,000 less his original $30,000 position and the $30,000 of borrowed money). In addition, Brad is now eligible to receive dividends on 2,000 shares of CDO stock rather than only 1,000 shares. (You should also note that Brad has increased the percentage return on his own funds from 33% where margin is *not* used—or $10,000 divided by $30,000— to 166% where margin *is* used - or $50,000 divided by $30,000. However, this increased percentage return is, of course, *before* the after-tax cost of borrowing the $30,000 from the broker-dealer is taken into account.)

There are also a number of disadvantages that investors need to consider before deciding to establish a margin account. These major disadvantages are as follows:

1) Investors can lose more funds than they deposit in the margin account. As we shall see in the upcoming Example 15-6, a decline in the value of securities purchased on margin may require investors to provide additional monies to the broker-dealer making the loan in order to avoid the forced sale of those securities.

2) The broker-dealer may sell the margined securities without contacting the investor. If the investor's equity in the margin account falls below the maintenance margin percentage required by the broker-dealer, the firm can sell the securities in the account and the investor has no legal recourse.

3) Investors are not entitled to a grace period or any other extension of time to satisfy a so-called *margin call*. While, as a practical matter, most broker-dealers will provide an extension of time for the investor to deposit additional monies, by law they are *not required* to do so.

Computation of Margin Call and/or Required Investor Equity

To understand the subsequent examples and computations, it is first necessary that you understand certain commonly-used terms with respect to margin trading. These are as follows:

- *Initial margin requirement*: The percentage of the original price of purchased securities that must be provided by the investor. This amount is established by the Federal Reserve Board pursuant to Regulation T of the Securities Act of 1934 and is currently 50%.

- *Maintenance margin percentage*: The level at which the investor will be required to add additional funds to the margin account established by his or her broker-dealer. This percentage is usually set at 35% of the current fair market of the margined securities but may differ among broker-dealers (for example, it could be as low as 25 or 30 percent of the current fair market value of the margined securities).

- *Debit balance*: The amount owed to the broker-dealer by the investor, including the original amount borrowed plus any interest accrued and due.

- *Equity / Actual Equity*: The current fair market value of the margined securities less the debit balance.

Accordingly, when using several of these terms, the formula for determining when a margin call to the investor by the broker-dealer will occur is:

$$\text{Margin Call} = \frac{(1 - \text{Initial margin requirement})}{(1 - \text{Maintenance margin percentage})} \times \text{Purchase Price of Stock}$$

You should also note that the numerator of this formula is equal to the amount owed to the broker-dealer and constitutes the debit balance of the investor (after accounting for any interest accrued and due).

Example 15-5: Jason buys 100 shares of Tripedia Company stock, currently trading at $40 per share, using a margin account with a 50% initial margin requirement. Therefore, Jason can actually purchase 200 shares of Tripedia since he uses $4,000 of his own money and borrows $4,000 from his broker-dealer. Jason is now concerned, however, about when he might receive a margin call. At which trading price do you tell him that a margin call will begin, assuming that a 35% maintenance margin percentage is established by the broker-dealer? The answer is $30.77 computed as follows:

$$\text{Margin Call} = \frac{(1 - .050)}{(1-0.035)} \times \$40.00 = \frac{0.50}{0.65} \times \$40.00 = 0.7692 \times \$40.00 = \$30.77$$

Example 15-6: Assume the same facts as in Example 15-5, but that the stock price of Tripedia company stock declines to $25.00. How much money is Jason now required to deposit with his broker-dealer so as to avoid a forced sale of the previously-purchased securities? The answer is $750 computed as follows (on a per-share basis):

Required Equity		Actual Equity	
Stock Value	$25.00	Stock Value	$25.00
Equity %	35%	Debit Balance	($20.00) [$4,000/200]
Required Equity $	8.75	Actual Equity	$ 5.00

Therefore, Jason will be required by the broker-dealer to deposit an additional $3.75 per share ($8.75 less $5.00) or a total dollar amount of $750 ($3.75 x 200 shares purchased) to maintain the equity position of 35%. In other words, the actual equity position must be compared to the required equity position to determine if there is a deficit or additional deposit that is due by Jason.

Finally, funds that are borrowed from a bank by the broker-dealer, and which are based on the firm's account balances, are referred to as *call loans*. The applicable rate charged on such loans by the bank (known as the *call loan rate*) may be determined by referencing a financial newspaper, such as the *Wall Street Journal*.

VALUE VS. GROWTH INVESTING

This chapter concludes with a brief look at the two primary styles of investing used by many investors today, value and/or growth investing.

Value and growth investing are really just different sides of the same "investment coin." In this case, however, the investment coin is the price/earnings (P/E) ratio of stocks. *Value investing* is a strategy that tends to concentrate on the *numerator* of that ratio (or price), while *growth investing* focuses on the *denominator* of that ratio (or earnings). Specifically, value investing assumes that the current P/E ratio is *below* its natural level and that an efficient market will soon recognize this and drive the stock price upward. Value investors are disciples of the late Benjamin Graham, who looked for stocks that sold for two thirds or less of their net current assets and stocks with high dividend yields and low P/E ratios, and the current mega-investor Warren Buffett. In contrast, growth investors assume that the P/E ratio will remain *constant* over the near term and the stock price in an efficient market will increase as the forecasted earnings growth of the issuing company is realized. Such investors look for *growth stocks*, that is, stocks of a company that has a significant ability to develop products with a minimum of marketplace competition. These stocks usually have a superior rate of earnings growth (usually 15 percent a year or more), low dividend payouts, and an above-average price to earnings ratio.

As with investment strategies generally, there is no absolutely correct answer regarding which investment style— value or growth— is best. In recent years, given the *flatness* of the broader secondary market, value strategies have come into prominence; however, previous to this time (for example, in the late 1990s), growth investing proponents seemed to dominate. It is likely fair to assert that an investor should consider *both* strategies in constructing his or her portfolio and, perhaps, weight the portfolio with a combination of each active-management strategy if so inclined.

IMPORTANT CONCEPTS

Investment policy statement

Benchmark

Value-weighted index

Price-weighted index

Dollar cost averaging

Averaging down

Share averaging

Dividend reinvestment plans (DRIPs)

Bond ladder

Bond barbell

Bond bullet

Bond swap

Market timing

Buy-and-hold

Passive portfolio management

Indexing

Active portfolio management

Short selling

Short selling against the box

Fundamental analysis of securities

Top-down analysis

Bottom-up analysis

Liquidity and solvency ratios

Current ratio

Efficiency ratios

Profitability ratios

Return on equity

Dividends payout ratio

Price multiples ratios

Technical analysis of securities

Dow Theory

Odd-Lot Theory

Short Interest Theory

Mutual Fund Cash Position Theory

Investment advisory opinions

Barron's Confidence Index

Leverage

Margin account

Margin call

Initial margin percentage

Maintenance margin percentage

Value investing

Growth investing

QUESTIONS FOR REVIEW

1. What are the two major components of a complete and thorough investment policy statement?

2. List five constraints that should be part of any investment policy statement.

3. What are the characteristics of an appropriate benchmark by which to judge investment performance?

4. What is the difference between a value-weighted and a price-weighted index? Give an example of each type of index.

5. What is the most common type of formula investing? Explain this technique and its practical importance for an investor.

6. When does dollar cost averaging work best? When does it not work well?

7. What is share averaging and how does it differ from dollar cost averaging?

8. Who offers dividend reinvestment plans (DRIPs) and why should an investor consider such a plan?

9. Describe the following types of investment strategies involving the periodic purchase of bonds:

   • Bond ladders

   • Bond barbells

   • Bond bullets

10. Why does an investor (or portfolio manager) engage in a bond swap?

11. Describe the following types of bond swaps and when each might be used by a fixed-income investor:

   • Substitution swap

   • Intermarket spread swap

   • Rate anticipation swap

   • Pure yield pickup swap

12. What is market timing? How does it compare to the portfolio rebalancing strategy currently practiced by many portfolio managers?

13. What type of investment theory or hypothesis is inherently being followed by a pure buy-and-hold investment strategy? Explain.

14. What are three advantages of the buy-and-hold investment strategy?

15. Indexing is a primary method of what type of portfolio management strategy? What is the goal of this type of portfolio management strategy?

16. Complete the following sentence: "_____ portfolio management is an attempt by the portfolio manager to outperform the benchmark portfolio or index on a risk-adjusted basis." Then list and describe several examples of this type of portfolio management.

17. What is selling short and what are the technical requirements that must be met before an investor may engage in this strategy?

18. Why does an investor sell short and what are the mechanics involved in doing so? Specifically, how does the investor profit from such activity?

19. What is an alternative to selling short and is it more or less risky? Explain.

20. What is meant by the term short selling against the box and why was it originally used? Now, what is the taxable result of such strategy?

21. Contrast the fundamental analysis of securities to the technical analysis of securities. Which of these two approaches uses company financial statements?

22. Assume that an investment advisor first examines the overall economy and selects an industry that she believes will outperform the market over the upcoming time period. She then screens a database of companies in whose stocks to invest. What type of security selection is she practicing?

23. What are four general categories of ratios that may be used in selecting securities based on ratio analysis?

24. If you divide a company's earnings available for common shareholders by the company's book value, what ratio is derived? What is a complementary ratio that may also be determined if ascertaining the company's earnings available for common shareholders?

25. What is a head and shoulders formation and what type of analyst uses this concept?

26. Explain the following types of theories used by a technical analyst:

      • The Dow Theory
      • The Odd-Lot Theory
      • The Short Interest Theory
      • The Mutual Fund Cash Position Theory
      • Investment Advisory Opinions
      • *Barron's* Confidence Index

27. Why does an investor engage in leveraging techniques? What is the most common form of this technique used in the securities industry?

28. List three disadvantages associated with the establishment of a margin account by an investor.

29. Define the terms initial margin requirement and maintenance margin percentage and explain how they are used in the computation of when an investor may expect to receive a margin call.

30. Contrast the focus of a value investor to that of a growth investor. What kinds of stocks are of interest to each type of investor?

SUGGESTIONS FOR ADDITIONAL READING

Tools and Techniques of Investment Planning, Stephen R. Leimberg, Robert T. LeClair, Robert J. Doyle, Jr., and Thomas R. Robinson, The National Underwriter Company, 2004.

Investments: An Introduction, 7th edition, Herbert B. Mayo, Thomson/ South-Western, 2002.

Investment Analysis and Portfolio Management, 7th edition, Frank K. Reilly and Keith C. Brown, Thomson/South-Western, 2003.

The Wall Street Journal Guide to Money and Investing, 3rd edition, Kenneth M. Morris and Virginia B. Morris, Fireside Publishing, 2004.

Hedging and
Options Strategies

• • •

For purposes of examination, CFP Board of Standards, Inc. is interested in you, the student, understanding the definition of *hedging* versus *speculation*. Furthermore, as a financial planner, you should attempt (presuming suitability requirements are met) to have your client *hedge* (not *speculate*) if concerned about minimizing his or her risk of investment loss. This chapter addresses certain popular hedging techniques, including the use of derivative or alternative investments. Alternative investments were previously introduced in chapter 7 of this textbook.

Upon completing this chapter, you should be able to:

- Contrast hedging techniques to those used primarily for speculation
- Explain the primary characteristics of a futures contract
- Describe basic option transactions
- Analyze a given situation in using options to protect or *hedge* an investor position
- Describe multiple option transactions
- Identify types of non-equity options and their use as a hedging technique
- Discuss the income tax rules that apply to equity option transactions

HEDGING VS. SPECULATION

A *speculator* is an investor (sometimes referred to as a *trader*) that does not typically own the underlying security in which he or she is speculating or, in the case of commodity futures, does not own the underlying product. In other words, a speculator is not currently *involved* in the investment in the same way as an individual who is simply trying to protect against the risk of significant loss. Indeed, a speculator is an investor who buys an asset and hopes to sell it rather quickly and for a substantial profit. Essentially, speculation is a means of *increasing* the investor's risk since he or she is attempting to outguess the market both in terms of time and direction.

On the other hand, a *hedger* is an investor who typically does own the underlying security or product in which he or she is hedging. In other words, a hedger *is* currently involved in the success or failure of the investment. Mechanically, a hedger tries to limit the risk of investment loss by taking an offsetting position from the position he or she is already in. For example, if a farmer already owns the commodity where he is trying to minimize the risk of loss, he is said to be *long* in that commodity. He would therefore go *short* by entering into a futures contract permitting him to sell the commodity at a specified price in the future (and minimizing his risk of how much he could lose if the price of that commodity went down in the meantime). Essentially, hedging is a means of *reducing* the investor's risk while trying to take advantage of market price fluctuations (and *not* attempting to outguess the market).

Hedging includes both investment strategies and investment tools. In terms of *strategies*, a hedger follows the basic principles of sound investing or: 1) portfolio diversification and management theory and 2) proper asset allocation. The investment *tools* of a hedger involve the use of derivative securities, notably 1) futures contracts, 2) the buying and selling (writing) of options, and 3) a combination of option contracts that are variations of the basic forms. The hedger's tools are the focus of the remaining sections of this chapter.

FUTURES CONTRACTS

A *futures contract* is an agreement between a buyer, seller, and some third party exchange (such as a commodity exchange) for the future delivery of an asset at a specified date and for a specified price. You should note that the same goal may be achieved between private parties without the involvement of the third-party exchange. However in that case, the agreement is known as a *forward contract*.

There are essentially three types of futures contracts, those involving: 1) commodities, 2) financial instruments, and 3) foreign currencies. Likely the most well known of these types of futures contracts involves the buying and selling of commodities. Therefore, all subsequent examples of how the futures market operates will involve commodities.

An investor or producer may become involved in the futures market when he or she desires a high degree of leverage in investing. This leverage derives from the low margin requirements of the futures market. For example, compared to margins of 50% on most securities (see chapter 15), margins on commodity futures are extremely minimal. Specifically, an investor can likely finance up to 95% of the value of the futures contract at the time of purchase, meaning that only a small cash deposit of only 5% needs to be made initially. In addition, unlike margins accounts for the purchase of securities that are interest bearing, the investor pays *no* interest on the unpaid balance in a commodities futures contract.

Operationally, an investor may also take part in a so-called *managed futures* program with a broker-dealer. Under this arrangement, the broker-dealer has the discretionary power to trade in the futures market for the investor's account. An additional characteristic of this program is that the broker may participate in the profits earned for the account in addition to any commissions that may be generated through the trading activity within the futures market.

A futures contract may be settled (*closed out*) by either *delivery* or *offset*. Delivery means (in the case of commodities) actual transfer of the commodity to the other party (normally, a speculator). Since delivery often proves to be practically imprudent (can you imagine dumping a load of corn at the doorstep of an urban speculator?) most futures contracts are settled by offset. This means that the buyer of the futures contract sells his or her position sometime prior to the date of actual delivery of the commodity and the seller of the contract buys that position.

> **Example 16-1:** Assume that a farmer plants soybeans in June and expects to harvest them during the month of September. In June, the cash (*spot*) price for soybeans is $5.00 per bushel. Also assume that the price of November soybean futures is $5.25 per bushel. The farmer, therefore, *shorts* his crop by selling a November soybean futures contracts at $5.25 per bushel. By the beginning of September, the soybean cash price has fallen to $4.74 per bushel. Accordingly, the farmer sells his soybeans to the local elevator for $4.74 a bushel and then purchases a November soybeans futures contract, currently priced at $4.95 a bushel. The 30-cent gain in the futures market ($5.25 sale price less $4.95 purchase price) *offsets* the lower price the farmer receives for his soybeans, thus allowing the farmer to receive a net selling price of $5.04 per bushel ($4.74 sale price plus 30-cent gain).

Finally, as you should have noted, Example 16-1 involves a farmer who is *hedging* his commodity investment. In the example, the farmer is *long* (owns) the soybeans in the first instance and, then, because he is concerned that cash prices may fall, sells (goes *short*) a futures contract on the commodity. This illustrates the offsetting positions that are fundamental to the concept of hedging and the attempt to minimize the risk of investment loss. Accordingly, you should analyze hedging transactions based on 1) what position does the hedger already occupy (that is, is he long or short) and 2) what position does the hedger need to assume in order to offset his or her original position. If one follows these steps, one will likely never be confused in trying to understand what may at times seem like an extremely complex set of transactions.

BASIC OPTION TRANSACTIONS

Similar to futures contracts, options contracts involve the delivery of a specified property (usually securities) at a specified time and at a specified price. Also, similar to the futures market, there is an offsetting long and short position in the options exchange. However, with options, one of these positions (the one purchasing the option) has only the *right* to buy or sell the security, while the other side (the one selling or writing the option) has the *obligation* to sell or buy if the other side exercises the option. In contrast, *both positions* in the futures market have the *obligation* to buy or sell depending on whether they are long or short.

There are four basic positions in the options market. They are:

1) Purchasing or buying a call

2) Selling (*writing*) a call

3) Purchasing or buying a put

4) Selling (*writing*) a put

However, any of these may be combined with another position to form a multiple option transaction, as we shall learn.

The amount that an investor (or speculator) pays for an option is called the option's *premium*. An option's premium reflects two types of value:

1) The option's *intrinsic value* of the amount by which the option is *in the money* (see chapter 7 in this text)

2) The option's *time value* or the market's perceived worth of the time remaining to the expiration date of the option

Example 16-2: Assume that a February 35 call option on MAD stock carries a premium of 4 1/2. From chapter 7, you will recall that a call option has intrinsic value whenever the stock's market price exceeds the exercise price of the option. Therefore, if the market price of MAD stock closed yesterday at 37 7/8, the intrinsic value of the stock is 2 7/8. We then also know that the time value of the call option is 1 5/8 since the option's intrinsic value (2 7/8) when added to its time value (1 5/8) must equal the option's premium (4 1/2).

Accordingly, an option has time value anytime the option's premium *exceeds* its intrinsic value. Time value represents the time remaining before the expiration of the option and the more time that remains, the greater the chance for a change in the underlying stock price. More distant expirations, of course, have greater time value. Since there is no intrinsic value when the market price of the underlying stock and the exercise price of the option are equal, the time value of the option is at its maximum at this point and, indeed, constitutes the *entire value* of the option's premium.

The factor with the greatest impact on the premium of an option, related to its intrinsic value component, is the *volatility* of the underlying stock. A stock that is highly volatile has the potential to experience greater price changes. However, as we have learned, this same stock also has the possibility for the greatest investor reward or profit. If the market price for such a stock falls from one day to the next, the premium for a *call* (or option to buy) would *fall* and the premium for a *put* (option to sell) would *rise*.

Buying Calls

An investor will buy a call option in hopes that the underlying stock will *increase* in value. In other words, he or she is *bullish* on the prospects for the underlying stock. By purchasing or buying a call option, an investor can profit from an increase in the stock price while investing only a relatively small amount of money (the option's premium). As a result, the maximum gain available to the call buyer or owner is, theoretically, *unlimited* with his or her maximum loss limited only to the option's premium.

Other reasons for buying a call are:

1) *Deferring a decision*: An investor can buy a call on a stock and lock in the purchase price until the option expires. In turn, this also permits him or her to postpone making a financial commitment other than the cost of the premium until the expiration date of the option.

2) *Diversifying holdings*: With limited funds, an investor can buy calls on a variety of stocks, therefore diversifying his or her portfolio.

3) *Speculation*: Investors can speculate on the upward price movement of the stock by paying only the premium when purchasing the actual stock would require a potentially far greater investment.

4) *Protect (hedge) a stock position*: Investors can use calls conservatively to act as an insurance policy against adverse market performance.

Selling or Writing Calls

An investor would sell— or write— a call in hopes that the underlying stock price will *decline* or at least stay the same. In other words, he or she is *bearish* on the prospects for the underlying stock. A call option is usually written on a stock that may have achieved a new high in price and is part of a trend that is not expected to continue. If the call is *uncovered* or *naked* (that is, if the seller does *not* already own the underlying stock), the seller's maximum gain is the premium received. His or her maximum loss is, however, theoretically unlimited since the seller could be forced to buy the stock at a potentially infinite price if the option is exercised against him or her.

Other reasons for selling or writing a call are:

1) *Receipt of income*: Premium income may be earned for a portfolio by writing calls. Investors then hope for expiration of the calls (that is, the underlying stock price does not rise), so that they can keep the premium income without any offsetting loss.

2) *Locking in a stock price*: If an investor has already made a profit from holding a stock and is interested in selling it, a call can be written at an exercise price that will ensure that the profit is realized.

3) *Speculation*: By writing calls an investor can profit if the underlying stock's price falls below or remains at the exercise price. The profit is the amount of the premium collected for the call.

4) *Protect (hedge) a stock position*: The premium that is collected from writing the call may be used to offset any loss if the underlying stock price rises.

Buying Puts

An investor will buy a put option in hopes that the underlying stock will *decline* in value. In other words, he or she is *bearish* on the prospects for the underlying stock. By purchasing or buying puts an investor can profit from a decrease in the stock's price while investing a relatively small amount of money. As a result, the maximum gain available to a put buyer is the exercise price of the option less the premium paid for the option. However, his or her maximum loss is limited to the amount of the premium paid for the put option.

Other reasons for buying a put are:

1) *Deferring a decision*: An investor can buy a put on a stock and lock in a sales price until the option expires. This allows him or her to postpone a selling decision until the expiration date of the option.

2) *Speculation*: Investors can speculate on the downward price of a stock that is not owned by paying only the premium for the option. (Note that this is akin to selling a stock *short*, but with much less risk, given that the loss to the put buyer is limited to the premium paid, whereas the short seller's loss is potentially much greater.)

3) *Protect or (hedge) a stock position*: Investors can use puts conservatively to act as an insurance policy against adverse market performance.

Selling or Writing Puts

An investor would sell or write a put in hopes that the underlying stock price will *increase* in value. In other words, the investor is *bullish* on the prospects for the underlying stock. Puts are usually written on stocks that have recently experienced a new market low in price and is part of a trend that is not expected to continue. If the put is uncovered, the put writer's maximum gain is the premium received. His or her maximum loss is the put option's exercise price less the premium received and occurs when the underlying stock price drops to zero.

Other reasons for selling or writing a put are:

1) *Receipt of income*: Premium income may be earned for a portfolio by writing puts. Investors then hope for the expiration of the puts (that is, the underlying stock price does not decline), so that they can keep the premium without any offsetting loss.

2) *Speculation*: By writing puts, an investor can profit if the underlying stock's price rises or remains at the exercise price. The profit is the amount of the premium collected for the put.

3) *Buying stock below its current price*: The premium received from writing puts may be used to offset the cost of the stock when and if the put is exercised against the writer. Accordingly, the writer buys the underlying stock at a price that is reduced by the premium received.

A summary of the maximum economic gain and loss with respect to basic option positions is shown in Figure 16-1 below.

Figure 16-1

Options Gains and Losses

	Max Gain	Max Loss
Buy Call	Unlimited	Premium
Buy Put	Exercise Price - Premium	Premium
Sell Call	Premium	Unlimited
Sell Put	Premium	Exercise Price - Premium

Using Options to Protect or Hedge a Position

An investor with an established stock position may use options to help protect (hedge) against the risk of that position. If the investor has a *long* stock position (that is, he or she already owns the underlying stock), he or she hopes for the price of the stock to *increase*. The risk of the position, a market price decline, may be offset either by buying a put (known in options language as a *protective put* or *portfolio insurance*), or by selling a call (a *covered call*). If the investor has a *short* stock position (that is, he or she does not own the underlying stock), he or she hopes for the price of the stock to *decline*. The risk of the position, a market price increase, may be offset either by buying a call (known in options language as a *naked call*) or by selling a put (a *naked put*).

The above paragraph and concepts are shown graphically in Figure 16-2 below.

Figure 16-2

Using Options to Protect a Position

	Buy = Long	Sell = Write = Short
CALL	↑ (Right to Buy)	↓ (Obligation to Sell)
PUT	↓ (Right to Sell)	↑ (Obligation to Buy)

If an investor is *long*, the risk is that the market will fall, which is a downward arrow. Therefore to hedge the position, select a position with a downward arrow. Accordingly, this is a *long put* or a *short call*. If the investor is short, the risk is that the market will rise, which is an upward arrow. Therefore to hedge the position, select a position with an upward arrow. Accordingly, that is a *long call* or a *short put*.

Sometimes, an investor may hedge his or her downside risk on a long position of stock by not expending any immediate out-of-pocket cash. This is known as a *cashless collar.* In this strategy, the investor sells an out-of-the-money covered call and uses the premium received to offset the cost of an out-of-the-money put option. The maturity date of this collar may range from several months to a number of years, and both options may be written to expire simultaneously. The concept behind the cashless (or *zero cost*) collar is to protect a gain on the underlying stock without the cost of purchasing a put option on the stock.

> **Example 16-3:** Assume that an investor is long 100 shares of WLA stock that is currently trading at $50.00 per share. He enters into a cashless collar by buying a put (long put) with an exercise price of $45.00 per share at 3 (or $300) and selling a call (short call) with an exercise price of $60.00 per share at 3 (or an offsetting $300). Therefore, his net cost of the option is zero. If the stock should decline, the investor can *put* the stock to the writer of the option at $45.00 per share. As a result, he knows that he can never lose more than $500 ($50 per share less $45 per share or $5 times 100 share round lot). However, his upside potential is also limited to only $500 ($300 premium income from selling the call plus the $200 difference between the $500 profit potential when exercising the put less the $300 cost of buying the put).

MULTIPLE OPTION TRANSACTIONS

Investors can also simultaneously buy or sell more than one option contract on the same or opposite sides of the market. Generally, these transactions are known as *spreads, straddles,* or *combinations* and, like basic option transactions, may be used either by traders (speculators) to speculate on a security's price movement or by hedgers to limit position costs and risks. Our focus, of course, will be on the use of multiple option transactions as a hedging strategy.

Spreads

A *spread* is the simultaneous purchase of one option and sale of another option on the *same* side or position within the market. For example, a *call spread* is the purchase of a call (a long call) and the sale of a call (a short call) at the same time. Similarly, a *put spread* is the purchase of a put (a long put) and the sale of a put (a short put) at the same time.

If an investor is fairly certain that the market will *not decline,* but nevertheless wants to limit the amount of possible loss on their portfolio of securities, he or she may enter into what is referred to as a *bull spread.* This is implemented in one of two ways:

1) By establishing a *debit call spread*, wherein the investor buys an in-the-money call and sells an out-of-the-money call with exercise prices roughly equally spaced above and below the current market price of the stock (see Example 16-4 below).

2) By establishing a *credit put spread*, wherein the investor buys an out-of-the-money put and sells an in-the-money put with exercise prices roughly equally spaced above and below the current market price of the stock (see Example 16-5 below).

Examples of each follow:

Example 16-4 *(debit call spread)*: Assume that a bullish investor, who is attempting to hedge, buys a QRM January 55 call for 6 and sells a QRM January 60 call for 3. (Note that because option contracts are issued to include a *round lot* of 100 shares, the total premium is calculated by multiplying the quoted integer by 100.) The current market price of QRM stock is $57.50 per share. Therefore, instead of paying $600 to buy the call, the investor/hedger has reduced his cost to $300 by also selling a call. In addition, the investor has the right to buy the stock for $55.00 per share, but must then sell the stock for $60.00 per share. As a result his total possible maximum gain or profit is $200 ($500 less $300). However, his maximum net loss is only $300 (or the net premium paid) since if the stock price falls below $55.00, both options will expire worthless.

Example 16-5 *(credit put spread)*: Assume that a bullish investor, who is attempting to hedge, buys an HDP January 55 put for 2 and sells an HDP January 65 put for 9. The current market price of HDP stock is $60.00 per share. Therefore, the net premium received is $700 ($900 less $200). If the stock price of HDP rises above $65.00 per share, both options will expire worthless and the investor/hedger will keep the net premium received ($700), which is also his total possible maximum gain. However, if the market price of HDP stock falls below $55 per share, his loss is also limited. Specifically, the exercise of the investor/hedger's short put will require purchase of the stock at $65.00 per share with his loss limited to $1,000 less the net premium of $700 received or a total of $300.

In contrast, if the investor is fairly certain that the market will *not increase,* but nevertheless wants to limit the amount of possible loss on his or her portfolio of securities, he or she may enter into what is referred to as a *bear spread*. This is implemented in one of two ways:

1) By establishing a *credit call spread*, wherein the investor sells an in-the-money call and buys an out-of-the-money call with exercise prices roughly equally spaced above and below the current market price of the stock (see Example 16-6 below).

2) By establishing a *debit put spread*, wherein the investor sells an out-of-the-money put and buys an in-the-money put with exercise prices roughly equally spaced above and below the current market price of the stock (see Example 16-7 below).

Example 16-6 *(credit call spread)*: Assume that a bearish investor, who is attempting to hedge, buys QRM January 55 call for 3 and sells a QRM January 45 call for 7. The current market price of QRM stock is $50.00 per share. The net premium received is, therefore, $400 ($700 less $300). If the stock price of QRM declines below the lower exercise price of $45.00 per share, both options will expire worthless and the investor/hedger keeps the net premium received ($400), which is also his maximum potential gain. If QRM stock rises above $45.00 per share, the investor/hedger's loss is also limited. His long call may be exercised to buy the stock at $55.00 per share with the loss limited to $1,000 less the net premium of $400 received or a total of $600.

Example 16-7 *(debit put spread)*: Assume that a bearish investor, who is attempting to hedge, buys an HDP January 55 put for 6 and sells an HDP January 50 put for 3. The current market price of HDP stock is $52.50 per share. Therefore, instead of paying $600 to buy the put, the investor/hedger has reduced his cost to $300 by also selling a put. If the market price of HDP stock falls below $50.00 per share, both puts will be exercised. The investor/hedger will sell the stock for $55.00 per share, but buy the stock for $50.00 per share. The $500 profit on the stock is, thus, reduced by the $300 net premium paid, for a net profit of $200. This is also the investor's maximum gain on the position. If the stock price increases to above $55.00 per share, both options will expire worthless and the investor will lose only his net premium paid ($300). Accordingly, the investor/hedger's maximum loss is only $300.

Straddles

A *straddle* is the simultaneous purchase of one option and sale of another option on *opposite* sides or positions within the market. For example, a *long straddle* is the simultaneous purchase of a call option and a put option with the same exercise price, usually at-the-money. Similarly, a *short straddle* is the simultaneous selling of a call option and a put option for the same exercise price; again, usually at-the money.

An investor who uses a *long straddle* expects substantial volatility in the price of the underlying stock, but is uncertain of the overall direction the price will move (either up or down). Therefore, to be ready for either possibility, the investor/hedger purchases both a call and a put. By doing so, if the market price of the stock rises significantly, the call will be profitable and the put will expire worthless. If the market price of the stock declines substantially instead, the put will be profitable and the call will expire worthless. In both events, however, the investor's gain is reduced by the premiums paid on the call and put.

Example 16-8 (long straddle) : Assume that an investor/hedger buys an RCC November 50 call at 3 and an RCC November 50 put at 4. The current market price of RCC stock is $44.00 per share. Therefore, her maximum potential gain on this long straddle is unlimited since the potential gain on the long call is unlimited. (Note, however, that the amount of total gain will be reduced by the $700 of premiums paid for the options.) The maximum loss is $700 or the total of the premiums paid for both the call and put ($300 + $400).

An investor who writes a *short straddle* expects that the underlying stock's price will not change or will change very little. If the market price of the stock changes little or not at all, both the call and put will expire worthless and the investor will profit by keeping the amount of the two premiums collected. Nonetheless, as would be expected since the gain potential on the long straddle is potentially unlimited, the maximum loss on a short straddle similarly has no limit.

Example 16-9 (short straddle): Continue with the facts of Example 16-7 and RCC stock, but now assume that the investor/hedger sells an RCC November 45 call at 4 and an RCC November put at 5. (Again, note that the current market price of RCC stock is $44.00 per share.) Therefore, her potential maximum gain is $900 or the total of the premiums paid for both the call and put ($400 + $500). The maximum loss on this short straddle is unlimited since the potential loss on the short call is unlimited.

Combinations of Calls and Puts

A *combination* is composed of a call and a put option with *different* exercise prices and/or dates of expiration. Combinations are similar to long straddles in investor strategy. That is, the investor/hedger will use a combination if he or she expects substantial volatility in the price of the underlying stock (upon which the options are written), but is not certain of the direction in which its price will actually move. Sometimes, the investor/hedger will use a combination rather than a long straddle because a combination is less expensive to establish if both the call and put option are currently out-of-the-money.

NON-EQUITY OPTIONS

An investor/hedger will use non-equity options for much the same reason as options purchased or written on equities—to offset the magnitude of his or her loss if the market value of the underlying asset declines. However, because the underlying asset is not a share of stock, non-equity options have different characteristics. We will briefly discuss three types of non-equity options, including 1) index options; 2) interest rate options; and 3) options purchased or written on foreign currencies.

Index Options

Options purchased or written on indexes allow investors to hedge against market swings. They may be based on broad-based or narrow-based indexes. Broad-based indexes are representative of the entire market and include the S&P 500, the Russell 2000, the Wilshire 5000 and the AMEX (American Stock Exchange) Major Market Index (XMI). Narrow-based indexes track the movement of market sectors, such as technology or health care.

There are some unique features of index options. Among them are:

1) *The multiplier*: Index options typically use a multiplier of $100 both to calculate the option's cost and the exercise price of the option.

2) *Exercise and settlement*: Index options settle in *cash* rather than in the delivery of a security (as do equity options). If the option is exercised, the writer of the option delivers cash equal to the intrinsic value of the option to the buyer or holder.

3) *Settlement price*: When index options are exercised, their settlement price is based on the closing value of the index on the day of exercise, *not* on the value at the time of exercise. For

example, if an investor exercises an option at 10 AM Eastern time, the settlement price is based on that day's later closing price (typically 4 PM Eastern).

4) *Position limits*: Unlike equity options that typically have position limits that may be assumed either by the buyer or by the writer, there are currently *no* position limits established for index option contracts.

An example of the exercise of an index option and the resulting profit or loss to the investor/hedger follows:

Example 16-10: Assume that an investor is long on an XMI January 410 call at 8 1/2. At the expiration date of the call option, the XMI is at 430. Accordingly, because this call is in-the-money by an index amount of 20, it would be exercised. The writer of the option must then deliver cash equal to the intrinsic value (in-the-money) amount to the holder. Thus, the amount that must be delivered is $2,000 (the 20 point spread times the $100 multiplier). The holder has a profit of $1,150, since the $2,000 cash received must be reduced by the $850 premium paid (8 1/2 times $100) for the call option.

Like equity options generally, if an investor/hedger believes that the market will decline in value, he or she can either buy an index put or sell (write) an index call. If the investor/hedger believes that the market will rise, he or she can either buy an index call or sell (write) an index put.

Interest Rate Options

Interest rate options permit an investor/hedger to protect against fluctuations of interest rates. There are two types of interest rate options: price-based options and yield-based options. *Price-based* options are options on U.S. Treasury securities and allow investors to protect against changes in the price of those securities because of interest rate changes. *Yield-based* options are also based on U.S. Treasury securities, but allow investors to protect against changes in yield, instead of changes in price. Yield-based options have a *direct* relationship to interest rates versus price-based options that have an *inverse* relationship to such rates.

Example 16-11: A yield-based option with an exercise price of 45 reflects a yield of 4.5%. If an investor buys this option at a premium of 2 1/2, and interest rates *increase* to 5.5%, he receives cash equal to the intrinsic value amount of 10 points here. Since the multiplier for yield-based options is also $100 (like index options and Example 16-10), 10 points of intrinsic value multiplied by $100 totals $1,000. Therefore, she will profit in the amount of $750 ($1,000 less the $250 premium cost to buy the option).

With respect to *price-based* options, an investor/hedger who expects interest rates to increase would buy a put or write a call on U.S. Treasury securities. If interest rates are expected to fall, an investor/hedger would buy a call or write a put. This is opposite of what we would normally think, of course, because bond prices move inversely with interest rates.

With respect to *yield-based* options, if the investor/hedger anticipates that interest rates will fall, he or she would purchase a yield-based put. If bond prices were expected to rise, he or she would also purchase a yield-based put, because as bond prices rise, yields fall.

Foreign Currency Options

Foreign currency options (FCOs) allow investors/hedgers to protect themselves against fluctuating currency exchange rates. Currency options are available on Canadian and Australian dollars, the British pound, the Euro, and the Japanese yen, among others. Importers and exporters frequently also use these options to hedge against currency exchange rates. The exercise prices for most of these options are quoted in U.S. cents. Thus, an exercise price of 180 British pounds means that the Pound must be bought or sold for 180 U.S. cents ($1.80) if the option contract is exercised. Finally you should note that an *inverse* relationship exists between the exchange rate of the U.S. dollar and that of a foreign currency.

If an investor/hedger believes that the value of a foreign currency is going to *rise*, he or she should buy a call option or sell (write) a put option on that currency. If the investor/hedger believes that the value of a foreign currency is going to *fall*, he or she should buy a put option or sell (write) a call option on that currency.

> **Example 16-12:** A U.S. importer must pay for Japanese television sets in the Japanese yen currency within three months. In the meantime, this importer is afraid that the value of the U.S. dollar will *fall* relative to the yen (and the value of the Japanese yen will rise costing him more money). Therefore, the importer should purchase a call option on the Japanese yen to lock in the purchase price of the amount of yen needed at the end of the three months.

It is important to remember the inverse relationship between foreign currencies and the U.S. dollar. If the U.S. dollar is *rising* (*strengthening*), the value of the foreign currency is *falling* in relative terms, so the investor/hedger should buy a *put* option (or write a call) on that currency. If the U.S. dollar is *falling* (*weakening*), the value of the foreign currency is *rising*, so the investor/hedger should buy a *call* option (or write a put)) on that currency.

INCOME TAX RULES FOR OPTIONS

There are three possible practical consequences of an investor/hedger that enters into an equity option transaction:

> 1) The option can expire unexercised (in other words, it is out-of-the-money and has no intrinsic value). If this happens, the buyer of the option loses the premium and the seller profits from the receipt of the premium.

> 2) The option can be exercised. If this happens, the investor/hedger either buys or sells the underlying stock depending on his position within the market.

3) The option may be *closed out*. This means that if the investor/hedger has *purchased* an option, prior to expiration he or she can *sell* the option. If the investor/hedger has *sold* an option, prior to expiration he or she can *purchase* the option. Notice that when *closing out*, the second transaction is always the *opposite* of the first transaction. In turn, whether the investor/hedger makes or loses money depends on the respective prices of the premiums paid or received initially.

For income tax purposes, options are considered to be *capital assets*, thus capital gains or loss treatment applies to the three practical consequences just described. Furthermore, the exercise of an option does not generate a capital gain or loss *until* a subsequent purchase or sale (a *closing* transaction) of the underlying stock takes place. Finally, the IRS does not allow the use of the normal nine-month option to postpone the sale of stock in order to generate long-term capital gains treatment. As you should surmise by now, the type of options that result in the sale of stock are long puts and in-the-money calls. If, at that time, the underlying stock has been held 12 months or less prior to the purchase of the put or sale of the call, the resulting gain is classified as *short-term* in nature.

While the tax consequences of options will be discussed further in chapter 18 of this text entitled the "Taxation of Investment Vehicles," Table 16-1 below summarizes the tax implications of option strategies according to each of the three possible practical consequences.

TABLE 16-1

Strategy	Option Expires	Option Exercised	Option "Closed Out"
Buy a call	Capital loss	Cost Basis = Exercise Price + Premium Paid	Capital gain or loss
Sell a call	Capital gain	Sale Proceeds = Exercise Price + Premium Received	Capital gain or loss
Buy a put	Capital loss	Sale Proceeds = Exercise Price – Premium Paid	Capital gain or loss
Sell a put	Capital gain	Cost Basis= Exercise Price – Premium Received	Capital gain or loss

IMPORTANT CONCEPTS

Hedging/hedger

Speculation

Futures contract

Commodities

Offset

Long position

Short position

Call option

Put option

Option premium

Intrinsic value of an option

Time value of an option

Bullish

Bearish

Buyer/holder

Seller/writer

Covered call

Uncovered/ naked

Protective put

Cashless collar

Spread

Bull spread

Bear spread

Straddle

Long straddle

Short straddle

Combination of call and put

Index option

Interest rate option

Price-based option

Yield-based option

Foreign currency option (FCO)

Closing out position

Capital assets

QUESTIONS FOR REVIEW

1. What is the difference between an investor who is speculating and an investor who is hedging? Which strategy is designed to reduce investor risk?

2. What are the three investment tools of an investor/hedger?

3. What is a futures contract and how does it differ from a forward contract?

4. What are the three primary types of futures contracts?

5. How does a futures contract differ from a securities transaction that is executed via the use of a margin account?

6. What is the primary method of settling (closing out) a futures contract?

7. If a farmer is long his crop, what does he do to "hedge" in the commodities market? Explain.

8. In the options market, which party has the obligation to buy or sell the underlying security? How does this differ from the futures market?

9. There are four basic positions in the options market. What are these positions?

10. What two types of values are reflected in the premium charged for an option? Explain each value.

11. Complete the following sentences: If an investor buys a call option, he or she is _____ on the prospects for the underlying stock. If an investor sells or writes a call option, he or she is_____ on the prospects for the underlying stock.

12. What are four reasons why an investor would purchase a call option? What are four reasons why an investor would sell a call option?

13. Complete the following sentences: If an investor buys a put option, he or she is _____ on the prospects for the underlying stock. If an investor sells or writes a put option, he or she is _____ on the prospects for the underlying stock.

14. What are three reasons why an investor would purchase a put option? What are three reasons why an investor would sell a put option?

15. What are a protective put and a covered call and why is each used by an investor?

16. What is a cashless or zero cost collar and why is it used by an investor?

17. Contrast a spread to a straddle.

18. If an investor is fairly certain that the market will not decline, but nevertheless wants to limit his or her amount of possible loss, what types of hedging strategies might he or she use? Explain.

19. If the investor is fairly certain that the market will not increase, but nevertheless wants to limit his or her amount of possible loss, what types of hedging strategies might he or she use? Explain.

20. When does an investor use a long straddle? In what circumstances is a short straddle used?

21. If a combination of calls and puts are used, what does this mean? When will such a strategy be used by an investor?

22. List three types of non-equity options.

23. What are four unique features of an index option?

24. What is the difference between a price-based and a yield-based option?

25. If an investor expects the U.S. dollar to strengthen against the Japanese yen, and he wants to protect against exchange rate risk, what should he do? Explain.

26. There are three practical consequences in any option transaction. What are they?

27. For purposes of federal income taxation, an option is considered what kind of asset? As a result, how are all gains or losses taxed?

SUGGESTIONS FOR ADDITIONAL READING

Tools and Techniques of Investment Planning, Stephen R. Leimberg, Robert T. LeClair, Robert J. Doyle, Jr., and Thomas R. Robinson, The National Underwriter Company, 2004.

Investments: *An Introduction,* 7th edition, Herbert B. Mayo, Thomson/ South-Western, 2002.

Investment Analysis and Portfolio Management, 7th edition, Frank K. Reilly and Keith C. Brown, Thomson/South-Western, 2003.

The Wall Street Journal Guide to Money and Investing, 3rd edition, Kenneth M. Morris and Virginia B. Morris, Fireside Publishing, 2004.

CHAPTER SEVENTEEN

Asset Allocation and Portfolio Diversification

• • •

This chapter takes up the tremendously important topics of asset allocation and portfolio diversification. There is likely no more important single factor contributing to the long-term investment performance of a portfolio than one that is structured using proper asset allocation principles. Further, diversification has been shown to be a key determinant in eliminating the unsystematic risk of a portfolio.

Upon completing this chapter, you should be able to:

- Explain the primary determinants of portfolio performance
- Describe the types of asset allocation
- Identify forms of asset allocation implementation strategies, including the use of a mathematical optimizer
- Identify strategies for managing concentrated investment portfolios
- Discuss factors that should be considered in the construction of a tax-efficient portfolio
- Summarize how asset allocation and portfolio diversification principles may assist in the tax efficiency of a portfolio

BACKGROUND/DETERMINANTS OF PORTFOLIO PERFORMANCE

What factors determine portfolio performance? A considerable amount of academic research has been conducted attempting to answer this question. Perhaps the most notable of these studies is a 1986 article in the *Financial Analyst Journal* by Gary P. Brinson, L. Rudolph Hood, and Gilbert L. Beebower, otherwise known as the (first) "Brinson study." This study uses a database of 91 corporate portfolios, ranging in size from $700 million to $3 billion in assets, over a 40-quarter time frame from the years 1974 through 1983. All portfolios were separated into three traditional asset classes: cash/cash equivalents, bonds (debt), and common stock (equity).

As a premise, the authors of the study hypothesized that there are, only three fundamental decisions that a portfolio manager makes that have a discernable impact on portfolio performance. These decisions are as follows:

> 1) *Security selection*: This is an outgrowth of the *active management style* of portfolio management discussed previously; that is, to what extent does actively selecting a specific security within the three asset classes contribute to overall portfolio performance?
>
> 2) *Weighting/timing*: This is the active decision by a portfolio manager to over- or underweight a specific asset class relative to the manager's *normal* or long-term asset allocation. It is also related to a market timing strategy since this weighting takes place according to changing market conditions.
>
> 3) *Investment policy*: An allocation among asset classes (and their respective weights) is a part of any credible investment policy. Such a policy is not really optional, since an investor has either implicitly (by default) or explicitly (in writing and as part of an investment policy statement) adopted some form of investment policy and asset allocation strategy.

After framing the study with the above decisions, the authors then ran a sophisticated quantitative analysis technique, known as *regression analysis*, to determine the contribution of each decision to the actual ending performance of a model portfolio. The results were quite striking, although discouraging to those portfolio managers who practice either active security selection or over- or underweighting among asset classes. Specifically, the Brinson study discovered that active security selection *reduced* the ending returns below a strictly passive portfolio by 0.36 % and weighting/timing also *lost* another 0.66 % from the portfolio's ending returns. Together, these two decisions resulted in an *underperformance* of the portfolio by 1.10 % as compared to passive management and a sound investment policy.

Instead, the Brinson study found that *over 93% of the variation* in the actual portfolio ending performance could be traced to the *investment policy (and, by extension, the asset allocation) decision.* To quote the conclusion of the study:

"Although active investment strategy may result in significant returns in some instances, these are *dwarfed* by the return contributions from investment policy, that is, the selection of appropriate asset classes and their normal weighting deriving from that policy."

Further, in 1991, Brinson updated his study based on data from 82 large pension (institutional) plans for the period between 1977 and 1987. This (second) updated study reconfirmed Brinson's earlier research and concludes thus:

"For our sample of pension plans, active investment decisions by plan sponsors and managers, both in terms of security selection and timing, did *little* to improve performance over the 10-year period from December 1977 to December 1987."

As a result, it is critical to recognize that the initial asset allocation decision (staying within the original weighting percentages deriving from this decision) is likely the *single most important factor* that determines actual portfolio performance over an extended period of time.

TYPES OF ASSET ALLOCATION

Strategic Asset Allocation

Strategic asset allocation is used to determine the long-term asset class weights in a portfolio. Typically, long-term historical average asset rates of return, risk, and covariance are used as estimates of future risk-adjusted performance. Efficient frontiers are generated using this historical rate of return information and the investor then decides which asset mix is appropriate given his or her risk tolerance and financial goals (over a pre-determined time horizon). As a result, a *constant-mix* (or weighting) asset allocation is determined with periodic rebalancing done to adjust the portfolio to the specified weights subsequent to actual performance.

Rebalancing is used in strategic asset allocation only in response to changes in the life cycle of the client or to reestablish the initial asset mix. Unlike in tactical asset allocation (discussed next), rebalancing is *not* done in strategic allocation due to changing market conditions. Rather, the portfolio manager determines the long-term asset allocation that is best suited for the particular investor by utilizing information from both the secondary market and from that investor. However, once the asset mix is established, the manager does not attempt to constantly adjust it in an effort to take advantage of market swings or overall investor sentiment.

Life-cycle 401(k) mutual funds are an example of rebalancing that is done in the context of a strategic asset allocation orientation. In these types of funds, portfolio managers will vary the initial asset allocation based on the client's advancing age and/or associated risk tolerance (for example, safety of principal becoming more important as the investor approaches retirement), but market conditions or timing does *not* play a part. The life-cycle adjustment that takes place is based on tried-and-true characteristics of investors proven over the years to generate the optimal risk-adjusted rate of return possible.

Tactical Asset Allocation

In contrast to the strategic approach, *tactical asset allocation (TAA)* continuously adjusts class mix in the portfolio in an attempt to take advantage of changing market conditions and overall investor sentiment. With TAA, these adjustments are driven *solely* by perceived changes in the relative values of the three traditional asset classes (cash/cash equivalents, bonds, and common stock). In effect, TAA is a *market timing approach* to portfolio management that is intended to increase exposure to a particular asset class when its performance is anticipated to be above average (and decrease exposure to this class when its performance is expected to be less than average).

Tactical asset allocation is fundamentally based on the concept of *mean reversion* which maintains that whatever a security's actual historical performance, the security will eventually revert or regress to its long-term average or mean value. This analysis is normally done on the basis of comparing one asset class to another. Therefore, for example, assume that the ratio of common stocks' historical return to that of bonds is 1.25. This means that stocks are perceived to have approximately 25% more long-term risk than that of bonds. However, if in the most recent investment year, common stock returns exceeded those of bond returns, the tactical investor or portfolio manager might determine that bonds are now undervalued relative to common stock. In response, he or she would then overweight (or re-adjust) the bond component of the portfolio from an initial 60-40 % stock-to-bond mix to a 50-50 % stock-to-bond asset allocation.

Finally, you should note that tactical asset allocation is characterized by a fundamentally *contrarian* approach to investing. Accordingly, the investor or portfolio manager will always be buying a traditional asset class- cash/cash equivalents, stocks, or bonds- that is not being purchased "by the herd" or the majority of marketplace investors.

Insured Asset Allocation

A third form of asset allocation strategy that is sometimes used is that of *insured asset allocation*. This form of asset allocation (like tactical asset allocation) results in continuing adjustments to the initial portfolio mix, but does so as the result of changes in the investor's *wealth position*. For example, increasing portfolio values increases the investor's wealth and, consequently, should accentuate his or her ability to handle risk. In turn, this means that the investor should be able to increase his or her exposure to risky assets. Conversely, a decrease in the overall value of the portfolio reduces the investor's wealth, meaning that his or her ability to handle risk should also decrease and the investor would likely reduce his or her exposure to risky assets.

Selection of a Type of Asset Allocation

The type of asset allocation to use likely depends on the investor's or manager's portfolio management style. Certainly, an investor or manager who believes in *active portfolio management* (and that the market is inherently *inefficient)* will tend towards *tactical asset allocation*. Alternatively, an investor or manager who adopts more of a long-term *buy-and-hold* strategy (passive management style) will find *strategic asset allocation* to be preferable. Finally, an investor who is very wealth-management oriented may find *insured asset allocation* to best meet his or her investment-planning goals. Regardless, as the Brinson studies show, a thoughtful analysis of which asset allocation technique to adopt, and then adherence to this technique throughout the investor's time horizon, is critical since it constitutes the primary factor impacting long-term portfolio performance.

ASSET ALLOCATION IMPLEMENTATION STRATEGIES

There are a number of practical strategies that investors or portfolio managers may wish to adopt to assist in implementing the asset allocation selected. Among these are model portfolios, judgmental intuition, multiple scenario analysis (MSA), and/or mathematical optimizers.

Model Portfolios

Perhaps the simplest solution for the investment advisor or portfolio manager in developing and implementing an asset allocation strategy is to adopt the use of a portfolio model. Such a model is often automatically provided by the sponsors of an investment product or family of products. Specifically, the investment advisor uses a questionnaire to determine the client's risk tolerance and, after answering a few additional standard questions provided by the model, inputs the answers and risk tolerance into a *black box* that, in turn, generates the appropriate allocation. For example, an individual who is 48 years old, who is just beginning to save for retirement, and who is self-supporting with a moderate risk tolerance, may find an asset allocation of 50% growth stocks, 20% income stocks, 20% investment grade bonds, and 10% cash equivalents to be appropriate.

However, there are several limitations on the use of any of these models, including:

1) The lack of specific customization to a client's particular financial goals and current cash flow situation

2) The prevalence of a *one size fits all* mentality; for example, when using a standardized model, the investment advisor may have no real appreciation of the specifics of the model's underlying assumptions, such as its expected returns, standard deviations, and correlation coefficients

3) The relevance of the *asset class* benchmark used by the model, tailored to the advisor's own investment style; for example, if the advisor has a pre-conceived bias against the use of corporate bonds, using the Lehman Brothers Bond Index as an appropriate benchmark may be impractical

4) The lack of tax efficiency of some models whereby they either ignore or do not properly attribute the impact of income tax factors involved in the construction of an optimal asset allocation

Judgmental Intuition

This is an approach that, while acknowledging the necessity of an asset allocation strategy, develops a solution based on all art and no science. In other words, historical qualitative data plays little, if any role, in determining the proper asset allocation and, instead, the advisor or manager implements his or her investment *hunches.* As an extension of this approach, sometimes an investment committee or investment club will try to determine the *turning point* in the performance of the traditional asset classes and thereby try to be "in the right (market) place at the right time."

Multiple Scenario Analysis (MSA)

This is an approach familiar to financial planners and investment advisors. In fact, a variation of the approach, Monte Carlo Simulation, was first discussed in chapter 9 of this textbook. In its most abbreviated form, Multiple Scenario Analysis (MSA) is based on projecting a best-case and worst-case analysis using a number of what-if scenarios and from, within that number, selecting a most probable or likely outcome.

The problem with the approach is the overwhelming amount of data that is generated and then, because of this fact, the tendency of portfolio managers to put an unfounded degree of confidence in the results. Furthermore, because MSA is so time consuming and expensive when generating this data, there is a bias *against* any short-term changes to the input factors. This, of course, makes the outcomes only as valid as the inputs used or, pejoratively, illustrates the dangers of a "garbage in-garbage out" strategy.

Mathematical Optimizers

A *mathematical optimizer* is the use of a computer software program that is designed to allocate investment assets and construct the *optimal portfolio.* It is analogous to the *black box* used by model portfolio providers to specify an appropriate asset allocation, but is more comprehensive in the inclusion of input variables. Depending on the belief of the investment advisor or the portfolio manager, such a tool is either the solution to the asset allocation problem or the problem itself.

The benefits of mathematical optimizers are as follows:
- They are exact.
- They provide solutions for an infinite number of efficient portfolios.
- They provide a mechanism for controlling the various components and sources of investment risk.
- They permit the manager to determine the portfolio's sensitivity to changes in expectations of market risk and return.
- They assist in the design of a procedurally prudent investment policy statement.

Nevertheless, mathematical optimizers may generate a result that is subject to *misleading exactness*. That is, the inputs may be subject to significant statistical errors and are, thus, fundamentally flawed. In addition, the conclusion of the optimizer may be counter-intuitive to the portfolio manager based on his or her knowledge of quantitative concepts and/or portfolio management theory.

STRATEGIES FOR DEALING WITH CONCENTRATED PORTFOLIOS

Currently, this is one of the most vexing problems of portfolio managers, particularly those who manage money for corporate executives. Specifically, many executives hold a disproportionate percentage of their investment portfolio in their own employer's stock. As a result, this exposes them to considerable unsystematic (business) risk. While this risk may be significantly minimized by diversification of the portfolio into other stocks or securities, many executives are reluctant to sell their employer's stock, believing strongly that their own efforts will increase the stock's future market value.

Therefore, strategies for dealing with a concentrated portfolio are both important and difficult to implement. Nevertheless, there are some basic strategies that may be used to manage such a portfolio, including the sale or gifting of some or all of the position, the use of options, variable prepaid forward contracts, a charitable remainder trust (CRT), and/or an exchange fund. Each is now briefly discussed.

Sale of Some or All of the Position

There are various forms of sales that may be used to minimize the unsystematic risk of the concentrated portfolio. Of course, the simplest of these is the outright sale of all or some of the executive's stock position. However, beyond the practical problem of obtaining the executive's agreement to do this, his or her basis in the employer shares is typically *very small*. Accordingly, there is usually a significant capital gains tax liability associated with the sale of these shares, a fact that merely encourages the executive to continue retaining them.

An alternative to the outright sale is the installment sale or, sometimes, the private annuity. However, the former (the installment sale) will also result in income tax consequences during the executive's lifetime as well as potentially disadvantageous estate tax consequences should the executive die during the term of the installment contract. In turn, while the disadvantageous estate tax consequences may be eliminated by executing a self-canceling installment note (SCIN), additional income tax liability results to the executive's estate with the implementation of the SCIN (consider the forgiveness-of-debt income tax rule). Finally, the entering into of a private annuity with a family member may prove a viable option for the executive, but the obligor of the annuity must be trusted longer-term to make good on the annuity payments due the annuitant since such a contract may not be *collateralized* with the underlying employer stock.

Gifting of Some or All of the Position

This alternative does avoid the income tax consequences associated with a sale of employer stock (as a gift is excluded from the definition of gross income). Nevertheless, unless proceeding carefully and with the advice of a competent tax advisor, gifting of the stock to others (likely family members) may result in the imposition of federal and/or state gift taxes. In addition, the income tax basis associated with a lifetime gift is usually carried over to the donee, meaning that he or she is ultimately responsible for the payment of income taxes due on sale. Unless the donee is in a lower marginal income tax bracket than the donor, this could result in a greater income tax liability being paid on the position than if it remained with the executive in the first instance.

The Use of Options

The use of options and derivatives has been discussed in previous chapters in this textbook and will not be reiterated here. However, the executive who uses options to minimize the investment risk of a concentrated position is now acting as a *hedger*, given the common understanding of that term. Specifically, he or she is taking an offsetting short position to the already-established long position generated by owning the employer stock. As a result, techniques such as the purchase of a protective put option or the selling of a covered call option to minimize the executive's downside risk of the employer stock decreasing in market value may prove valuable.

Variable Prepaid Forward Contracts

When using a variable prepaid forward contract, the executive agrees to sell a variable number of shares at some point in the future, typically between one and five years, in return for receiving an up-front cash advance. This cash advance is usually between 75 and 90 % of the stock's current fair market value, and does not have to be repaid. Therefore, the executive can immediately reposition these funds to work in a diversified portfolio. The contract is then settled at expiration by delivery of a portion of all of the shares pledged in the contract, to be determined by the stock price at expiration. Taxes are also deferred until the contract's expiration, at which time the executive pays capital gains taxes on the difference between the proceeds from the cash advance and his or her cost basis (if any) in the employer shares.

The variable prepaid forward contract is structured similarly to an option collar (see chapter 16) such that the executive's downside exposure is protected by a floor amount and the appreciation potential is capped by a ceiling. The executive retains ownership of the underlying employer shares and also retains rights to any dividend payments from the shares, although the dividend is considered to be *non-qualified* for income tax purposes.

Charitable Remainder Trust (CRT)

A charitable remainder trust (CRT) is fundamentally an estate planning strategy and is best left for a detailed discussion in an estate planning textbook. But when a CRT is established and assets are transferred to its trustee, a charitable income tax deduction is afforded that may be used to offset currently taxable income. In addition to the charitable deduction that is created, the asset transferred to the trust may be sold without any income tax liability since the CRT is a non-taxable (tax-free) entity. The proceeds from the sale can then be reinvested to diversify the concentrated portfolio and generate income for the executive. As such, the CRT may prove to be the solution for the corporate executive who is looking to diversify out of a portfolio heavily invested in employer stock, and at the same time may afford the executive the income from the stock that would be available if he or she retained some or all of the shares.

Exchange Fund

Some financial institutions offer so-called *exchange funds* that may be used in the management of a concentrated portfolio. Specifically, these funds permit the corporate executive (or any investor, for that matter) to contribute shares of his or her publicly-traded employer stock to the fund. In exchange, the executive receives a percentage income interest in the overall fund. Because the exchange is tax-free for income tax purposes, there are no immediate income tax consequences to the executive. In addition, because the fund also owns numerous securities other than the executive's employer stock, he or she receives an interest in a diversified fund.

There are some drawbacks, however, to the use of an exchange fund. Such fund is inherently illiquid; for example, investors must generally hold the shares of the fund for seven years to avoid incurring a tax liability. Further, federal income tax law mandates that 20% of the fund's assets be invested in relatively illiquid assets like real estate. Finally, the portfolio that the executive eventually owns may not be optimal, providing inefficient diversification plus a less certain expected rate of return.

CONSTRUCTION OF A TAX-EFFICIENT PORTFOLIO

One of the goals of any financial planner in creating a properly constructed and diversified portfolio should be to ensure that it is tax-efficient. That is, while it is imprudent in most instances to establish a completely tax-free portfolio (for example, a portfolio consisting entirely of municipal bond funds), it is a realistic goal to strive to maximize the amount of after-tax income possible from the portfolio. Accordingly, several variables and assumptions (as follows) make up the foundation of any tax-efficient portfolio.

Variables and Assumptions in Portfolio Tax Management

A number of variables and assumptions impact the after-tax return of an investment portfolio. These include:

1) *The marginal income tax bracket of the investor*: Most academic studies divide taxpayer/investors into low and high income tax brackets when evaluating the after-tax rate of return of a particular investment. The maximum marginal income tax rate is currently 35% and the lowest is 10% (a spread of 25%). Historically, the spread between the highest and lowest rates is relatively small, but there is no doubt that a taxpayer in a higher marginal income tax bracket benefits proportionately more from a tax-free or tax-deferred investment than does the lower-bracket investor. This is shown in our previous discussion about computing the *taxable equivalent yield* (TEY) of a municipal bond. Accordingly, the marginal income tax bracket of the taxpayer/investor should be an important factor in portfolio development and analysis.

2) *The holding period of the investor*: This is simply the length of time a particular investment is likely to be held without a significant change or repositioning of the portfolio. Currently, an investment (or *capital asset* for income tax purposes) needs to be owned by the taxpayer for a period of one year and a day in order for it to be eligible for preferential tax treatment as a *long-term* asset. As a result, any gains from the sale of the investment will qualify for either a 15% or 5% tax rate depending on the taxpayer/investor's marginal income tax bracket (a taxpayer in the 25% or higher marginal tax bracket pays capital gains taxes at the rate of 15% and a taxpayer in the 10 or 15% marginal tax bracket receives the 5% rate). The eligibility for this lower potential tax rate should, of course, be considered when analyzing whether to sell an investment. However, this consideration should *not* override the economic determination that a stock that has otherwise performed poorly should likely be sold.

3) *Relative interest, dividends, and capital gains*: The term *relative* here refers to the assumption that is made regarding the income tax components of the investment's total return. Specifically, each of these three components (interest, dividends, and capital gains) receives different tax treatment. For example, interest is taxable as ordinary income, so-called *qualifying dividends* are taxable as ordinary income but are entitled to a preferential rate, and capital gains derive a tax advantage from the sale of a capital asset. Therefore, an investment's return in the form of its taxable component(s) needs to be analyzed carefully by the investor or portfolio manager. Indeed, one of the fundamental principles of effective tax management is to *convert income* from an ordinary income form (such as interest) to that of capital gains (deriving from the sale or disposition of a capital asset).

4) *Turnover of assets*: This variable primarily applies to assets that are *pooled* or combined together. The most common example is that of the open-end investment company or mutual fund. Generally, the more frequently that the assets within a pooled fund experience *turnover* (the more frequently they are bought and sold within a given period of time), the less tax-efficient is the fund. That is, if the mutual fund portfolio manager frequently sells or disposes of the investments within the fund, there is often a greater income tax consequence to the mutual fund shareholder. This is because, by law, a mutual fund must *pass through* its tax gains or losses to its shareholders to avoid certain disadvantageous tax consequences at

the fund level. Accordingly, a mutual fund investor that is interested in a tax-efficient fund should look closely at its *turnover ratio* of assets. The *greater* this ratio, the *less* income tax efficient is the fund.

Timing of Capital Gains and Losses and the Netting Process

As most financial planners and investment advisors are aware, a *netting* process occurs with respect to the reporting of capital gains and losses. That is, gains or losses are first grouped according to whether they are short term (an asset sold after being owned for only one year or less) or long term (an asset sold after being owned for at least one year and a day). Then, short-term capital losses are applied to reduce short-term capital gains, resulting in a net short-term capital gain or loss for the year. The same procedure then applies with the application of long-term capital losses against long-term capital gains.

Taxpayers who have capital losses (whether short term or long term) that exceed their capital gains in a given year must follow a special set of rules. Specifically, losses from the sale of capital assets are allowed *only* to the extent of a taxpayer's net capital gains for the year of sale *plus* up to $3,000 of excess losses. If the net capital loss for the year exceeds $3,000, the taxpayer may carry forward the excess amount to future years until it is completely depleted. Any capital loss that is carried forward retains its original short-term or long-term character in that year. Finally, when both a net short-term capital loss *and* a net long-term capital loss exist, the allowable $3,000 net capital loss is first treated as an offset to the short-term capital loss.

> **Example 17-1:** Assume that during the taxable year 2006, Joseph incurs a short-term capital loss of $1,000 and a long-term capital loss of $12,000. Based on this assumption, Joseph's total net capital loss for the year 2006 is $13,000. Of this amount, $3,000 is available to offset Joseph's other or *ordinary* income. Since the first $3,000 offsets the short-term capital loss, Joseph will fully utilize all of his short-term capital loss in the year 2006. He will then apply $2,000 of long-term capital loss in 2006 and will carry forward a $10,000 long-term capital loss to the next taxable year 2007 and beyond.

Because of these special rules, it is very important that the taxpayer/investor consider the *time* at which he or she sells (or otherwise disposes of) an investment. A major advantage of investing in most securities is that the choice of this time is within the discretion of the investor. That is, there is no taxable event recognized unless the taxpayer chooses to incur one. For example, if the taxpayer is a pure *buy-and-hold* investor, it is unlikely that he or she will ever incur a capital gain or loss of his or her own choosing during his or her lifetime. Rather, assuming that the security appreciates in value, the taxpayer's heirs will likely receive a *step up* in the basis of the security, free of any capital gain taxation. It will then be up to the taxpayer's heirs to either continue to postpone recognition of a taxable event regarding the inherited securities or to sell the investments at some future date.

Regardless, the critical time frame for the taxpayer/ investor to keep in mind is that of the *one-year-and-a-day* period mentioned earlier. If the taxpayer has owned (held) the investment asset for at least this amount of time, he or she will be entitled to a tax preference in the form of a reduced tax rate on any gains resulting from the sale of the asset. Alternatively, if the taxpayer has not yet held the asset for at least this time period prior to its disposition, ordinary or regular income tax treatment will apply. As noted, depending on the taxpayer's marginal income tax bracket, the sale of an investment prior to a *year and a day* may mean an additional tax rate of 20% (35% less 15%). Further, when translated to dollar terms across the broader portfolio, the taxable impact of multiple asset sales that are considered *long term* in nature may be significant.

Wash Sale Rule

Under the so-called *wash sale rule*, a taxpayer who realizes a loss on the sale or other disposition of stock or securities may *not* claim the loss as a tax deduction. Specifically, this rule operates to disallow the claiming of a tax loss on the sale of the stock *if* the investor/taxpayer purchases substantially identical stock within a period beginning 30 days before the date of the sale and ending 30 days after that date. Similarly, a loss realized on the closing of a short sale of stock or securities is disallowed if, within 30 days before or after the closing, substantially identical stock or securities are sold or another short sale of substantially identical stock or securities is entered into. The term *substantially identical* is defined in the Treasury Regulations, but is based on a test of facts and circumstances that takes into account the characteristics of one security as compared to the security with which it is replaced. Bonds or preferred stock are not ordinarily considered substantially identical to the common stock of the same issuer; however, they may be considered as such when the bonds or preferred stock are convertible into the common stock of the same corporation.

> **Example 17-2:** Sarah buys 200 shares of XYZ stock for $10,000. She sells all of these shares for $7,500 on December 2, 2006 and on December 30, 2006 she purchases 200 more shares of XYZ stock for $8,000. Therefore, because Sarah purchased *substantially identical* stock, she cannot deduct her loss of $2,500 on the sale of XYZ shares on her 2006 personal income tax return. (Note that the result would be the same if Sarah had purchased a $10,000 convertible bond issued by XYZ Corporation and had converted the shares into the 200 shares mentioned and had then sold—and repurchased—those shares in the same time frame.)

When a loss is disallowed because of the wash sale rule, the disallowed loss is subsequently added to the cost of the new stock or securities. The result is that the investor/taxpayer acquires a new adjusted basis in the reacquired stock or securities. Accordingly, this adjustment effectively operates to postpone the loss deduction until the sale or disposition of the new stock or securities beyond the prohibited time frame.

> **Example 17-3:** Continuing with the facts of Example 17-2, Sarah subsequently adds the disallowed loss of $2,500 to the cost of the new 200 XYZ shares that she purchased. As a result, her adjusted basis in the new shares is $10,500 ($8,000 original cost plus the $2,500 loss she could not claim under the wash sale rule loss prohibition). Subsequently, as long as Sarah does not sell the new shares prior to January 30, 2007 (and once again reacquire substantially identical shares), she can recognize the originally disallowed loss on a subsequent sale of the XYZ shares.

Finally, when there has been a wash sale, the holding period of the new securities *includes* the period that the taxpayer held the securities on which the loss was not deductible.

Qualified Dividend Income

A dividend is the most common type of corporate stock distribution and is a distribution to the shareholder of either cash (a cash dividend) or property (a stock dividend) payable from the C corporation's current or accumulated earnings and profits. A dividend distribution is considered as ordinary income to the investor/taxpayer and is not deductible by the distributing corporation. Therefore, *double taxation* of the corporation's earnings and profits occurs, first at the corporate entity level and next at the shareholder/investor level. However, effective January 1, 2003, *qualifying dividend income* to the shareholder/investor is taxable at a preferred rate of 15% or 5%, depending on the shareholder's marginal income tax bracket. Shareholders who are in the 25% or greater marginal income tax bracket receive a preferred flat rate of 15% on qualifying dividends, while those shareholders in the 10% or 15% bracket are eligible for the 5% flat rate. The 5% and15% taxable rates also apply to stocks that are held for more than one year before being sold at a taxable gain (the so-called *long-term capital gain preference*).

So what requirements must be met before a dividend is considered to be *qualified* for these favorable rates? Under the rules, qualified dividend income is that received by a shareholder during the taxable year from both domestic and qualified foreign corporations. A qualified *foreign* corporation is one that is incorporated in a U.S. possession (such as Puerto Rico) or that is eligible for benefits of a comprehensive income tax treaty with the United States. In addition, corporations whose shares are traded as American Depository Receipts (ADRs) on an established U.S. securities market also are qualified foreign corporations. Qualified foreign corporations do *not* include foreign holding companies or those companies that are incorporated outside the U.S or a U.S. possession solely for purposes of investment (and not as an ongoing operating concern).

Most dividends payable from real estate investment trusts (REITs) are *not* eligible for the reduced or favorable rates that apply generally to qualified dividends. This is because most REITs do not pay corporate income taxes and, instead, are only *pass through* entities (like an S corporation) to its shareholders. Nevertheless, a small number of dividends paid by REITs may be qualified and are eligible for the preferential rates. These exceptions include dividends paid by a REIT that are attributable to dividends received from a non-REIT corporation, such as a taxable REIT subsidiary, and income that was subject to tax at the REIT entity level when it distributes less than 100% of its taxable income.

Finally, in order to be a *qualified* dividend for income tax purposes, a separate holding period applies. Dividends received from a stock or mutual fund are not eligible for the reduced rates if the shareholder does not hold the share of stock for more than 61 days during the 121-day period beginning 60 days before the ex-dividend date of the stock. The ex-dividend date is the date following the record date on which the issuing corporation finalizes the list of shareholders who will receive the dividend. In the case of preferred stock, this holding period is extended to more than 91 days during the 181-day period beginning 90 days before the ex-dividend date. In turn, the ex-dividend date is defined as the first date following the declaration of a dividend on which the purchaser of the stock is not entitled to receive the *next* dividend.

Tax-Exempt Income

The best of all possible results is to not have the income from an investment taxed *at all.* This is referred to as *tax-exempt income.* Unfortunately, there are not many of these types of investments available. There are, however, several forms of debt instruments (bonds) that do generate income that is tax exempt for either federal, state, or local income tax purposes (and sometimes all three).

The first of these types of investments is a municipal bond issued by a state or local government. As discussed previously in chapter 2 of this text, these bonds usually come in one of two forms: either a *general obligation* (G.O.) bond used to finance the everyday operational needs of the state or local government or a *revenue* bond that is floated to finance the expense of a special project, such as an airport. In both instances, the interest income earned on these investments is excluded from the recipient's taxable income for regular income tax purposes. This exclusion usually applies for both federal and state income tax purposes if the bondholder is also a resident of the state or local government issuing the bond. (You should note, however, that the interest from certain types of state or local government bonds issued for a private business purpose, such as the construction of an office park, is potentially subject to the federal alternative minimum tax. These are sometimes referred to as *private activity bonds* or, more colloquially, *AMT bonds.*)

There is also a second form of debt instrument that will produce tax-exempt income for some taxpayers. These are obligations issued by the U.S. Treasury in the form of Treasury bills, notes, and bonds (see chapter 2 of this text). While the interest earned on all of these obligations is subject to federal income tax, this same interest is exempt from income taxes levied by any state or local government. In common parlance, this result occurs because of a theory known as the *doctrine of reciprocity.* In other words, certain obligations issued by the federal government are taxable only at that level and not by the state. Conversely, certain obligations, such as a municipal bond investment that is purchased by a non-resident, may be taxable by the state, but not by the federal government.

Finally, before investing in tax-exempt issues, the taxpayer/investor should be aware that (due to the tax advantage) the nominal rate of return on such issues is often *less than* that of taxable obligations. However, in computing the tax-equivalent yield for individuals who would otherwise incur tax (particularly those in the higher marginal income tax brackets), the after-tax return of tax-exempt issues may well be *greater.*

TAX EFFICIENCY AND ASSET ALLOCATION

The frequency with which Congress changes marginal income tax rates is very familiar, particularly to financial planners and portfolio managers. Certainly, the most obvious impact of an increase in marginal tax rates is a reduction in the after-tax return on most investments. But, what about the impact of the rate increase on the relative desirability of bonds (as a proxy for a fixed-income type of investment) versus stocks (or a capital-appreciation type of investment)? It would seem clear that if a portfolio manager, in response to an increase in marginal tax rates, recommends an increase in the percentage of stocks, he or she is also recommending a higher risk portfolio. However, is this really the case? A particular study, commissioned by SEI Investments Company in July 1993, attempted to provide a definitive answer to this question.

The SEI study developed a ratio that measures the *rate of tax return to risk* for stocks and bonds. Accordingly, this ratio, referred to here as the *SEI ratio*, subtracted the inflation rate from the rate of investment return for the portfolio (for both the before- and after-tax return of stocks and bonds) and divided the result by the investment's standard deviation (or measure of absolute risk). Then, SEI calculated the *SEI advantage factor* (*SEI factor*), a measure of the real rate of return of the investment per each unit of risk, as: SEI Ratio for stocks less SEI Ratio for bonds. The results are as shown in the following Table 17-1 below:

Table 17-1: Rate of Tax Return to Risk

	Before Tax Return		After Tax Return (Current)[1]		After Tax Return (New)[2]	
	Equity	Bonds	Equity	Bonds	Equity	Bonds
Real Rate of Return	6.50%	2.50 %	3.35 %	0.55 %	3.35 %	-0.10 %
Risk (S.D.)	21.00	7.00	14.70	4.90	14.70	4.20
SEI Ratio	0.31	0.36	0.23	0.11	0.23	-0.02
SEI Factor	-0.05		0.12		0.25	

[1]For current after-tax rates, assumes a combined 30% ordinary and capital gains tax rate
[2]For new after-tax rates, assumes a 40% ordinary income tax rate (capital gains tax rate is unchanged)

Table 17-1 shows the relative advantage of stocks (or equity) over bonds in terms of a resulting before- and after-tax return. However, the startling fact about the findings of the study is that, as the table demonstrates, an increase in tax rates not only reduces the total investment return of stocks, but also reduces the total *risk* associated with such investment (from a standard deviation of 21.00 to one of only 14.70). In addition, the relative advantage of stocks over bonds (as measured by the *SEI advantage factor*) increases as the assumed ordinary income tax rate becomes greater (for example, from 0.12 with an assumed 30% ordinary and capital gains rate to 0.25 with an assumed 40% combined rate). Of course, this makes sense given that the interest return from bonds (or fixed-income types of investments) is taxable as ordinary income, so that the higher the ordinary income rate, the less the relative tax advantage of bonds as compared to stocks.

While the goal of portfolio income tax management is often debated (is the goal to maximize the after-tax rate of return of the portfolio or to avoid as much tax liability as possible?), there is little doubt that taxes are the greatest artificially imposed impediment to wealth accumulation. As such, the financial planner that specializes in investment management and portfolio asset allocation ignores the impact of annual taxes only at the risk of his or her client's potential dollar loss. In addition, if the client assumes this income tax risk without being informed by the planner of the basic taxation of investments, the long-term relationship of planner to client is likely to be severely jeopardized.

IMPORTANT CONCEPTS

Asset allocation

Brinson study

Strategic asset allocation

Rebalancing

Tactical asset allocation

Insured asset allocation

Model portfolio

Multiple Scenario Analysis (MSA)

Mathematical optimizer

Concentrated portfolio

Charitable Remainder Trust (CRT)

Exchange fund

Tax-efficient portfolio

Asset turnover

Netting process

Holding period

Wash Sale Rule

Qualified dividend income

Tax-exempt income

Doctrine of Reciprocity

SEI study

QUESTIONS FOR REVIEW

1. What are three decisions that a portfolio manager could make that would have a discernable impact on portfolio performance? Which of these decisions have academic studies shown is likely the most important?

2. What is the conclusion of the Brinson study with respect to the asset allocation decision?

3. In strategic asset allocation, what is the role of portfolio rebalancing? Give an example of a type of mutual fund that uses these principles.

4. In tactical asset allocation, are the financial goals more important or are changing market conditions more important? Explain.

5. Define insured asset allocation and explain how it differs from both strategic and tactical asset allocation.

6. There are four types of asset allocation implementation strategies discussed in the chapter. What are they and what are several limitations on the use of any of these strategies?

7. Explain the following sentence: "Mathematical optimizers may generate a result that is subject to 'misleading exactness.'"

8. What is usually meant by the term *concentrated portfolio*? List six strategies that may be used in managing such a portfolio.

9. How is a charitable remainder trust (CRT) used in minimizing the unsystematic risk that is inherent in a concentrated portfolio?

10. What is an *exchange fund* and how does it differ from an *exchange traded fund*? (Note: See chapter 4 of this textbook to review the application of an exchange traded fund.)

11. What are four underlying variables and assumptions that impact the after-tax rate of return of an investment portfolio?

12 How is each of the following components of investment return taxed?
    • Interest
    • Dividends
    • Capital appreciation

13. Complete the following sentence: The _____ the turnover of assets within a mutual fund, the _____ income-tax efficient is the fund. Explain your sentence completion.

14. What is meant by the phrase "netting of capital gains and losses"?

15. What is the holding period that applies before an investment sold at a gain qualifies for favorable income tax treatment? What tax rates apply in such situation?

16. What is the practical effect of an investment loss tax deduction being disallowed because of the so-called wash sale rule? What triggers the application of this rule?

17. What requirements must be met before a dividend distribution is considered to be qualified for favorable income tax treatment? What tax rates apply in such situation?

18. What are two types of investments that generate tax-exempt income?

19. What is the doctrine of reciprocity and why is it important in the taxation of investments?

20. What was the conclusion of the SEI study and why is it important in portfolio tax management and asset allocation?

SUGGESTIONS FOR ADDITIONAL READING

Tools and Techniques of Investment Planning, Stephen R. Leimberg, Robert T. LeClair, Robert J. Doyle, Jr., and Thomas R. Robinson, The National Underwriter Company, 2004.

Investments: An Introduction, 7th edition, Herbert B. Mayo, Thomson/ South-Western, 2002.

Investment Analysis and Portfolio Management, 7th edition, Frank K. Reilly and Keith C. Brown, Thomson/South-Western, 2003.

The Wall Street Journal Guide to Money and Investing, 3rd edition, Kenneth M. Morris and Virginia B. Morris, Fireside Publishing, 2004.

CHAPTER EIGHTEEN

Taxation of Investment Vehicles

• • •

This textbook concludes with a discussion of the taxation of investment vehicles. While much of this is best reserved for a formal textbook on income taxation and income tax planning, because of its importance to the financial planner, the basic principles involved in tax planning with investments are presented here

Upon completing this chapter, you should be able to:

- Identify the basic concepts of our income tax system, including types of income
- Describe how to take advantage of tax-advantaged accounts in investing
- Explain the income tax treatment of investment interest expense
- Define personal interest expense and why it is important for investment tax planning
- Describe how distributions from a mutual fund are taxed
- Explain the general rules associated with the taxation of a stock or bond
- Identify characteristics of the taxation of insurance-based investment products
- Explain the three basic forms of real estate ownership and their taxable consequences
- Identify the taxable principles that apply to the sale or disposition of collectibles
- Describe the taxation of derivative investment vehicles, most notably options and/or futures

BASIC CONCEPTS

A fundamental income tax strategy is the conversion of ordinary income into capital gains income. However, to do this, the taxpayer first needs to invest in a *capital asset.* Fortunately, the majority of assets held for investment purposes easily fall within the Internal Revenue Code's definition of a capital asset and, therefore, typically qualify for preferential tax treatment. (The most notable exception to the definition of a capital asset is a life insurance product, which generates ordinary income for tax purposes.) In addition, in order for this preferential treatment to occur, a capital asset must be owned or held for a specified period of time, referred to as the *holding period* for the asset. Currently, this period is more than 12 months or one year, commonly referenced as *one year and a day.* Accordingly, if a capital asset (investment) is held for more than the required 12-month holding period, it becomes a *long-term* asset and is subject to lower income tax rates (either a flat rate of 5% or 15% depending on the taxpayer/investor's marginal ordinary income tax bracket).

Additional income tax management or strategies include the avoidance of income and/or its deferral to a subsequent year. Avoidance techniques are best left to a course or textbook on income tax planning and will not be further discussed here. However, deferral techniques take advantage of tax-exempt trusts or accounts to postpone the recognition of taxable income from the current taxable year to a year or years into the future. Likely, the most notable of deferral techniques is an employer-sponsored, *qualified* retirement plan or a taxpayer's individual retirement account (IRA). In recent years, other deferral-of-income techniques, such as the Roth IRA, have also been added to the Internal Revenue Code to encourage individuals to save for their own retirement. All of these techniques operate from the basic tax principle that it is better to defer taxable income into a future year and use the magic of compound interest to accumulate as many before-tax dollars as possible before mandatory minimum distribution rules apply.

TYPES OF INCOME

As noted, for income tax purposes, there are two basic types of income that are possible: ordinary income and income from capital gains. However, three additional types of income are defined in the Treasury Regulations accompanying the *passive loss* rules and of which the taxpayer should be aware. These types of income are referred to as:

1) Active income

2) Portfolio income

3) Passive income.

Certainly, *passive income* is the most important for purposes of the passive loss rules, as only that type of income may be used to offset losses that are *passive* in nature, such as those deriving from a limited partnership investment. However, the definition of *active* income and *portfolio* income may also help us understand the difference between ordinary and capital gain income for tax purposes.

Active income, by definition, is any income that is *not passive*, or income from an investment activity in which the taxpayer *materially participates* (as defined in the Treasury Regulations). But more specifically, active income includes a taxpayer's salary and wages or any income from a trade or business. Roughly, this also equates to *ordinary income* for tax purposes, whereby withholding also applies, as does taxability at the taxpayer's highest marginal tax rate under the progressive tax system.

On the other hand, *portfolio income* includes interest, dividends, annuities, and royalties, as well as gain or loss from the disposition of investment property that is *not* derived in the ordinary course of the taxpayer's trade or business. Roughly, this equates to income from investments or *capital gain income*, although we often need to go further and classify the kind of return that is generated in order to determine the precise tax treatment. For example, interest and dividend income from a security are taxed at ordinary income rates whereas gain upon disposition of that security (or capital appreciation) will enjoy capital gains rates.

As noted previously, gains (or losses) from investment property may be either long term or short term in nature. Only long-term gains, however, receive a preferential rate of taxation. Generally, the maximum rate on long-term capital gains for investment property sold before January 1, 2011 is 5%, to the extent that the taxpayer is taxed at the 10 or 15% marginal income tax brackets, and 15%, to the extent that he or she is taxed at higher marginal rates (currently, through the year 2008, either 25%, 28%, 33%, or 35%). These rates are used for computing the regular income tax as well as the alternative minimum tax. Finally, short-term gains retain their character as capital-gain income (and, thus, must first be used to offset any capital losses), but are taxed at the same marginal rates as if the income were *ordinary* in nature.

DEFERRAL OF INCOME/TAX ADVANTAGED ACCOUNTS

Assume that, as a financial planner, you are advising a client who holds individual stocks and bonds in addition to both taxable and tax-deferred or tax-advantaged accounts, such as a traditional deductible or Roth IRA. What type of account do you recommend that the client use to position these individual stocks and bonds? Conventional wisdom suggests that the client should position his or her stock holdings in the taxable accounts and bonds in the tax-advantaged accounts for several reasons:

1) The highest ordinary income-generating investments (or here, bonds) should be protected from current taxation by placing them in the tax-advantaged account.

2) The lowest yielding investments (or here, stocks generating capital gains or qualifying dividends at lower rates) should be placed in the taxable account.

3) Capital gains may be deferred at the discretion of the taxpayer/investor. In other words, because the imposition of the taxable event at the date of sale is chosen by the taxpayer, he or she should position currently taxable income in the type of account with the least tax exposure to the investor.

As enticing as this wisdom is in theory, however, its practical implementation is often the subject of considerable discussion and analysis.

Some financial planners and portfolio managers argue that this approach to tax-efficient investing overlooks two very important points: 1) the economic goal of attempting to achieve the *maximum* possible total return for the investor, and 2) the existence of tax-free alternatives in the investment marketplace. With respect to the first point, the goal of any portfolio manager should be to maximize the efficient use of the tax-advantaged account. This may be accomplished by positioning the investments generating the *highest* taxable return in the tax-advantaged account (and not the lowest return as the conventional wisdom theory maintains). Further, the second point addresses the choice in the investment world between bonds that pay taxable income and bonds that do not (for example, municipal bonds). There is no similar choice for equities. Therefore, some planners and portfolio managers argue that the real choice is between sheltering income from *stocks*, whose qualifying dividends and capital gains are taxed at the same low rates, and *municipal bonds* whose return is in the form of tax-free income.

Tax-Advantaged Account Investing

While the positive impact of tax deferral through tax-advantaged accounts likely cannot be understated, this advantage comes at a price. Specifically, in most instances, when achieving tax deferral through the accumulation of investment wealth in a tax-advantaged account (including an employer-sponsored retirement plan) potential capital gain income is converted *back* into the ordinary income form. In other words, investment income that may otherwise be taxed to an investor as capital gain income (like stocks or mutual funds) is now taxable at potentially higher ordinary income marginal rates. This point is important to realize when the planner is doing both investment and retirement planning.

There is one major exception to this dilemma, however. This is the concept of *net unrealized appreciation (NUA)*, which applies in the case of lump-sum distributions made from certain types of qualified employer plans where employer securities are part of the distributable assets. These types of distributions are normally made in stock bonus types of retirement plans, including the well-known *employee stock ownership plan (ESOP)*. In these types of plans, the appreciation in the value of employer securities while held in the retirement plan trust is not taxable to the recipient at the time of *distribution*, but rather at the time of subsequent *sale* of the stock. The appreciation is, thus, *unrealized* for income-tax purposes and, accordingly, non-taxable. Further, once the employer stock is sold and the taxpayer/investor chooses to incur a taxable event, the previously untaxed appreciation in the stock *retains* its character as capital gain rather than as ordinary income. As a result, this is a significant tax-related reason why employer stock is an attractive component of any retirement portfolio, although investors do need to pay attention to prudent investment practices, such as the proper diversification of his or her retirement asset portfolio.

An example of the application of the net unrealized appreciation (NUA) concept follows:

Example 18-1: Bruce participates in his employer's employee stock ownership plan (ESOP) and has recently received a lump-sum distribution of employer stock valued at $500,000. The market value of the employer stock that was contributed to Bruce's account over the years was $100,000 (basis to the qualified plan trust). Therefore, at time of distribution of the stock, Bruce has net unrealized appreciation in the stock of $400,000 ($500,000 less $100,000). This appreciation is not taxed to Bruce until he subsequently sells the shares of employer stock in the secondary market, with any resulting gain taxable to Bruce at capital gains rates and on the excess of the amount realized upon sale over his basis in the stock. The amount of basis to the qualified plan trust ($100,000) is taxable to Bruce as ordinary income at time of distribution.

Finally, you should note that, if the employer stock appreciates after the time of distribution to Bruce, the net unrealized appreciation portion of his gain is *always* taxed at long-term capital gain rates, regardless of his actual holding period. (In Example 18-1, this would be the $400,000 amount.)

INVESTMENT INTEREST EXPENSE

Investment interest expense (such as margin interest) on an investor's individual income tax return (IRS Form 1040) is deductible only to the extent of *net investment income*. Therefore, the determination of what constitutes net investment income is important in the computation of tax and in tax planning for the investor. If a taxpayer borrows money from his or her broker-dealer using a margin account and, subsequently, uses the proceeds to buy investment property, the interest paid on the debt is a miscellaneous itemized deduction for income tax purposes and deductible only to the extent that its total exceeds 2% of the taxpayer's adjusted gross income (AGI). Any non-deductible portion of investment interest expense is carried forward to a future taxable year.

Net investment income means the excess of investment income that exceeds investment expenses. Investment income includes portfolio income (such as interest, dividends, and royalties), net short-term and long-term capital gains, and ordinary income gains from the sale of investment property. However, a dividend will qualify as investment income only if the taxpayer elects *not* to use the preferred tax rates discussed in chapter 17 of this text (i.e., the 5% or 15% qualifying rates). In other words, the taxpayer must *elect out of* the qualifying rates and, instead, choose to have the dividends taxed using the higher marginal ordinary income tax rates (i.e., 10%, 15%, 25%, 28%, 33%, or 35% rates). In addition, long-term gains may only be included if this same (*opting out*) election is made.

Example 18-2: Andy and his wife, Carol, have earned income of $100,000 this year. They also have portfolio income of $10,000, consisting of $4,000 of interest from their certificates of deposit (CDs), $3,500 of dividends, and $2,500 of royalties. They also have incurred $20,000 of margin interest expense. Therefore, if they elect to treat the dividend income of $3,500 as ordinary income (that is, if they *elect out of* the qualifying rates), they can potentially deduct up to $10,000 of investment interest expense. Alternatively, if Andy and Carol take advantage of the qualifying dividend rates, they *cannot include* the dividend income of $3,500 among their portfolio income, meaning that they may potentially deduct investment interest expense of only $6,500 ($10,000 less $3,500).

You should note that if, in Example 18-2, Andy and Carol had also incurred net short-term gains of $4,500 and net long-term gains of $5,500 (with their portfolio income thereby equaling a total of $20,000 net investment income), they could only elect to use the net long-term gain income of $5,500 to offset investment interest expense if the preferential long-term rates were not used. This would mean that they would have to use ordinary income tax rates on *both* the dividends and on the long-term rates if they want to offset the entire $20,000 of margin interest expense. Otherwise, net investment income of $9,000 ($3,500 of dividend income and $5,500 of net long-term gains) would have to be carried forward and deducted against investment expense in future years.

Finally, it is generally *not* to a taxpayer's advantage to opt out of the qualifying dividend rates for dividend income (or long-term capital gain income) solely to take advantage of a greater investment expense deduction. In part, this is because the deduction is subject to the miscellaneous itemized deduction *2% AGI floor* in the first instance. Nevertheless, in some instances, it is preferable to opt out of the reduced rates and tax dividend income at the higher marginal rates. The planner should work closely with a tax advisor to determine when this is the case.

PERSONAL INTEREST EXPENSE

Individuals are also *not* generally permitted to deduct any personal interest paid or accrued during the taxable year. Most often this means that individuals are not allowed to deduct interest paid on credit card debt or automobile loans. However, like most everything else associated with income taxes and the Internal Revenue Code, the definition of what is and what is not personal interest is not nearly so straightforward.

Specifically, personal interest is defined to include all types of interest *except*:

1) Interest incurred in connection with the conduct of a taxpayer's trade or business

2) Investment interest expense (as just discussed)

3) Interest expense taken into account in computing a taxpayer's income or losses from passive activities

4) Qualified residence interest

5) Interest on qualified educational loans

Likely, the most important of these exceptions is the exception for *qualified residence interest*, since this includes both home mortgage acquisition indebtedness interest and interest incurred as a result of a home equity loan or line of credit. Indeed, home mortgage interest will probably make it more advantageous for taxpayers to elect to itemize their deductions than to claim the standard deduction available for their filing class (for example, married filing jointly). However, the details of this exception are beyond the scope of this text and best reserved for discussion in an income tax textbook, such as Kaplan University's text entitled *Individual Income Tax Planning, 2ⁿᵈ edition* by Mershon and Fevurly.

MUTUAL FUNDS TAXATION

Investors in a mutual fund typically receive annual income in one of three forms: 1) ordinary taxable dividends; 2) exempt interest dividends (for example, dividends from a municipal bond fund); and 3) capital gain distributions. Shareholders who receive either short-term or long-term capital gain distributions from the fund report these distributions on Schedule D of IRS Form 1040 (dividends are reported on Schedule B of this same form). Occasionally, shareholders will also receive a distribution that is a tax-free return of capital arising out a sale of shares by the fund; these will be labeled as non-taxable distributions on their Form 1099-DIV. Finally, mutual fund investors often have a dividend reinvestment option under which dividend income and capital gain distributions are used to purchase additional shares for the investor's account. See chapter 15 of this text discussing *dividend reinvestment plans (DRIPs)*. While the investor receives no cash payments for these shares, he or she is nevertheless in *constructive receipt* of the dividends reinvested on his or her behalf and must pay income tax on this distribution as well. The same concept applies with respect to the receipt of reinvested capital gain distributions; that is, they are currently taxable.

You should note that, while dividends paid from a tax-exempt fund (such as a municipal bond fund) are non-taxable annually, a sale or exchange of shares from such fund does result in a taxable event. However, to the taxpayer's benefit (consistent with the general tax rule applying to taxable funds), the original cost basis of tax-exempt fund shares is *increased* by the amount of any reinvested dividends. This rule applies even though the distribution is considered as an exempt-interest dividend and is not otherwise reportable in the taxpayer's annual income.

Taxable distributions are one of the biggest drawbacks to investing in mutual funds (compared to owning stocks or bonds directly). When a taxpayer buys a stock or bond, no taxes are currently owed (except for those on dividends or interest) until he or she sells the security. Therefore, the taxpayer controls the timing of the taxable event with an individual stock or bond. This is *not* the case with mutual funds. The law requires that gains from the sale of securities within the fund—those remaining after taking offsetting losses—*must* be distributed by December 31ˢᵗ of the taxable year. Some funds can, and often do, take steps to minimize taxable distributions to shareholders by practicing buy-and-hold strategies or by taking whatever losses they can early in the taxable year. However, taxpayers are generally at the mercy of the mutual fund manager in the timing and implementation of these strategies. Accordingly, this means that the taxpayer's best strategy is to find out about the timing of these potentially taxable distributions *before* they occur. Another strategy is to avoid those mutual funds that historically buy and sell their holdings frequently (referred to as mutual fund *turnover*) and instead invest in more stable funds.

Of course, if a taxpayer/investor sells shares of a mutual fund, there is income tax due on any gain. This gain is measured by the sale price received for the shares (after deducting any expenses of sale) less the investor's basis (adjusted cost) in the shares. The calculation of the shareholder's total basis in the shares sold is relatively complicated, particularly if, as is often the case, these shares have been accumulated at different times over different years. In this instance, there are three methods the taxpayer/investor may use to calculate basis: 1) the specific identification method; 2) the average cost method; and 3) the first-in-first-out (FIFO) method. Generally, of the three methods, the specific identification method will prove *most favorable* for the investor (that is, result in the *highest* basis and, therefore, the *least* amount of income tax due upon sale of the shares), assuming a steadily appreciating secondary market in share prices. However, this method does require extensive taxpayer record keeping. Conversely, the FIFO method is usually the *least favorable* alternative for computing mutual fund shareholder basis and is the method used by the IRS when the taxpayer/investor cannot identify the actual shares sold. Finally, the average cost method is usually the most frequently-used means of computing shareholder basis. In this method, the taxpayer pools all of his or her purchased shares in one account and divides its total cost by the number of shares held. Accordingly, all shares have the *same* unit cost or basis for purposes of computing any gain (or loss). Many mutual funds provide the average cost basis of shares to their investors as part of the fund's shareholder services.

STOCKS

Consistent with the general rules previously discussed, when an investor sells individual shares of stock, he or she recognizes a capital gain or loss. Whether such gain is long term (thus qualifying for preferential tax treatment) or short term depends on how long the investor has owned the shares before selling them. When shares of stock are sold, the amount of gain or loss is the difference between the net sales price of the shares (referred to in tax language as the *amount realized*) and the shareholder's basis in the shares. If these shares were a one-time purchase, the shareholder should have little difficulty in establishing his or her cost basis. However, similar to the mutual funds problem in identifying which shares were actually sold, basis determination becomes more problematic when the shares were acquired at a different time and price. In this instance, the shareholder will need to adequately identify the *round lot* (100-share increment) from which he or she acquired the shares or will need to rely on the FIFO method and attribute the basis of the shares to the earliest of the lots purchased or acquired.

A *dividend* is the most common type of publicly-traded corporate stock distribution (closely held stock normally does *not* return a dividend) and is a distribution to the shareholder of either cash or property out of the corporation's current or accumulated earnings and profits. Such a distribution is treated as ordinary income to the taxpayer/investor (not capital gains) and is also not deductible by the distributing corporation. However, effective January 1, 2003, and as previously discussed, so-called *qualifying* dividend distributions are eligible for the same 5% or 15% rates as long-term capital gains if they meet certain conditions.

If a corporation *redeems* its stock (buys the shares back), it may be treated as an exchange of the stock (rather than as a dividend) if the transaction satisfies one of four tests. The significance of this *sale and exchange* treatment to the shareholder is that he or she is entitled to recover his or her basis in the shares and pay capital gains only to the extent of any excess corporate distribution. However, this treatment is not easy to achieve and is generally available only if one of the four following situations exists:

1) The redemption is substantially disproportionate with respect to the shareholder

2) The redemption terminates the shareholder's *entire* interest in the corporation

3) The redemption is not substantially equivalent to a dividend

4) The redemption consists of stock held by a non-corporate shareholder and is made in a partial liquidation of the redeeming corporation

When a corporation distributes shares of its own stock as a dividend, the distribution is referred to as a *stock dividend* and, unlike a cash distribution, is generally not taxable. However, the planner should distinguish between a stock dividend, which *may be* taxable in some instances (for example, if the shareholder had the option of receiving stock or taxable cash), from that of a stock split, which is *never* taxable. A stock split is not considered a distribution of a corporation's current or accumulated earnings and profits and, thus, does not carry with it any taxable consequences to the taxpayer/investor.

BONDS

One of the three major categories of bonds—municipal bonds—and its primary form of return have already been discussed in connection with the discussion on tax-exempt income (see chapter 17). Accordingly, only government issues (U.S. Treasury securities) and corporate bonds remain relevant to our discussion here.

U.S. Treasury Securities

As you should be aware by now, there are three basic types of U.S. Treasury securities: bills, notes, and bonds. Treasury bills (with a maturity date of one year or less) are issued at a discount from face value and are redeemable at the bill's face value at maturity. Unless an investor chooses to accrue the amount of this discount daily and include it in his or her income, the amount of this acquisition discount is taxable in full at the maturity date of the bill. Therefore, an investor holding the bill as of the date of maturity includes the amount of the discount as ordinary income. A taxpayer/investor who sells the Treasury bill prior to its maturity includes as ordinary income only the portion of the acquisition discount proportionate to the total time he has held the bill.

The taxation of Treasury notes (with maturity dates of more than one year up to 10 years from date of issue) and Treasury bonds (more than a 10-year maturity date) to a taxpayer/ investor is much more complex than that of Treasury bills. If the bond or note was originally issued at a discount (that is, at a price below its face value) after July 1,1982, any investor who did not pay more than the face value of the obligation must include in his or her income each year a calculated share of this *original issue discount(OID)*. This calculation is very complicated and will not be dealt with here, but you should note that the taxpayer/investor is paying tax on income that he or she has not yet received in the form of cash (so-called *phantom income*). The taxpayer's basis is then increased by the amount of OID he or she includes in income each year.

If the Treasury note or bond is subsequently sold prior to its maturity date (the usual case), proceeds from the sale must then be segregated into the following components:

- An amount equal to the taxpayer's adjusted basis in the note or bond is recovered income tax free; this amount is usually the purchase price of the obligation plus the addition of any accrued OID.

- If the sale occurs prior to the interest-reportable date of the note or bond, the seller receives from the buyer an amount separately stating interest accrued but not yet due; this amount is reported by the seller as accrued-interest income on his or her income tax return for the year of sale.

- The excess (deficiency) of any sale proceeds received over the seller's basis and accrued interest is treated as capital gain (or loss) per the previously discussed general rules applying to capital assets.

Finally, any interest received from Treasury bills, notes and bonds is subject to federal income tax at ordinary income rates. However, under the *doctrine of reciprocity*, this same interest is entirely exempt from all state and local taxes.

Corporate Bonds

The taxation rules regarding corporate bonds are somewhat similar to those of U.S. Treasury securities, but probably even more complex. This is because of another type of discount (or premium) that is commonly associated with the buying and selling of corporate obligations. For income tax purposes, this discount (or premium) is known as *market discount* or *market premium*.

As we know, bond prices in the secondary market fluctuate as the level of the interest rate changes and as the issuer's bond rating varies. Therefore, bonds may be purchased at a discount from the face or par value of the bond because of an increase in interest rates subsequent to the bond's issue. A bond acquired at a discount in the secondary market (as contrasted to one *issued* at a discount) is known as a *market discount bond.* The corporate bond that is issued at a discount is taxed similarly to that of a U.S. Treasury bill. That is, the discount is *accreted* or accrued annually over the term of the bond. However, the amount attributable to a market discount is generally *not* includible in the taxpayer/investor's income until the sale or disposition of the bond. That portion is subsequently treated as ordinary income with any sale price excess over and above the bond's par value treated as capital gain. Instead of recognizing interest income (the portion attributable to the market discount) at the date of sale, the taxpayer may elect to include the market discount annually using either the so-called *ratable accrual method* or the *constant interest* method. However, once this election is made, it applies to *all* market discount bonds acquired during and after the tax year of the election.

Example 18-3: Assume that George has purchased two $1,000 par value five-year corporate bonds at a discount in the secondary market for $965 each. He sells both these bonds prior to their maturity for $1,020 each. Therefore, in the year of sale, George must report interest income of $35 on each of the two bonds ($1,000 less $965) and pay capital gains on the $20 excess of the sale price over the par value of the bonds ($1,020 less $1,000). Note that if George had elected to include the market discount of $35 annually using either the *ratable accrual* or *constant interest* method, he would have had to apply this method to both of the bonds and not just one. However, this method would have *increased* his basis in the bonds and thereby lowered the amount of interest income that he would have had to report at time of sale. George might choose to ratably accrue the market discount if he anticipated being in a higher marginal income tax bracket in the future. In such event, George would pay more tax today, but less in the future at his anticipated higher rate.

When a bond owner has paid a *premium* over the par or face value of the bond, he or she has the option of 1) amortizing the premium until the maturity date of the bond and reducing his or her basis in the bond by the amortized amount or 2) not amortizing and treating the premium as part of the bond's basis. Most investors will elect to amortize the premium annually, using a constant yield method. See the Treasury Regulations to IRC Section 171. This is because investors pay tax at their ordinary income marginal brackets as the interest is paid on the bond, but have to wait until they sell the bond to recover the amount of the premium. As a result, if investors hold the bond until its date of maturity, redeeming it at par, they must treat the amount of the premium as a long-term capital loss. In addition, instead of offsetting ordinary interest income, this loss usually must offset capital gains that are generally taxable at a more-favorable (lower) tax rate. Consequently, investors will typically recover *less* in tax benefits than they have already paid on the portion of the interest payments attributable to the bond premium.

Finally, although an investor may elect to amortize the premium on a *taxable* corporate bond, any premium paid on a *tax-exempt* bond (such as a municipal bond) may *not* be amortized. Instead, such premium must reduce the taxpayer/investor's basis at the time of purchasing the bond. However, this makes sense when remembering that the interest from a municipal bond is not subject to taxation annually and must be recovered as ordinary income upon sale of the bond.

INSURANCE-BASED PRODUCTS

In recent years, the life insurance industry has implemented products with less of an insurance orientation and more of an investment focus. Nonetheless, the tax treatment of life insurance is considerably different than that of a security. For example, the cash value increases resulting from investment income on a life insurance policy are *not* subject to current taxation. These increases in cash value remain exempt from income tax if the policy terminates in a death claim. In addition, dividends payable from a life insurance policy are typically considered a return of premium by the policyholder and are also not taxable. This tax-free accumulation each year is known as the *inside buildup* in the policy and is *unique* to life insurance. In contrast, if an individual invests in security products in a taxable account, interest, dividends, and recognized capital gains are all currently taxable and generally *not deferrable*.

Because of the tax-favored treatment of life insurance, Congress has adopted certain rules to ensure that a life insurance policy is what is says it is; most notably, in 1984, several tests known as the *cash value accumulation* test and the *cash guideline and premium corridor* test were adopted to define an insurance policy. These tests were expanded in 1988 with the implementation of the *modified endowment contract* (*MEC*) rules designed to curb the use of single premium life insurance policies masquerading as insurance (versus security) products. The major taxable consequence of the application of the MEC rules is that loans or withdrawals from a single premium life insurance policy (or other policy that has failed the so-called *7 pay test* which is part of the 1988 rules) are *immediately taxable* as ordinary income. In other words, the taxable earnings within the policy are treated as having been distributed *first*, which is the opposite of the general rule where a loan or withdrawal from a life insurance policy is considered to be drawn, at least initially, from the policyholder's non-taxable basis.

Another form of life insurance product that may serve as an investment is an annuity. Individuals purchase annuity contracts from commercial insurance companies to protect themselves from the risk of *superannuation* or the risk of outliving one's money during his or her lifetime. The owner of the contract makes one or more payments to the insurance company; in return, the owner is provided with the professional money management skills of the company and the guarantee of a periodic payment during lifetime. This payment may begin immediately or may be deferred to some point in the future. If deferred, tax is postponed until the owner starts to receive the periodic payments, which, in turn, represent the beginning of the *distribution stage* (versus *accumulation stage*) of the annuity.

On receipt of the annuity payments (or *annuitization* of the annuity) over the chosen time period, the portion of each annuity payment representing an accumulation of the deferred earnings is taxable as ordinary income. The portion representing the return of the owner's after-tax investment (if any) is treated as a non-taxable return of capital. Finally, to determine the amount of the payment that is *not* taxable annually, a so-called *exclusion ratio* is used. This ratio is established by dividing the amount of the owner's after-tax investment (in the form of premiums paid under the terms of the annuity contract) by his or her *expected return* in the contract. This percentage is then multiplied by the amount of the annuity payment to determine the income-tax free portion of each payment. An example of the application of the ratio follows:

> **Example 18-4:** Assume that Joan, age 60, purchases an annuity contract from an insurance company for $40,000 that will begin to pay her a fixed amount of $500 per month at age 65. Her life expectancy at that age (or when she begins to *annuitize* the annuity) is 20 years. Therefore, her *expected return* in the contract is 20 × $500 × 12 or $120,000. Since Joan's investment in the contract is $40,000, the applicable exclusion ratio is .3333 or 33.3%. When multiplying this ratio by the monthly payment of $1,500, we determine that $500 of the payout is income tax free (and that the remaining $1,000 of the monthly payout is taxable). Should Joan outlive her projected life expectancy, the annuity payments are fully taxable once she has fully recovered her basis in the contract.

The above example illustrates the taxable consequences of a so-called *nonqualified annuity* that was annuitized by the owner of the annuity contract. However, less than 10% of non-qualified annuities are actually paid out in this manner. The remaining majority are either taken in a lump sum or random withdrawal by the annuity owner or left to the owner's beneficiaries at his or her death. If withdrawn in a lump sum or random withdrawal, *last-in, first-out* (*LIFO*) taxation rules apply, resulting first in taxability of the earnings portion of the annuity (as ordinary income) and second, in recovery of the owner's non-taxable basis/after tax contributions. If the annuity owner dies while still holding the annuity, the greater of either the contract's cash value or the guaranteed death benefit is payable to the owner's beneficiary; in either case, income tax consequences result from the selected payout or distribution of the annuity contract.

REAL ESTATE

As previously discussed in chapter 6 of this textbook, real estate may be owned either directly or indirectly, for example, through ownership shares in a real estate investment trust (REIT). However, the Internal Revenue Code (IRC) does not distinguish between forms of real estate ownership and, instead, taxes real estate according to the character of its income. We will now briefly consider the three basic forms of real estate ownership and the taxable consequences of each.

Undeveloped Land

This form of investment does not usually generate significant current taxable income or cash flow to the investor. Rather, the primary tax advantage to the owner/investor is that the capital appreciation in the market value of the land is not recognized as income until the owner disposes of the land in a taxable transaction (note: it is possible to do a non-taxable *like-kind exchange* with undeveloped land). At such a time, any capital appreciation in the land's value, from the time the owner purchased the property, is taxed as capital gain. The primary exception to this taxable treatment is if the owner is also considered to be a *dealer* in real estate by the I.R.S., in which case ordinary income tax treatment will result.

Finally, the payment of real estate taxes on undeveloped land is normally tax-deductible by the owner during the entire period of his of her ownership.

Rental Real Estate

Unlike undeveloped land, in rental real estate ownership, current income is typically received by the owner in the form of rents. Accordingly, these rents are taxable to the owner as ordinary income and any net profit (after deductible expenses) is reported on Schedule E of his or her IRS Form 1040. Since an annual depreciation deduction is also afforded the owner who invests in either residential or commercial rental real estate, he or she may recoup some of the investment dollars expended through claiming such a deduction. However, you should note that the depreciation allowance is only a tax benefit and does not impact the actual cash flow generated from the rental real estate to its owner. This effect was observed when performing the *net operating income* (NOI) computation in chapter 6, leading to an estimated intrinsic value of the rental property and the basis for an appropriate investment decision regarding possible purchase by the investor.

REIT Ownership

In this form of indirect ownership of real estate, the investor/shareholder is taxed very similarly to that of other mutual fund investors. Notably, all distributions in the form of dividends are taxable as ordinary income *unless* these distributions are specified otherwise by the REIT entity. In addition, as mentioned earlier, dividends generated from the REIT normally do *not* constitute a *qualifying dividend* for income tax purposes and the preferential 5% or 15% rates.

For taxable years beginning in 2001, a REIT is required to distribute only 90% of income (down from the previous 95%), therefore making such investment very similar to that of a mutual fund. However, unlike a mutual fund, losses from a REIT investment may not be passed through to the shareholder. In contrast to this treatment, losses from a direct investment in real estate (either in undeveloped land or in rental property) may be passed through to investors, although limitations may exist in the case of rental real estate.

Finally, assuming that the REIT distributes at least 90% of its income to shareholders, there is no corporate-level entity tax. In turn, this permits REIT shareholders to enjoy the benefits of limited liability with respect to their real estate investment, while avoiding the disadvantageous consequences of double taxation associated with corporate ownership.

COLLECTIBLES

Unless the investor is considered a dealer, an individual who invests in collectibles (art, coins, stamps, and the like) is normally purchasing a capital asset. Therefore, any gain on the sale of a collectible is subject to long-term capital gain treatment, assuming it is owned for the requisite *one year and a day* period from the date of purchase. However, there is a special flat tax rate accorded to the sale of a collectible; currently, this rate is either 15% or 28% (depending on the taxpayer's highest ordinary income marginal tax rate) and constitutes an exception to the normal lower capital gains rates imposed. Nonetheless, any loss on the sale of a collectible is treated as a long-term or short-term capital loss and will offset any other long-term or short-term capital gain without separate treatment.

Like stocks generally, there is no maturity date on a collectible. Accordingly, this makes it possible for the investor to time the recognition of a taxable event and postpone any gain into a year in which he or she has experienced losses on a collectible or, alternatively, when his or her total income is low. Of course, the investor pays no income tax on the annual gain from the collectible (if there is any) until he or she chooses to sell.

DERIVATIVES (OPTIONS AND FUTURES)

This is a very complicated area of the Internal Revenue Code (IRC) that is similar to bonds. While the taxation of options is discussed previously in chapter 16 of this textbook, no mention has yet been made of the taxable consequences of a futures contract. Specifically, futures contracts are referred to in the IRC as a *Section 1256 contract* and enjoy their own unique set of tax provisions known as the *marked-to-market rules*. A detailed explanation of these very complex rules will not be attempted here, except to state that futures contracts generally are treated as a capital asset and are taxed at their fair market value at the end of any given year of ownership. This is the case even if the contract is not yet complete or the maturity date has not yet been achieved. Under the marked-to-market rules, 60% of the gain or loss from a regulated futures contract is treated as long-term capital gain or loss and 40% is treated as short-term gain or loss on the last business day of the taxable year when the contract is owned. This treatment occurs *regardless* of the actual holding period of the contract and underlying property.

In the taxation of options, an investor realizes *no* taxable gain or loss on the purchase of a put or call. As noted in chapter 16, both puts and calls are capital assets, so that if either of these options is sold prior to exercise or expiration, capital gain or loss will result. To figure out the taxable consequences, however, the planner must first differentiate whether his or her client is the *holder (buyer)* of the option or is its *writer (seller)*. In this regard, it is also helpful to review the taxable consequences to either position as outlined in the previous Table 16-1.

If a taxpayer/investor *writes (sells)* the option, the amount received for doing so is not taxable at the time of receipt. Rather, the amount received is carried in a deferred account until the obligation expires, or the writer sells (in the case of a call option) or buys (in the case of a put option), the underlying stock when the option is exercised. If the option expires unexercised, the amount received for writing the option is short-term capital gain. If a *call* is exercised and the writer sells the underlying stock, he or she *increases* the amount realized on the stock sale by the amount of the call premium. If a *put* is exercised and the writer buys the underlying stock, he or she *decreases* his or her basis in the stock by the amount of the put premium.

For the *holder (buyer)* of the option, if the option expires, it is considered sold at the end of the standard nine-month period and a short-term capital loss is created. If the holder exercises a *call* option, its cost or premium paid is added to the basis of the underlying stock purchased. This means the premium paid may be treated as a long-term capital gain if the underlying purchased security was held more than 12 months (otherwise, the premium paid is treated as a short-term capital gain). In exercising a *put* option, the holder is obligated to sell the stock to the writer of the put. Therefore, it is the sale of the underlying stock (not the put option) that is taxed. Accordingly, in order to determine his or her gain or loss on the sale of the stock, the holder of the put offsets the total option premium paid against the price received for the stock to arrive at the net amount realized. If this net amount realized exceeds the holder's basis in the stock sold, the excess is capital gain and, like the call option, is considered as either a short-term or long-term capital gain depending on how long the underlying stock has been held prior to sale.

IMPORTANT CONCEPTS

Capital asset

Holding period

Capital gain or loss

Ordinary income

Active income

Portfolio income

Passive income

Tax deferred or tax advantaged account

Net unrealized appreciation (NUA)

Investment interest expense

Net investment income

Personal interest expense

Constructive receipt of income

Specific identification method

Average cost method

First-in-first-out (FIFO) method

Cash dividend

Stock dividend

Stock redemption

Stock split

Original issue discount (OID)

Market discount bond

Market premium bond

Inside buildup

Modified endowment contract (MEC)

Annuitization

Exclusion ratio

Expected return of contract

Last-in-first-out (LIFO) taxation

Capital appreciation

Rental income

REIT

Collectible flat rate of taxation

Marked-to-market rules

Taxation of options

QUESTIONS FOR REVIEW

1. For income tax purposes, how is an investment generally classified and why is this important?

2. What is the time period that an investment must be owned for it to qualify as a long-term asset?

3. What are the three types of income for purposes of the passive loss rules and to what general type of income (ordinary or capital) is each roughly equivalent?

4. What does conventional wisdom suggest as to where an investor should position an investment in stocks versus bonds? Why do some financial planners disagree with this approach?

5. When can an investor take advantage of the net unrealized appreciation (NUA) income tax concept? What is the benefit to the investor in applying this concept?

6. Complete the following sentence: Investment interest expense may be deducted to the extent of _____.

7. What items typically constitute net investment income? Which one(s) of these items may or may not be included at the discretion of the investor?

8. Is personal interest expense always non-deductible? Explain.

9. How (in what form) do mutual fund investors typically receive annual income? If they participate in a DRIP, are distributions from that plan currently taxable? Why or why not?

10. How does a taxpayer/investor potentially minimize taxable annual distributions from a mutual fund?

11. What are the three methods for calculating a taxpayer's basis in mutual fund shares? In a rising secondary market, which one of these is the most favorable to use?

12. How is a dividend distribution from a stock generally taxed? How is this different from a distribution that constitutes a stock redemption?

13. Contrast the potential tax treatment of a stock dividend to that of a stock split.

14. How does the concept of original issue discount enter into the resulting taxation of a U.S. Treasury bill?

15. If a U.S. Treasury bond or note is sold prior to its maturity date, how must the proceeds from the sale be segregated for income tax purposes?

16. Explain the taxable significance of a corporate bond that is selling in the secondary marketplace at a discount to its par value.

17. If a corporate bond is selling in the secondary marketplace at a premium to par value, how do most investors choose to account for this premium for income tax purposes? How does this differ in the case of a municipal bond that is selling at a premium?

18. Contrast the taxable consequences of the annual accumulation of earnings within a life insurance policy to that of an annual return from a security. Which one is taxed more favorably? Explain.

19. What is a proxy for application of the modified endowment contract (MEC) rules to an insurance product? What is the practical consequence of the MEC rules?

20. How is the distribution of an annuity taxed to the investor if he or she chooses to annuitize the payout? How does this taxable treatment differ from a lump sum or random withdrawal from an annuity?

21. Contrast the taxable treatment to a taxpayer from each of the following three types of real estate investments:
    - Undeveloped land
    - Rental real estate
    - Shareholder in a real estate investment trust (REIT)

22. What is the special flat tax rate that applies if a collectible is sold at any time?

23 What unique tax concept applies in the taxation of a futures contract?

24. Summarize the taxable consequences to the *writer* of an option in each of the following circumstances:
    • The option expires unexercised
    • The option is exercised

25. Summarize the taxable consequences to the *holder* of an option in each of the following circumstances:
    • The option expires unexercised
    • The option is exercised

SUGGESTIONS FOR ADDITIONAL READING

Individual Income Tax Planning, 2nd edition, Jeffrey B. Mershon and Keith R. Fevurly, Kaplan, Inc., 2005.

U.S. Master Tax Guide, most recent annual edition, CCH Editorial Staff Publication, CCH Incorporated.

Index

• • •

C

U

V

Valuation of securities. *See* Bond valuation;
    Equity securities valuation

Value investing, features of, 228, 234-35

Value line enigma, and efficient market
    hypothesis, 146

Value stocks, 49

Value weighted indexes, 219

Variable annuities
    features of, 67-68
    taxation, 52, 66
    versus mutual funds, 51-52

Variable life insurance policy
    features of, 64
    taxation, 62

Variable prepaid forward contracts, 266

Variable universal life (VUL) insurance policy
    death benefit options, 65
    features of, 64-65

Venture capital limited partnerships, 58

VIPERs, 54

Volatility, market risk, 110, 118

W

Warrants, 39-40

Wash sale rule, 270-71

Weak-form efficient market hypothesis, 145

Weighted beta, 128

Wildcatting, 99

Wilshire 5000, 219, 251

Working interest, 100

Wrap accounts, 48

Writing options, 245-47, 291

Y

Yield-based interest rate options, 251-52

Yield curves, 191-92
    flat curve, 191
    humped curve, 191
    negative/inverted curve, 191
    positive/normal curve, 191
    shape, basis of, 192

Yield ladder, 162, 190-91

Yield to call (YTC), 162-63

Yield to maturity (YTM), 20, 162, 190, 193, 223

Yield to worst, 163

Z

Zero cost collar, 248

Zero coupon bonds
    corporate issued, 24-25
    defined, 19
    duration and maturity, 194
    features of, 24-25
    and portfolio immunization, 200
    tax exemption, 24
    Treasury STRIP, 13-14

Zero growth, 175-76